KONGLISH

KONGLISH

The Ultimate Survival Guide for Teaching English in South Korea

MATTHEW WATERHOUSE

iUniverse, Inc.
Bloomington

KONGLISH
The Ultimate Survival Guide for Teaching English in South Korea

Copyright © 2012 by Matthew Waterhouse.
Author Credits: Matthew Waterhouse

All rights reserved. No part of this book may be used or reproduced by any means, graphic, electronic, or mechanical, including photocopying, recording, taping or by any information storage retrieval system without the written permission of the publisher except in the case of brief quotations embodied in critical articles and reviews.

iUniverse books may be ordered through booksellers or by contacting:

iUniverse
1663 Liberty Drive
Bloomington, IN 47403
www.iuniverse.com
1-800-Authors (1-800-288-4677)

Because of the dynamic nature of the Internet, any web addresses or links contained in this book may have changed since publication and may no longer be valid. The views expressed in this work are solely those of the author and do not necessarily reflect the views of the publisher, and the publisher hereby disclaims any responsibility for them.

Any people depicted in stock imagery provided by Thinkstock are models, and such images are being used for illustrative purposes only.
Certain stock imagery © Thinkstock.

ISBN: 978-1-4697-8642-1 (sc)
ISBN: 978-1-4697-8643-8 (ebk)

Printed in the United States of America

iUniverse rev. date: 05/04/2012

This book is dedicated to my darling Dayna,
the most amazing thing I discovered in South Korea.
Long may she love me.

ACKNOWLEDGEMENTS

It goes without saying that this book wouldn't exist if not for the help and support of my family and friends. First cab off the rank is M & M, who got me on a plane to Korea when I was unemployed and barely educated. Then there's Director, who kept renewing my contract regardless of how messy my apartment became. Big thanks to Captain Kerr who offered me alcohol and info, and my parents who visited and never asked when I was coming home.

Of course there is my marvellous Editor Di, who put up with much and offered more. Last but not least are Isabelle and Jason, who heard I was sitting on a stalled book and ordered me to get off my ass and finish it. Obviously there are others, but like a good Oscar speech I gotta keep it short, so I apologise if you aren't listed here by name. Thank you all very much.

CONTENTS

INTRODUCTION

Hello curious customer,

If you're taking the time to read this introduction and aren't in one of those funky bookstores that encourage you to lounge around for hours, then you've probably just purchased Konglish or are thinking about doing so. Congratulations on having the foresight and good taste to invest in your future and my mortgage.

Teaching English in South Korea is one of the most exciting, rewarding and downright incredible things you'll ever do. It's not however the easiest job, and the unique challenges that accompany it are compounded by the fact that the people who live there possess a culture that's often at right angles to wherever you're from. This can be a source of frustration and despair but it's also what makes it so damn interesting.

Hospitable inhabitants, fiery cuisine, imposing palaces, excellent infrastructure, Confucian customs, ancient arts, vibrant cities, shamanistic rituals, hi-tech industries, marvellous mountains, acres of orchards, beautiful temples and a recent history that includes monarchy, assassination, invasion, occupation, civil war, dictatorship, democracy and unprecedented economic growth are just some of the factors that make this tiny nation a complex and intriguing option for both teachers and tourists alike.

While this book was written with prospective teachers in mind, much of its content addresses Korean history, culture and customs, and will be of use to anyone seeking to know more about living and working in this fascinating country.

The structure is simple and follows a natural and intuitive order. It starts by questioning your sanity and quickly moves on to help identify who your ideal students might be and where you should base yourself. After this come simple things like finding the perfect job, acing the interview, negotiating a favorable contract and securing the coveted E-2 visa.

The next section deals with things you should know before you depart. These include, amongst other topics, accommodation, cross cultural communication, social faux pas, home sickness and what to pack for a bag that weighs less than your mother.

Further on are a number of chapters dedicated to the different needs of your various students, everyone from nearly newborns to ancient artefacts, plus a section on the illegal pleasures of private tuition. These are followed by a host of other erudite scratchings, covering everything you could possibly ever need to know about the culture and customs of South Korea—including the stuff nobody wants to discuss.

I wrote Konglish because I was dissatisfied with the quality of information available on the subject. Most of what I read was out-dated, incomplete or as boring as bat shit. Some of the printed publications were nothing more than tarted up ESL handbooks without a single shred of social context, while others were so politically correct that they failed to provide the reader with any meaningful advice on the hard realities of living and working abroad.

South Korea is an amazing place, brimming with smart students, fantastic food and vibrant traditions, so it should come as no surprise that many writers are content to stick with safe subjects like lesson plans, barbequed beef and Buddhist temples. I however, wanted to create a book that while addressing these fundamentals would also take a look outside of the box. I wanted to write about the other Korea that teachers experience, in order to prepare readers for the drunken businessmen, racist remarks, vomit strewn streets and aching bouts of loneliness and dislocation.

As the full title implies, the purpose of Konglish is to ensure that the reader possesses the knowledge necessary to survive the challenges of teaching English in South Korea. I feel that this is vitally important, in that each year hundreds of new teachers quit their jobs after only a few months because they aren't adequately prepared for the intensity of the experience. But survival doesn't mean just scraping by, it's knowing how to successfully cope with the inevitable lows of the job in order to appreciate the mind blowing highs that come with this incredible country.

I honestly believe that if an individual arrives in South Korea armed with the right attitude and information, he or she will have an enjoyable time and be a better teacher regardless of what life throws at them. I also feel that the best way to pass this knowledge on is through honesty and humor. Honesty because I think we all want to be warned about the potential pitfalls in our path, and humor because it's always easier to accept advice if we're laughing with the fool who's already stepped on the banana skin.

Though no text is perfect, this one has turned out better than I dared imagine. At just over thirty five chapters, I feel that Konglish strikes the right balance between fact, fun, anecdotal evidence and serious subject matter.

Choosing to live and work overseas is a significant decision and not one to be entered into lightly. That said, teaching English in South Korea was the one of the best things I've ever done. I met my wife, made great friends, helped thousands of people improve their English, learned a second language, experienced a unique culture, saved some money, found a vocation and gained a deeper understanding of myself and the world I inhabit. I have no doubt that you'll find it equally rewarding. I hope this book meets your expectations and helps you succeed in your journey. Have a pitcher of lemon Soju for me and don't forget to try the squid.

Yours sincerely,
Matthew Waterhouse

LOOKING FOR MR. GOODJOB

Luckily for you, looking for Mr. Goodjob is a lot easier than finding true love, though there's the very real possibility that you'll wake up after a year long affair to find that the boss has never respected you and the money on the dresser isn't quite what he promised. That said, if you go into these kinds of sordid business transactions with your eyes wide open, you stand a good chance of ending up with a teaching position that doesn't outwardly resemble abject slavery.

As with all relationships, the chances of fulfilment are greatly enhanced if you're honest about what makes you happy. This sounds logical, but sadly a lot of people apply for the first job they encounter, without giving this important decision the thorough consideration it deserves. It's too late once you're in South Korea to realize that what you really wanted was a NGO position showing third world farmhands how to pollinate peanut plants.

This isn't rocket science, it's just common sense. Before you start emailing recruiters and employers, it's wise to think about your own personality and whether any kind of teaching position offers you the possibility of job satisfaction.

Please answer the following questions to see if you're psychologically suited to teaching English in South Korea, a job with one of the highest rates of depression, schizophrenia and alcoholism on the planet:

- Do you like repeating instructions ad infinitum?
- Derive satisfaction from hours of unpaid planning?
- Enjoy blank stares and meaningless paperwork?
- Love eating dinner in under five minutes?
- Can't resist spending your own money on supplies?
- Get excited working split shifts?
- Delight in substandard accommodation?
- Take pride in being underpaid and overworked?
- Relish isolation and sexual abstinence?
- Don't mind being treated like a second class citizen?

If you answered yes to some or all of these questions then you were born to be an ESL teacher. (There are actually loads of good things to recommend the job, but it's best to weed out the weak and unsuitable before they become deranged co-workers.)

First you need to determine if you're actually eligible for a visa. The rules state that to teach in South Korea you must be a native English speaker who has attended an English speaking university and received a Bachelor's, Master's or Doctoral degree. French or Afrikaans just won't cut the mustard, nor will a certificate in Hamburgology. Specifically they're looking for educated and erudite individuals from Canada, the US, Australia, the UK, Ireland, and South Africa. (Technically speaking, New Zealanders are allowed in, but it's best if they're not actively encouraged.) On a purely theoretical basis it's possible for Jamaicans, Ghanaians and Nigerians to work in South Korea but the Korean government doesn't seem to issue a lot of visas to applicants from those three countries.

It may strike you as a bit sloppy that any old university degree will do. You might think that four years of molecular chemistry or philosophy wouldn't really prepare you for the challenges of teaching English and you'd be right. That's why it's a good idea to take some kind of ESL or TEFL training before you go. ESL stands for English as a second language and TEFL is teaching English as a foreign language.

If you are committed, cashed up and have some spare time then nothing beats a CELTA certificate course from Cambridge University or Trinity College. These can be completed in the UK or at various other locations around the world. They take around a month of full time study to complete or several if attempted part-time. These are intense and extremely thorough programs intended for serious students, so don't bother signing up for one if you don't really know what you want.

Of course any form of ESL study will help you become a better teacher and there are plenty to choose from. They range from weeklong, evening and weekend programs at your local community college to very basic online offerings. Even a good book or two on the subject is better than nothing. That said, if you have a brain in the basket, speak English and are willing to learn along the way, you'll survive, so don't let a lack of training stand in your way.

The next thing to determine is which kinds of students are the ones for you. Most teaching positions advertised will be for Hagwons. These are private educational institutions that offer a variety of subjects, though by far the greatest demand lies in the field of supplemental English study. Some Hagwons located in larger urban areas focus exclusively on one specific age group but most conduct lessons for a wide range of students. A typical Hagwon will provide classes in the morning for housewives, a preschool program during the day, elementary in the afternoon, middle and high school in the early evening and conversation classes for businessmen at night.

Positions are often advertised as teaching only adults or children but be advised that these job descriptions have a funny way of changing once you're in the country. Don't be surprised when your adult conversation class morphs into a room filled with screaming imps hell-bent on plucking your arm hair without anaesthetic.

If you happen to posses better qualifications, (real or imagined), perhaps you should consider becoming an instructor at one of the country's many universities and colleges. These kinds of positions generally offer improved accommodation, higher wages, a more stimulating academic environment, fewer split shifts and a student body less inclined to leak.

Another possibility is snagging a job with a large corporation. A number of big companies run their own Hagwons with the aim of improving their employees' English skills. The focus tends to be business related, although some also offer basic classes for the wives and children. They usually provide better working conditions than those found elsewhere but tend not to be situated in idyllic rural locations—think Posco steel works or Hyundai shipyards.

Last but not least, there are a number of positions, organized through both private and governmental channels that allow you to work in the public school system. Here your time is shared between the classroom and the staffroom, for as well as teaching students you are expected to help improve the English skills of your fellow teachers. Working conditions are good, the pay is always on time and unlike other jobs you won't ever have an evening class, though you may be asked to accompany a weekend school excursion. These positions are probably best suited to those individuals who have proper teaching qualifications, however for some of these programs an education degree is not a prerequisite.

Of course there is one more option on the cards but it's highly illegal. Some people who just don't meet the nationality or education requirements, choose to work between the cracks. They enter on a tourist visa and support themselves through a combination of private tutoring, and short term engagements at shonky Hagwons. They run the risk of being ripped off by their employers and being fined and deported by the government. It's not an easy life, but if you thrive on fear and uncertainty, it's definitely more exciting than collecting unemployment cheques from the isolation of your parents' basement.

Once you know who you're going to teach, the next question is where. Do you like big cities? If your answer is yes, then Seoul, the fifth largest metropolis on the planet, with a population of over ten million people should keep you busy. If you fancy something full of life but not quite so intimidating, then Busan, Incheon, Daegu, Daejeon, Gwangju and Ulsan are all options worth investigating.

It comes down to personal taste. If you love noisy malls, world class museums, huge markets, amazing theatres, discount shopping and can cope with a personal space bubble the size of a basketball, then Seoul is a good fit. If on the other hand you like fresh air, quiet streets, open vistas, friendly neighbors and the option of riding a bike to work, then door B, a country town of less than 150,000 is probably the correct choice. The pay tends to be a bit poorer outside urban areas, but then the cost of living is dramatically lower once you enter the rice belt.

If you're after a really peaceful existence, there are always a few jobs available down amongst the islands of the far south. They're great places, with rocky beaches, lots of seafood and stunning sunsets, the only drawback being that access to the mainland is by ferry, which can be a major pain in the ass during storm season. Of course if a typhoon lands directly on your island you also run the risk of becoming one of those weird statistics you read about on the internet, but true seafood lovers are never intimidated.

It's interesting to note that most people who bug out before the end of their first contract tend to be living in Seoul. It seems there's something about the place, perhaps the staggering weight of humanity that just erodes people's sanity. So if you've got some major debts and are planning to stick around for a few years it may be wiser to ignore the lure of the big city until you're well broken in to the ways of Korea.

After you've sorted out the big three: students, schools and location, you need to understand job offers in detail. Because as the saying goes, that's where the devil dwells.

Of prime importance is accommodation. A simple way to deal with this is to reject any position that does not offer private, single accommodation, which is usually the norm. Your workmates could very well turn out to be retired cordon bleu chefs or attractive massage therapists looking for adventure but they might just as easily be psycho whack-jobs with limited cleaning skills, so always say no to any offer that includes the word 'shared'.

Another factor to keep in mind is distance, because a humid hour or two spent daily on public transport quickly abrades the soul. And don't just assume that the apartment is free and furnished, make sure you have it in writing. (For more disturbing information regarding housing please refer to the chapter entitled 'But Director my apartment has fleas!')

Of course the issue of remuneration is never far from mind. Inflation rages, currencies fluctuate and economies falter, so the best way to get an up-to-date understanding of wages is to compare a wide selection of current job advertisements. Korean employers begrudgingly accept the fact that potential employees will shop around, so most positions are within a few hundred thousand won of each other, the difference on average being about two hundred dollars per month. Most Hagwon salaries are around USD $2,000 per month, some a bit more, depending on exchange rates and location. Universities and the like often pay more but the difference is linked to educational qualifications and previous teaching experience. This basic wage might not seem a lot of money for a month's labor, but with no major costs except for beer and bratwurst, it's quite feasible to save the majority of your pay packet.

Equally important is how many hours you must work to earn the dough. If you're foolish enough to sign a contract that doesn't clearly state this then God help you. Look to see how many hours you're expected to work per week, at what point overtime kicks in, whether the pay rate then increases, whether you'll be working split shifts and if you have the option to refuse excess hours. If these things haven't been mentioned, or aren't clear, then it's your responsibility to enquire after them.

Standard practice is to recompense employees for their flights and pay a bonus at the end of the contract. Flight costs are often reimbursed in one or two instalments throughout the year and the bonus is almost always one month's salary. Wages are paid monthly, often in cash. Receiving this gangsteresque wad is a rite of passage for new employees, though the Korean government is considering the introduction of larger denomination bills, which will certainly make payday less of a physical challenge for bank tellers and Hagwon owners.

Almost everyone who has taught in Korea has a horror story about missing wages, crazy hours or crappy accommodation, though happily the majority of them aren't first hand accounts. This unfortunate situation arises from an unholy amalgam of rumor, cultural misunderstanding and the sad fact that a high percentage of morons find themselves mysteriously drawn to the idea of running a Hagwon. This last factor isn't really surprising in that Hagwons are considered to be a license to print money.

This erroneous belief in easy income continues to attract financial incompetents to the dynamic field of Hagwon management like flies to the proverbial turd.

The only way you can reduce the chances of becoming the central character in one of these stories is to do your research. Any school that has treated its staff well should be happy to assist you in speaking with its current and past employees. If they can't or won't put you in contact with their English teachers then forget about it, no matter how inviting the job description sounds.

Don't be embarrassed to ask these teachers lots of gritty questions, because it's going to be a year that you'll never get back. How old is the school? How many teachers does it employ? How many have quit in the last year? Will you have a Korean assistant? Are the student numbers fairly stable? How big are the classes? Does the school only have one building, or are you expected to work at multiple locations? Have teachers ever been lent out to other schools? Do you get paid for preparation and planning? Are you expected to work weekends or engage in unpaid promotional work? Are holidays honored? Have there ever been problems with getting paid? Was it a once off situation or a regular occurrence? Is collecting overtime an issue? Were airfares recompensed as specified? Was the full bonus paid on completion? Is the boss clearly deducting tax and pension payments? Did you ever see your health insurance book? This may all seem a little pedantic but if you don't know the answers to most of these questions then think twice about signing a contract.

That said, you will be working in Asia, and over there a contract is seen more as a conversation than a cast iron agreement. Just because you have it in writing doesn't mean that things won't change! The important thing is to remain flexible, as it's almost guaranteed that your working conditions will alter at some time during your stay—they may even be different upon arrival. Try to balance paranoid fears with commonsense and good faith, as the majority of employers aren't evil bloodsuckers. If you scream blue murder when asked to work an extra hour and wave the contract around like it's the constitution, you will not prosper in the long run. This is Korea, where bosses expect a certain amount of respect and for the most part those that play the face game end up the better for it.

Far too many new teachers gorge themselves on chat room horror stories and completely burn any chance of good relations with their boss by freaking out at the first sign of change. Don't stand for getting ripped off on the big ticket items like wages and accommodation, but when it comes to the little stuff it pays to compromise.

If something untoward does happen once you're working in Korea, take a second to breathe and talk to your co-workers before launching an attack. More often than not they've been through similar events and will be able to offer some advice and perspective, which may save you from making a costly mistake that cannot be rectified. Nobody wants their paymaster as their enemy, so be sure to exercise a little caution when it comes to these matters, as Koreans don't easily forgive if they feel insulted or wrongly accused.

But before you get stressed about these kinds of tricky diplomatic situations, you first need a job. One way to go about this is through a recruiter. The recruiter basically finds you the best position available and you don't pay a cent. The money moves from the employer to the recruiter when you arrive to take up the job. You provide them with a photo, resume, copies of degrees, etc and they get back to you with the job offers.

Just like employers, there are a wide variety of recruiters out there looking to make money from your innate English ability. Some see you as little more than a commodity, and will happily sell you into slavery if it means a quick buck. Others hold a more long term outlook and are interested in maintaining a strong, supportive relationship with both you and the schools they're serving.

The trick is working out which ones are credible and which ones are used car salesmen on sabbaticals. With over one hundred recruiters online at last count, it pays to do your homework. Contact recruiters and ask questions. Visit ESL forums, blacklists and websites that offer first hand accounts from teachers who have gone down the recruitment path. If you're in a university education program you'll probably be approached at your graduation job fair by some friendly strangers, but that in itself doesn't guarantee that they're lovely human beings with your best interests at heart.

Keep in mind that recruiters are there to make money by helping schools locate employees. They aren't there to hold your hand or help you when things go pear shaped. It's up to you to ask the right questions before you sign a contract. Once you're working they aren't that interested in hearing about your broken hot water heater or the fact that the boss wants you to tutor his brats every weekend.

A lot of prospective employers like to save money and so choose to advertise directly as opposed to paying substantial fees to recruiting agencies. An internet search for 'esl jobs Korea' will yield around 260,000 results. There are heaps of different sites that offer information, and while it can be amusing to trawl the cyber seas in search of wisdom, one of the best places to start is Dave's ESL Café, www.eslcafe.com. This excellent website, in addition to providing all kinds of helpful resources, has a number of boards advertising teaching positions around the world. Of particular importance to you is that on any given day there are approximately 500 current job postings on its dedicated Korean job board.

All job postings that appear there have a title that lets you know who the employer is, where the position is and what kind of classes you'll be teaching. If you see something that catches your eye, you just click on it to read in further detail all the wonderful reasons why you should work for that employer.

Most postings will give details such as location, starting date, contract period, basic salary, overtime, housing, student level, working hours, holidays and benefits. This is usually followed by a list of requirements necessary for application. These may include a cover letter, statement of teaching philosophy, resume, recent photographs, copy of passport, reference letters from past employers, university transcripts, a copy of your diploma, a criminal record check and of course an email address and phone number.

After first contact is made, providing they're interested, you'll most likely be invited to attend a telephone interview, though a Skype chat wouldn't be out of the question in tech savvy South Korea. Some schools will have you speak directly with the owner; others leave everything up to a Western manager or member of staff.

The interview is their chance to establish whether you'll be an asset or a liability to their organisation. The following is a list of questions they're trying to answer.

- Does the applicant speak clearly
- Can they express themselves without difficulty
- Do they sound outgoing and friendly
- Will they fit in with other employees
- Are they committed to working for a whole year
- What motivates them to seek this kind of work

If they're happy with the interview and the material you've sent them they'll no doubt get a couple of contracts off in the mail. All that remains is the tiny hurdle of getting your E-2 visa. The next chapter should see you through that painful process relatively unscathed but if you're religious a few Hail Marys or quick prayer in the direction of Mecca probably wouldn't hurt.

DAS PAPERWERK

So you've done your research and selected South Korea as the perfect place to experience the joys of indentured servitude. You've made the right enquiries, perhaps signed your soul over to a recruiting agent and found a smooth talking employer happy to whisper sweet contractual nothings in your ear. Now all you need to do is get cracking on those pesky forms. Welcome to the living hell that is Das Paperwerk.

Like all good bureaucracies, the Korean Government maintains an almost religious faith in the efficiency of paper documentation, despite recent technological advances such as the computer chip and the internet. In order to secure the coveted E-2 working visa, you're required to prove your worth by demonstrating your ability to correctly fill in countless forms, attain and attach certified copies of various documents, and coordinate their transfer to various embassy and government offices. Those unfamiliar with the idiotic intricacies of inter-departmental paperwork may feel they share a kindred spirit with the Greek hero Theseus, however only some of you will face a bloodthirsty monster at the end of your journey.

The first thing you need to accept is the inevitability of change. Even as you read this, some unknown office drone in Seoul is sending out updates to the various consulates around the globe alerting them to last minute modifications to the visa program. This chapter attempts to give an accurate overview of the current process but don't be surprised if after reading this you find that the hoops have been raised a few more meters or lined with razor wire instead of flames.

The next news flash is that Koreans are big believers in the notion of collective punishment. Unfortunately, over the last few years the actions of a few isolated idiots have screwed things up for everyone. 'Toking Teachers Caught in Café!' exclaimed the headlines. Say hello to a comprehensive health examination that includes a urine and/or blood test to ascertain whether you've been naughty.

South Korea has always been a bit leery of outside influence (you don't earn the title Hermit Kingdom for being a social butterfly) and this inclination towards xenophobia has remained a constant factor in policies regarding immigration. When you're issued a piece of ID entitled Alien Registration Card you know you're not exactly a welcome visitor, but up until recently obtaining a working visa has been more inconvenience than inquisition.

The real spanner in the works came about when a bunch of Western knobs got together and started boasting about all the Korean girls they'd slept with. They posted explicit photographs on the web and invited their mates to share and compare—not a good idea in a country that's still a little touchy about subjects like foreign exploitation and sexual slavery.

In the proverbial blink of an eye the country was in an uproar. What started as an internet blog bite quickly became a major news sensation. Preachers pounded pulpits, right wing commentators fanned the flames, and it soon became obvious to everyone that all foreigners, regardless of their gender, age or marital status were a threat to the nation's moral order.

Although some sections of the public favored execution, or at least mass deportation, the government was forced to admit that for the foreseeable future English teachers were a necessary evil. To appease concerned citizens they've done their best to transform the visa application process into an expensive, time consuming and excruciatingly painful experience.

Once a school has decided to hire you there are a number of things that have to be done at your end before you can head to the airport. It all starts with a comprehensive national criminal background check in your country of residence. This means making contact with the heavy hitters of the acronym community like the FBI or the RCMP. After filling in lengthy forms and being fingerprinted, you get to pay for the privilege of finding out what you already know. Be warned that while these documents can take ages to process they can't be older than six months when submitted.

The next things on the wish list are officially verified copies of your university degree, passport and criminal background check. For American citizens this means an Apostille stamp, a form of internationally recognized notarization, and this must be done in the jurisdiction of the embassy closest to where you reside. For everyone else it's usually just a quick trip to the nearest public notary but that may have changed by the time you read this. While these things take time they're actually a pretty good idea, as in the past all kinds of freaks used to slip in under the radar.

You'll then send off by courier your police check, notarized copies of degree and passport, one set of unopened university transcripts, a signed contract, a signed resume and two signed and dated passport photographs to your employer or recruiter. Oh and don't forget the self-declared health form, an inoffensive little document designed to help the Korean government identify psychotic, AIDS ravaged, tuberculosis patients wishing to enter the workforce.

Once your school or recruiter in Korea receives these documents they then add their own contribution and drop them all off at their local immigration office. After these things have sat in a filing cabinet for the approved period of time, the coveted visa authorization number will be issued.

When this arrives you're ready for the next round. Either in person or by mail you need to get the visa authorization number, along with a visa application form, original passport, notarized copy of passport and degree, one set of sealed university transcripts, visa application fee, two signed and dated passport photographs, another health form and a consul checklist to your local Korean embassy. Just remember, you don't want the one marked Democratic People's Republic of Korea, as those are the guys in charge of coalmining, famine and synchronized sports. If you're mailing this material make sure you include a self-addressed envelope with sufficient stamps, and ask for a multiple entry visa if you're planning on any travel outside the country during your stay.

If and when this has been approved you'll need to attend the embassy for an interview. This is the time to get a haircut, remove the visible piercings and dress neatly. During the interview you'll be asked a series of cunning questions designed to trap you into revealing your deviant ways. Although Mother always said that honesty was the best policy, it's advisable to give a clear and resounding negative when they pop the one about illegal drug consumption. Any answers they don't like, as well as attitude and appearance can be grounds for refusal. Be warned that Korean embassy employees endure mandatory Botox treatments on a regular basis, so don't expect a lot of smiles or facial movement.

If you get through the interview without screwing things up, you'll receive at some point your passport with an E-2 visa annoyingly pasted somewhere towards the back. Of course this doesn't mean the paperwork is finished. Once in Korea you'll have thirty days to submit to a complete health check performed at a nationally recognized hospital. This will include among other things tests on your hearing, vision, cardio vascular system, urine and blood, as well as chest x-rays, measurement of your height and weight and an oral interview conducted by a trained physician.

If you bomb any of these you must undergo a more expensive and exhaustive examination. If you fail that it's bye-bye. If you pass with flying colors the results will be forwarded along with your other documentation to the nearest Immigration office where they'll be processed. At some point thereafter an Alien Registration Card will be dispensed to your unworthy person. Needless to say it's not a good idea to lose it or your passport.

This entire chapter should only be seen as a rough guide to the process. Your employer or recruiting agency will help you along the way. The time it takes for each of these steps to be completed will vary with individual applications and locations. The following list is included for the purposes of wishful thinking and should under no circumstances be considered reliable.

- Criminal check—from a few weeks to as long as six months
- Verified copies—an hour or so excluding travel time
- First processing in Korea—roughly two weeks
- Embassy processing—one week
- Interview—half an hour
- Health examination—three hours plus travel time
- Final processing—eight to ten days

If you wish to renew your contract or transfer to another employer then most of these steps, according to the new rules, must be carried out all over again, even those that are supposed to be done outside of Korea. This is a major concern for employers, as they like to rehire old hands who know the drill, but if the government makes it too difficult or expensive, teachers may be inclined not to renew their contracts.

How the laws will stand when you're ready to apply is anybody's guess, as they seem to change on a weekly basis. Sometimes even the officials in charge can't answer your questions. So be prepared for the worst, hope for the best and don't quit your job anytime soon.

PREPARATION K

Worries about what to take on a big trip have plagued mankind since Noah set sail without the unicorns. After language, abstract thought, and an unhealthy obsession with tools, the fourth defining characteristic of Homo sapiens is undoubtedly the impulse to over-pack. While this chapter won't stop the urge, it can hopefully help you to make some informed decisions as to what to bring and what to leave behind.

An easy way to approach the problem is to consider what you'll have waiting for you upon arrival. Any reputable employer will provide accommodation containing the following articles: a bed frame, mattress, sheets and blankets, wardrobe or chest of drawers, table, chairs, cook top, pots, pans, cutlery, dishes, glasses, cups, kettle, fridge, TV, DVD player, mirror, washing machine and clothes drying rack.

Although most of this material will be second hand and mismatched, your basic food and shelter requirements should be covered. There isn't really much more in the homewares department that you'll need, and anything else can be purchased locally for a fraction of the cost, so save your back and dump everything domestic at your parents' place.

That said, one thing that can make the first week a little easier to handle is a good night's sleep. If you aren't the world's greatest snoozer you might want to consider importing your pillow. Of course Koreans do sell them but there's something comforting about lying down with a familiar friend. Ear plugs are also a wise investment if you tend to be troubled by barking dogs, fighting couples and noisy nightclubs.

While on the subject of sleep, sheets are another item to consider but only if you're one of those bed linen snobs who chafe at anything less than 500 threads per square inch. If you are an educated individual who knows their percale from their pima, make sure you find out what size of bed you'll be sleeping on, as most teachers end up with only a single or double bed.

Undoubtedly the most important things to bring are clothes. You don't need a whole year's worth of wardrobe, but you'll want enough respectable work wear to get you through the first month, and some casual clothes if your contract allows you to leave the school grounds after dark. On the job think neat, tidy and a little conservative. Most employers don't demand Windsor knotted ties or skirts with Victorian hemlines, but neither are they keen on ragged skater shorts and see through blouses. Likewise, no one is interested in your particular brand of underwear or bra, so buy a belt and save the spaghetti straps for clubbing in Seoul. (For more information please read the chapter entitled 'Thou shalt not wear old clothes'.)

South Korea experiences the classic four seasons, so if you're coming from a sunny location you might want to pack some warm clothes, but don't go crazy buying gear, as you'll pick up jackets and gloves for a lot less when you get there. Winters can get down to minus 20°C, however minus 5°C is much more common. Summer temperatures average in the mid to high 20s but can climb into the 30s come August. That might not seem particularly hot, but with monsoon rains and a million rice paddies the humidity can make you feel like you're marinating in your own sweat. A simple climactic guide is:

- Spring—cool, sunny, a little rain
- Summer—hot, uncomfortably humid, a lot of rain
- Autumn—crisp, clear, sunny
- Winter—cold, clear, snow in some locations

Again the indigenous people of the peninsula do wear clothes, so unless you exist outside the bell curve when it comes to body shape or size you can replace most items in Korea. Anyone who is very tall or large will have difficulty finding clothes to fit them. The same goes for shoes, wide as well as long. Ladies who require bras larger than Ds are advised to come prepared.

Cosmetics and toiletries are something else to think about, as most Korean products are designed with local complexions and concerns in mind. You probably don't want a moisturiser that contains a skin bleaching component. Likewise it may be difficult to purchase sanitary products that are 100% organic, non-bleached, unscented cotton. Ditto for deodorant that can handle foreign funk. In Seoul's big department stores you'll find imported cosmetics, toiletries and perfumes but they're prohibitively expensive, so you might want to arrange for a care package to be mailed part way through the year.

The following true story is an example of why it's a good idea to bring a little backup. A certain teacher once ran out of toothpaste and had to go shopping for a local alternative. He unfortunately chose a herbal brand made from powdered bamboo and found to his amazement that it smelled exactly like dog feces blended with mint. This was probably an anomaly, but if you know that Colgate Gel or Lady Speed Stick is integral to your daily grooming routine then don't leave it to chance.

Medications fall into the same basket. As long as you enter the country with a valid prescription and what you're carrying isn't 2,000 tablets of Valium you should be fine. Things like Epi-Pens, acid reflux reducers or acne medications are all examples of things more easily brought than bought in South Korea. So for the sake of both simplicity and safety, visit your doctor before you leave.

Electronics are generally fine, but if you're not a member of the 220-240 volt club then you'll need to check all of your electronic devices to make sure that they're compatible. If they aren't there's a good chance you'll end up with an expensive fire starter, so check the label in regards to input. Most modern rechargeable battery operated gadgets are designed for international travel but it's best to read the fine print. Anything that can't handle the juice will need a converter, thus it's best just to leave your hair dryer at home.

Everybody, regardless of voltage, will need to bring travel plug adapters so they can access the power. These plugs are available in Korea but they can be a real pain in the ass when it comes to finding the right socket combinations, so pick them up before you leave. Computers, tablets, cameras, e-books and music players should all be fine but mobile phones generally won't work or if they do, the roaming fees will be outrageous.

Gifts are good. Everybody likes them and they're a great way to ingratiate yourself with the boss. Think distinctive local produce. For Canadians that means anything maple flavoured, Aussies could bring chocolate covered macadamia nuts and Kiwis need look no further than a nice fluffy sheepskin. The rest of you will have to come up with your own ideas.

A photo album or PowerPoint presentation consisting of family, friends and your local environment is a great way for students and co-workers to gain a deeper understanding of who you are and where you come from. Like everybody else on this screwy planet, Koreans can have some pretty strange ideas about foreign places and cultures. This is one way to open their eyes and let them see that the similarities are greater than the differences.

If working with kids it's a good idea to bring heaps of flashy stickers as rewards for good behavior and excellent work. These can usually be had for a few bucks at your local dollar store. Hold off on buying bigger purchases like board games or flashcards until you've had the opportunity to talk with someone on staff, as there's no point duplicating what they've already got.

Little treats for you aren't a bad idea either. A jar of Vegemite, a kilo bag of Reese's Pieces or a duty free bottle of Baileys can help take the edge off a day spent fighting the evil forces of kindergarten. They also come in handy when trying to lure a love interest into your lair, though to be honest a spread made from brewer's yeast probably has limited appeal compared to chocolate or alcohol.

Things have changed dramatically over the last decade when it comes to accessing foreign food, so you no longer need to import the contents of your spice rack or 40 boxes of Mini Wheats. Most larger cities now have Western owned and stocked supermarkets that carry a variety of familiar products.

Books come in two distinct categories—those for work and those for pleasure. Education-related publications can be anything from ESL textbooks to esoteric epistles dedicated to the finer points of grammar. Bring whatever you feel is necessary, but remember that between the school library, your fellow teachers and the internet, most questions can be answered. As for pleasure it can be difficult to source new books outside of the major cities. Of course many of you will be digitally literate and have access to thousands of titles online, but for those who aren't yet ready to abandon the printed page it's a good idea to bring some new material for the community slush pile.

Even though you've come for a job you'll need to bring some money, about $1,000 cash, or a credit card. This will ensure financial liquidity until your first payday, which will be at least a month away. That may sound like a lot of dough but it's better to have too much than too little during the early days.

Sports equipment is again the same refrain. Unless you are a semi-professional athlete on track for Olympic glory you're better off picking up gear when you get there. Tennis racquets, snowboards, mountain bikes and everything else under the sun are available in South Korea, so don't bring it unless it's really necessary.

With a few exceptions, this whole chapter boils down to three easy questions. Is this item essential? Will I use it? Can I buy it there? If you rigorously apply this line of reasoning to everything you're thinking of bringing you should be able to pack two bags that won't blow your luggage allowance.

Incidentally, there are a few more things that will make your trip an enjoyable and rewarding experience but they are by their very nature difficult to obtain: a sense of adventure, an open mind, a kind heart, a tolerant attitude, a practical disposition and a flexible view of the world. Luckily the conditions under which they develop are often found when you leave the safe confines of your everyday life, so don't let a few personal imperfections scare you off making the journey of a lifetime.

BUT DIRECTOR MY APARTMENT HAS FLEAS!

Yes, the title does refer to events that actually took place, only the identities have been changed to protect the innocent. If you suffer from Parasitophobia, an unreasonable fear of parasites, you are strongly advised to skip this chapter and go make yourself a cup of tea, preferably with cream and lots of sugar.

Once upon a time in Korea, a certain teacher crawled into bed only to find he could sense minute movements beneath the sheets, as if someone was sprinkling his naked body with a tiny salt shaker. He turned on the light, conducted a thorough inspection but found nothing. He chalked it up to work-related stress, laid back down and drifted off into a somewhat broken sleep.

Over the course of a few days the nightly disturbances grew worse. Sleep became impossible and he had to accept the evidence at hand; either he was going mad or his bed was infested with some kind of invisible vermin. He foolishly asked his boss for local insight regarding the mysterious midnight visitors. A rather cool reply informed him that parasites only appeared in the rooms of exceptionally dirty Westerners and that extermination by chemical means was the lone solution.

With that resounding stamp of disapproval, he wandered off to the local family drugstore to make his shameful purchases. He bought a can of environmentally friendly insect spray recommended by the curious clerk and headed home, confident that his problems would soon be over.

He diligently stripped the sheets and washed them on the hot cycle. He held his breath, squinted his eyes and saturated the apartment in slow even strokes until the can was empty and his eyes were burning.

That night he slept undisturbed, blissful in his unbroken solitude, but within a few days the invisible invaders had returned. This time he didn't give a damn about his reproductive health, or that old hag Mother Nature, and took home for himself the most toxic product he could find. A sinister contraption the size of a grapefruit, the self-proclaimed 'Bug Mega Bomb' was painted army green, covered in grimacing skulls and came with a long list of warnings regarding pregnant women, nursing babies and goldfish.

Following the directions exactly, he removed the plastic and vinyl items from the room due to their propensity to combust on contact with the fumes, disposed of all foodstuffs, set his plants on the porch, sealed the windows with tape, pulled the pin and spent the next 24 hours in a nearby hotel waiting for the carcinogen levels to reach minimum third world standards.

Upon return, the issue seemed resolved and the blurry vision, blinding headaches and random diarrhea attacks seemed a small price to pay for a bug free boudoir. However within days the enemy rallied, and his resounding victory proved merely to be a temporary respite in the battle for the bed. The life force that had colonized his room was evidently resistant to chemical attack and able to regenerate its numbers at a staggering rate.

Each night was a haze of agonized scratching, and with little sleep the students were beginning to wear him down. Their inane questions and nervous smiles began to grate upon his nerves and he knew without a doubt that if he did not find an answer soon he would snap in spectacular fashion, no doubt going postal with a ruler in one hand and a whiteboard marker in the other.

But where could he turn? What else could he do? The store bought stuff just wasn't working, and though he desperately longed for sleep he wasn't yet prepared to douse his bed in kerosene or buy black market DDT from the local rice farmers.

Perhaps he was just crazy, suffering from some kind of unknown psychosis or stress induced delusion. He'd heard of drug addicts feeling cockroaches burrowing beneath their scabby hides, why not tiny invisible ants that emerged only at night to dance on the beds of insane English teachers? Maybe Nancy Reagan had been right, maybe he should have just said no. Those hazy weekends spent watching foreign films and gorging on nachos didn't seem so funny now.

At a loss one night and searching for some kind of solace, he decided to head up onto the roof to enjoy the moonlight and contemplate his strange situation. Imagine his surprise when he opened the door to find several dozen scrawny chickens roosting directly above his apartment.

Eureka! A close inspection in the morning revealed that the nesting boxes were positioned around a drain that ran down from the roof and passed directly through his kitchen. It appeared that bird lice were marching down in their hundreds and entering his apartment through a gap between the pipes, which explained why they reappeared no matter how much poison he pumped into the place. A few dollars spent on silicon sealant and visiting hours were over, though his boss seemed somewhat disappointed to learn that poultry, not racial inferiority, was the source of infestation.

The point of this story isn't to suggest that you need to scope out the roof of your new abode for covert poultry farms, (though it probably wouldn't hurt), but rather to drive home the point that anything can happen when it comes to housing in the land of the morning calm.

The first thing you need to accept in order to understand the various accommodation issues that plague teachers in Korea is that supplying you with a place to live is a costly proposition for your employer, and he or she will do whatever they can to minimize that expense. They aren't really out to screw you; it's just not in their interests to set you up in the sweetest pad on the peninsula. What they're aiming for is the perfect compromise, a place that comes close to flouting Geneva Convention standards for prisoner housing while still offering you enough comforts to keep you in the country. This means you can forget stainless steel appliances, hand rendered stucco walls and gorgeous views of the mountains—think more along the lines of greasy gas tops, stained wallpaper and a window facing a busy intersection.

In terms of space, the average teacher's apartment is about as big as a large bedroom back home, with a minimalist kitchen and bathroom tucked away in the corners. If you're a serial soaker you're bound to be visiting hotels on a regular basis, as showers are much more common than tubs.

The good news is that almost all bathrooms come with Western toilets, so you can leave the squatting for school. Some teachers never develop the bulging thigh muscles required to carry out this operation successfully, and more than a few regularly walk home at lunch to 'rest' in the comfort of their own homes.

Most apartments come decorated in pastel pink or green wallpaper and are floored in standard issue oatmeal linoleum. The furniture is usually an eclectic mix that looks like it was scooped up during the closing minutes of a charity auction by a blind bidder. In the electronics department you'll get a TV of some description, a video or DVD player and a fan to circulate the mosquitoes if you happen to miss out on insect screens.

Your kitchenware will likely be comprised of assorted cutlery orphans, a few chipped bowls, some mismatched plates and a pot or two that last saw service cooking popcorn during the Korean War. Gas top burners are the norm and stoves are rare, as baked goods don't feature prominently in Korean cuisine. If you do strike it lucky and get a place with an oven, you can look forward to making friends or enemies depending on how far your charity extends when it comes to sharing freshly baked treats. Fridges come in two types, either immaculate new energy efficient models that still smell like the showroom, or rattling monstrosities that need to be chained down at night so they don't shift and crush you in your sleep.

If you end up living within a few blocks of your school you can count yourself lucky. This isn't so much an issue in smaller country towns, but those in larger urban areas may find the distance between home and work to be a gross abuse of the phrase 'a short stroll'. Before you take a job, talk with past and current employees about everything, including your accommodation and its location, as the quality of your life away from the job is important too.

Koreans don't seem to have any problems with second hand noise, so accordingly, local architects and builders have given the subject little thought when it comes to designing and constructing apartments. It might be wise to bring some earplugs, as echoing down your hallway at all times of the day and night will be the sounds of your neighbors above, beside and below you engaged in every possible activity. Fighting, farting, snoring, skipping, screaming, barking, crying and hearty humping are just some of the acoustic delights you'll encounter.

Staying warm isn't a problem, due to the radiant floor heating system used in Korea. This is where hot water is circulated through the floor in pipes, keeping everything toasty warm. After walking back from work on a cold winter's day, there's nothing quite like coming home and lying down on the floor to soak up the heat. Caution is advised though, as some floors are hot enough to melt candy bars in your pockets, kill your plants and boil your guppies but they're just about perfect for fermenting yogurt or running a small home brew operation.

The only real disadvantage is that if they have been turned off or up too high, they can take quite a while to heat back up or cool down. Koreans are quite proud of this modern twist on their traditional heating system, so be careful what you have to say about it. A newly arrived teacher once left her hosts speechless by declaring that her uncle 'had floors just like these on his ostrich farm.'

Summer can get unbearably hot, but you'll have to make do without air conditioning unless you want to pay for it yourself, though it may be worth trying to convince your boss to share the costs, as he'll inherit the setup once you're gone. Most other mortals survive the stifling hot summer nights by taking cold showers, turning on their portable fans and dragging their beds over to the window.

As for mod cons like cable TV, telephones, computer access and state of the art sound systems, they are available in Korea, just don't expect your employer to provide them. If they do, say three Hail Mary's and don't tell a soul about your good fortune. Even if you miss out on a benevolent boss, the majority of school owners will usually help you navigate the bureaucratic labyrinth of forms and fees that must be mastered in order to get anything hooked up.

Most school owners aren't really evil; they're just trying to save a few won, as the following story illustrates only too well. A couple of teachers once had a pretty good boss and the apartments they had were quite the catch. They were situated only a few blocks from work, and were spacious, open plan arrangements with plenty of natural light. They had terracotta floors, walls paneled in honey tinged pine and a large roof top balcony that overlooked the local Russian strippers' apartment, where the poor girls liked to sun bake after a hard night of dancing. Word soon got out about its enviable ambiance, and other teachers would often drop by just to savor a beer, marvel at the decor and appreciate the view.

When the boys learned of plans to build a new school with self contained teacher accommodation they were naturally disappointed. They knew the Russians were not transferable, so they spoke of how the wood paneling was the talk of the town and a pleasure to behold. Their Director told them that he appreciated their input and that he'd pay extra attention to the interior design of the new apartments.

As the moving date grew closer, so too did the boys' sense of unease. They knew their Director was a good guy, but they also understood that the construction was a big investment, and that something like their precious wood paneling might easily be forgotten.

After a few restless nights they mustered up their courage and confronted him, demanding to know how the decorating was proceeding. Smiling smugly, he assured them that all was well, and that he'd secured a special type of wood paneling that was actually cheaper than the tongue and groove pine that currently graced their lives. 'Ominous' was all they could say when they left the meeting, especially in regards to his use of the words 'special' and 'cheaper'.

They had good reason to be wary, as when they moved they were greeted by a decorating scheme that was hard to comprehend, let alone actually look at. The walls and ceilings of every apartment had been paneled in chipboard and carefully coated in high gloss Shellac. Imagine if you can a million golden flakes of pine all randomly flashing beneath the might of a single megawatt bulb. It was a retinal assault of unprecedented power, and one that those teachers would never forget.

After reading this you're no doubt worried and probably wondering if it can get any worse. It can. This is because the accommodation issues mentioned so far have only pertained to the lucky buggers who live in single apartments. All kinds of other strange and harrowing problems may arise but no matter what else happens they're captain and commander once they cross the threshold and return to the privacy of their quarters.

Others are not so fortunate because they failed to consider the words "shared accommodation" in their contract. For God's sake don't let this happen to you! Whatever falsehoods they tell you, whatever lies or fairytales they fabricate, don't believe it for a minute. It's all bullshit, nothing more than a crafty attempt by your employer to save money.

Anyone who has ever lived in a shared house knows the frustrations. The last bottle of beer vanishes without a trace, your favorite cereal disappears before breakfast and milk levels drop quicker than the Nile in summer. Under normal circumstances these things would be annoying, but here in Korea it's a recipe for murder. Could you honestly resist throttling your roommate if you woke in the middle of the night to find the greedy cow stuffing your last home baked cookie into her quivering cakehole?

Then there's everything else; bad music, body odor, shaving scum around the sink, singing in the shower, stray toe nail clippings, unwashed dishes, tumbleweeds of pubic hair and worst of all, the disgusting sounds of lovemaking as you lie alone in your own empty bed.

Oh and the cleaning, let's not forget the cleaning! How many conventional marriages have been torn apart by the issue of household hygiene, let alone the bizarre polygamy that is group habitation? It's bad enough having to negotiate cleaning duties with loved ones, but it is moral and spiritual suicide to do it with the people you work with. It doesn't matter what you're like or where you stand, it always ends in tears.

Positions become polarized and in someone else's eyes you're either a sanitation Nazi high on bleach, or a filthy pig that would rather roll in its own feces than clean the bathroom. OK, perhaps that last one was a bit extreme, but if you value your mental health you'd do well to steer clear of any job that that mentions shared accommodation.

So now you're probably thinking that shared housing is the worst it can get, but you'd be wrong, horribly, sadly, wrong. Picture, if you can, the following hypothetical situation: a new school owner so determined to save money and make his business venture a success that he organizes for his first teacher a special 'cultural home-stay program'.

That's right, the poor new chum has unknowingly traded her own loving parents and large suburban home for a group of weird strangers in a cramped apartment. They will count on her to be home every night for dinner, tutor the children on demand and never stay out past midnight. They'll expect her to eat rice at every meal, help with the cleaning and accompany them to church on Sunday like some prize winning show pooch.

Throw in the possibility of a drunk husband and a hormonally deranged teenager determined to set up a secret webcam and you may begin to see why this is not a good idea. Again this is merely a hypothetical situation, but most teachers would agree that it is far better to suffer the odd bout of homesickness alone than go mad living with the locals.

Admittedly there are exceptions to these rules but they are few and far between. A small number of Hagwon owners have clued in to the fact that happy teachers finish their contracts, and go out of their way to ensure that the accommodation they provide is both comfortable and appealing to Western tastes but they are sadly in the minority.

The level of respect and associated creature comforts you receive also relates to what's known as the totem pole effect. This is where the new teachers get the oldest TVs and worst apartments, whilst the weirdo long lifers get whatever they want from their grateful employers. Those working for international schools, universities and private corporations receive bigger, better, and much more wholesome housing than the plebs down in Hagwon town, so consider aiming high when you apply for your first job.

Hopefully this chapter hasn't scared you off teaching English in Korea, because the place has many things to offer the adventurous soul. There are all kinds of opportunities for personal growth, spiritual discovery and financial reward, just remember that none of them are worth trading away the right to live alone in a crappy, one room apartment. It's completely legitimate to love your workmates but nobody in their right mind should have to live with them, so stay strong and always demand a womb of one's own.

CULTURE SHOCK OR SHOCKING CULTURE

Korea is not like home. This may seem a pretty obvious statement to make, but far too many people assume that living here for a year will be no different from taking a job in Sydney or New York. Just because the younger generation likes to wear Western clothes, play computer games and eat junk food doesn't mean that you're going to fit in or feel comfortable. This is one country where you will always be the outsider.

Anyone who lives in a foreign culture for an extended length of time goes through a period of personal adjustment, and it's not just nerds and losers who get wacked with the homesick stick. Culture shock happens to everybody. The important thing is to recognize the symptoms, understand why it occurs, and possess the tools to manage it. If you don't know how to do these things, there's a very good chance you'll be buying an early ticket home.

The term culture shock was coined by the anthropologist Kalvero Oberg in an attempt to describe his own feelings in reaction to being immersed in a foreign cultural environment. Culture shock describes the mix of negative emotions that are often felt when a person leaves the security and emotional safety of their own culture to live in another.

The most common feeling experienced is that of anxiety, of not knowing what to do and how to do it. Simple acts like accessing your bank account, ordering a meal or shopping for groceries can become daunting tasks. Even the most self assured and confident person can find themselves stressing out big time over something that wouldn't even merit a swear word back home.

As culture shock deepens, it may be expressed in more visceral emotive responses. People may find themselves feeling inadequate, depressed, angry and resentful. They may experience physical symptoms such as stomach aches, insomnia, muscle pain and headaches. They may begin to display certain behaviors that are indicative of the stress, uncertainty and emotional discomfort they are experiencing. These include, but are not limited to, denigrating the local culture, idealizing home and family, withdrawing from social interaction, making stereotypical or racist remarks, drinking excessively and worrying unduly about health and cleanliness.

Culture shock often occurs as a series of stages, though of course not everyone will experience the same stages in the same order, nor will the duration and severity of any one stage be identical to anyone else's. Your personality, life experiences, finances, education and outlook on life will all play a part in how you're affected and how you respond.

The first stage is often referred to as the honeymoon period. During this time everything about your new home will seem amazing. The people will seem incredibly genuine and friendly, the food tasty, the scenery exotic and the customs charming. Everything about Korea will be more interesting and exciting than the boring old life you left behind. You may feel sorry for your friends back home and wonder why it took you so long to make the break. Many people liken this early stage to being high or falling in love, due to the feelings of euphoria and excitement that accompany it.

The second stage is the one that most people associate with culture shock. This phase is usually characterized by feelings such as annoyance, frustration, anger, loneliness, melancholy, inadequacy, and vulnerability. These emotional responses arise due to an individual's inability to function smoothly in a foreign culture. Most often they emanate from a person's inability to communicate their wants and needs effectively due to the language barrier.

Compounding this communication divide is an absence of cultural knowledge. The newcomer doesn't know all the unspoken rules that govern daily life and often feels unsure about themselves and their actions. Without understanding why something happens you can feel powerless to avoid it reoccurring. This can quickly result in the mistaken belief that the new rules don't make any sense. People at this point often begin to use the familiar standards of home to make unfavorable comparisons in regards to the local culture.

A common symptom during this stage can be deep feelings of loneliness and isolation, otherwise known as homesickness. Many people, especially men, are surprised by the intensity of these episodes. You might think that this kind of thing only affects women or slender guys in Mohair sweaters but it can knock around the biggest blokes with ease.

To top things off you're forced to operate under these trying circumstances without your usual support network. Far from friends and family, you lack the emotional safety net that's often taken for granted. The absence of a sympathetic ear, a cup of tea and a dozen chocolate biscuits cannot be underestimated when it comes to dealing with the injustices of life.

The third stage is marked by a positive swing away from these negative emotions towards a more balanced outlook on life. The individual begins to 'get' some aspects of their new home and experiences a corresponding sense of achievement and security. You start to feel more positive and are better equipped to respond with humor to situations that before might have resulted in feelings of anger or hostility.

You begin to believe that you're capable of successfully navigating the challenges of the new environment and find yourself less likely to criticize circumstances you don't understand. You're able to look beyond your own immediate situation and recognize that other people are experiencing similar problems.

The fourth stage is really just a continuation of the third, but at a deeper level. The individual becomes proficient in adapting to new situations, accepts that they'll continue to make mistakes and finds their own place of balance within the existing social structure. You understand that your new home has both positive and negative aspects and acknowledge that it isn't better or worse, just different.

It's only through this ongoing cultural and social integration that the individual begins to feel at home. One sign of this deepening emotional security and sense of connection is that you stop viewing life in terms of just getting through the day and instead begin to set long term goals. A good indicator is that you're motivated to take up new interests or hobbies that are part of the local culture.

Another is when you feel less of a need to associate with other expatriates. This may cause some ill feelings, but a sure sign that you've kicked culture shock is the fact that you no longer feel the need to spend every moment of your free time anaesthetized in the local pub discussing the stupidity of Koreans.

The fifth stage won't be felt until you've left the country, and it's much more common if you have been away for a couple of years.

It's known as reverse culture shock, and people say that this is the one that really gets you because no one expects to feel out of place where they 'belong'.

You hop on a plane at the end of your contract and all you can think about are the things you'll do when you get home. The first few days seem a blur as you eat and drink in the company of friends and family. It's only after the dust settles that you notice things are a little strange.

Everything is the same and yet everything is different. Firm handshakes feel oafish, pouring your own drink seems rude and nobody appreciates a good bow. People don't wave in the street because you're blonde, nobody wants to take your photo, and being an English teacher does shit all when it comes to impressing members of the opposite sex. Everyone seems fatter, whiter and hairier than you remember. The fabled homeland of yore ain't quite so rosy once you're back living in it.

You know you're experiencing reverse culture shock when you head down to Chinatown just to be with people who don't look weird. You know it's bad when you want Kimchi and rice for breakfast. You know it's chronic when you'd rather hang out in the local Korean grocery store cracking jokes than spend time at home. Again, the thing to remember is that this too shall pass.

Now you're familiar with the five stages of the beast, the next thing you need to know is how to triumph over it. One of the secrets is staying fit. You wouldn't attempt to tackle Everest unless you were in top form, and you'll have a similar advantage in Korea if you keep your mind and body in good condition.

Run, swim, walk, wiggle—do whatever it takes to keep the blood moving and the body grooving on those most excellent endorphins. The same goes for the brain. Find some way to relax and get out of the stress zone. Read a book, listen to music, meditate, medicate or masturbate, (it doesn't really matter) the key is just to get off that mental hamster wheel for a few moments every day.

Learn the language. You don't have to become fluent, but getting a handle on the local lingo will make life easier and much more interesting. Attending some language lessons is a great way to speed up the process, with the added benefit of meeting other people in the same boat. Just knowing that you aren't the only one out there can make a big difference when it comes to getting through the week.

Speaking Korean will give you a definite advantage when it comes to dealing successfully with a variety of stressful situations. It will help you bargain in the street, ask for directions, control your students, butter up the boss, order take away, sweet talk the opposite sex and psych out opportunistic taxi drivers.

Just remember to give it some time. Things won't magically get better but they will improve with every passing day. Be patient, both with yourself and others. Relax. Don't expect to understand everything or for others to know exactly how you're feeling. Be reasonable. It takes months to feel comfortable at home when you move locations, why should it be any less painful when you move half way around the globe?

Get outside. Don't lock yourself away in your room, as this just compounds those feelings of loneliness and isolation. Meet some people. Make some friends. Go out with other expats and have some fun in the sun.

On the same note, try to find a way in which you can interact with Koreans outside of school hours. Go bowling, attend church, join a hiking club, study Tae Kwan Do or volunteer in the local community. Go forth and investigate Korean life, so you can identify all the things that you have in common with the locals, instead of focusing on all the superficial differences.

Be kind to yourself. If something is stressful and emotionally tiring, consider not exposing yourself to that situation until you feel better prepared to deal with it. If your first trip on Seoul's metro is a claustrophobic nightmare, then be smart and look over the free map a few times before you next attempt to perform a solo circumnavigation of the city during rush hour.

Keep in contact with friends and loved ones back home. It may be painful to hear their voices but it will help you get through the hard times if you have someone who genuinely wants to listen to your problems. That said, don't spend every moment of the day pouring your pain down the receiver or you'll miss out on all the amazing opportunities this country has to offer.

Don't deny your emotions. Be willing to accept the sadness and loneliness you feel but don't get caught in a self enforcing mind melt. Remember that you always have the ability to alter your perceptions. Try to look at your situation from different angles and salute the fact that you're actually here. You pulled up stakes from a comfortable life and stepped outside the box to do something quite amazing. You're living in Korea, and no matter what else happens you got yourself here and that's something to be proud of.

Review all of your past hardships and remember your successes. Chances are the most meaningful moments in your life were not the easiest of achievements. It's usually the ones where you suffer a little that prove to be the most rewarding. True growth comes not from comfort and familiarity but through challenge and discovery.

Too many people flee Korea after only a few months. This needn't be the case. Armed with the knowledge and wisdom inscribed within this veritable tome of information, you have everything you need to overcome the inevitable bout of culture shock. Make some friends, get active and before you know it you'll be surprised you ever wanted to go home.

SO SHELL FOE PAWS

Mistakes are part of life, and when living overseas some of the easiest ones you can make are those that arise from cultural differences. Coming in cold means that you have the potential to commit numerous social faux pas on a daily basis. While the information contained within this chapter is by no means encyclopedic, it will hopefully allow you to avoid most of the basic mistakes. They aren't arranged in any particular order due to the fact that all of them can get you into trouble.

Let's start with the body.

Blowing your nose is bad. Adjectives like horrid and revolting are applicable when the act is carried out in public, especially during a meal. It marks you out as a cultural cretin, an oaf and an idiot. The basic rule to remember is if you gotta blow, you gotta go. Just get up and head to the bathroom, because if you do it in the presence of Koreans eating you will make them physically ill. (Of course snorking up a nasty nasal drip or spitting in a cup doesn't exactly spell sophistication either but the issue at hand is your table manners not theirs.)

If you can't give up the blow, restrict the habit to disposable tissues in private, and don't even think about carrying around a crusty handkerchief unless you're comfortable with the term 'filthy barbarian'. The way Koreans regard the snot rag is akin to how Westerners might feel towards the concept of reusable toilet paper.

This charming introductory topic leads on to the wonderful world of spitting. If you hack back some mucky mucus, the accepted local response is to spit it out on the nearest patch of pavement, as understandably nobody wants to swallow the stuff. (Of course nobody really wants to step in it either, but that problem is neatly addressed through a shoe taboo that you'll learn about shortly.)

Try not to become visibly upset when you encounter a spit fest on your way to work, as most people don't consider what they're doing to be offensive. The habit is so engrained that some countries have even put up signs in their airport arrival areas reminding Korean tourists that spitting is unhygienic.

Unfortunately these saliva storms only intensify during the winter months, when it seems like half the nation's smokers are in the process of expelling a lung. The cold, dry air irritates the bronchial tubes, predisposing the body to longer and more violent bouts of coughing. Watch out for the shiny patches of yellow ice that dot the footpaths as they're slipperier than hell in a pair of leather soled shoes.

This phlegm filled wonderland explains why wearing street footwear inside a Korean house is such a no-no. Most people in the West don't appreciate crusty trainers tramping across their shag either, but in Korea it's even more disgusting because many people sit and sleep on the floor. To help get a lock on the Korean mindset, just imagine how you'd feel if you caught some guests jumping on your bed in their muddy shoes.

Always remember to take off your footwear without exception unless you're told differently. This goes not just for homes but also temples, churches, restaurants and other intimate interior public spaces. If in doubt just look for the mound of shoes near the entrance.

Bare chests are another area that needs to be discussed. Asians in general have a modesty taboo that prohibits the flaunting of the flesh in public, be it men or women. Sure there are places where you'll see more than you bargained for, like the hot baths for example, but that is expected behavior in an acceptable location amongst the same sex. This doesn't mean you have to wear an overcoat when swimming at the beach, it just means that you should follow the lead set by the locals.

Whipping the old shirt off just because you're baking in the sun at a sporting event is no excuse to inflict your hairy beer gut on Korean society. The same goes for that teeny, tiny sports bra/top you brought for jogging. While it might be perfectly acceptable back home to show off your ironing board abs, it isn't here.

Don't point with your index finger. If you need to indicate something, use your whole hand. The same goes for calling someone over. The polite way to do so is to put the hand out, with the palm facing down, and then raise and lower it at the wrist. If you do it with the index finger or palm out and up, you're giving the command reserved for animals, which is never a good idea when seeking to establish a respectful relationship with your students.

The 'got your nose trick' with the thumb between the fingers is another banned hand action. That particular arrangement of digits has its own unsavory meaning, and performing it for the Kindie kids will not endear you to their parents.

The act of eating is an important part of Korean life, and as such there are more than a few practical considerations to be aware of. While none of them are on par with the left handed Indian food fiasco, knowing how to avoid them will help to ease your way into Korean society.

After a meal don't pick your teeth openly, as it's considered disrespectful, especially in front of older people. The Korean method still requires the same action but it involves tactfully turning away and covering your mouth while you are engaged in locating the offending material. By playing out this social charade you're saying "I know this is rude, but please bear with me until this unpleasant business is concluded."

Another interesting one is not to walk while eating. To fail to do so says, "I am too busy to stop, nor do I care about how I look to others." Of course you'll see Koreans doing it occasionally but people generally don't eat while on the go. With a busy teaching schedule you sometimes won't have a choice, but at least you'll know why people are looking at you strangely.

Koreans are big on sharing. Which is generally a good thing, unless you're a bit of a germ phobe. They'll dip into the same bowl of soup and swig away from the communal cup without a second thought, so be prepared for some hurt feelings if you feel strongly about not imbibing group saliva.

After a big meal, don't lie down or sit with your legs pointing out in front of you towards other diners. This again spells disrespect, especially in the presence of the boss or those more senior to you. Sit up with your legs crossed or folded under you. If you find your legs ache when you sit on the floor for extended periods of time, grab more than one cushion at the start of the meal. Admittedly, it will look a bit odd when you do your Princess and the Pea routine, but comfortable eccentricity beats disrespect any day.

There will be Korean behaviors that annoy you, even when they are born out of a desire to treat you as an honored guest. One of these is not being allowed to cook the meat at the barbeque table. Koreans will see it as their job to cut, flip and cook the marinated manna and will struggle with the concept of letting you get in on the action. This is because to them it says, "I did not fulfill my responsibilities and obligations. I am such a crappy host that I let my guests do the cooking."

Basic rule of thumb is let them take care of it in the beginning, but once you're friends it's time to take back the tongs. Bringing a choice strip of mouth watering meat to its perfect moment is a joy that must be experienced directly. Letting someone else do all the grilling just isn't living up to your potential.

The same rules apply when it comes to paying the bill. Don't fight the boss when it's time to settle, but be sure to take your turn at the register when it's a meal between friends or if you've organized the outing. To pay for the meal is an honor, to avoid it is a disgrace. And don't even think about trying to split the bill, as this will only insult your fellow diners and confuse the serving staff.

Superstitions are another area where it's easy to offend. While many of these beliefs may seem old fashioned, strange or downright ridiculous, they still possess the power to disconcert even the most Westernized Koreans. Relatively speaking they're no different from the crazy things people believe in back home. Everybody knows at some abstract level that these kinds of events don't have any logical effect on future outcomes, but that doesn't stop you from choosing to walk around ladders as opposed to going under them.

It's the same with Koreans. While they might not consciously believe in superstitions, they aren't exactly thrilled about you doing some bad ju-ju in their presence. Knowing which things to steer clear of saves you the trouble of having to work out for yourself why the room has gone ominously silent.

Many of these beliefs relate to death, as in the case of the missing fourth floor. The number four sounds like the word death, thus a simple homonym becomes responsible for the fact that many buildings, especially hospitals and hotels, have no floor that corresponds with the number four. Of course it's still there, but skipping an ordinal allows everyone to avoid saying that particular word. This seems quite reasonable when you think about it, as nobody really wants their sick child to spend the night on the 'death floor'. The same thinking applies to those on their honeymoon.

Ditto for writing people's names in red. It doesn't matter whether it's to mark the roll or to make a list on the whiteboard, it's a deeply disturbing action. This interesting phenomenon comes from the fact that red ink was, and still is, used to record the names of the deceased in family registers. Thus when you scribble a late students name in red you are basically stating to the whole class that you wish they were dead. While this may temporarily relieve the stress that arises from teaching middle school classes, it's not recommended as an effective technique to influence student punctuality.

Another deadly blunder is sticking your chopsticks upright in the rice bowl. This should be avoided as it resembles the sticks of incense that are burned during funerals and at the altars of the deceased. If you're finished and haven't eaten all your rice, just lay your chopsticks on the table where they belong.

When you give a present don't expect the person to open it in front of you and remember to behave in a similar manner when you receive one. This cultural behavior ensures that neither party is made to feel uncomfortable or embarrassed by the gift or the reaction to it. The correct response is to politely thank the person for their thoughtfulness and open it later in private. This may initially prove difficult but you're more than a Manchurian Candidate activated by the sound of rustling paper.

Handshakes are a social nicety, not a testosterone fueled crushing contest to prove who is compensating for the smallest penis. Nor are they a chance to practice your patented dead fish grip. A gentle but firm handshake is all that is required. The only major difference in Korea is that the left hand gets to be involved. While you are shaking with the right, the left comes across so that the left palm cups the underside of the right forearm. The shake usually occurs simultaneously with a bow.

The bow should hold the middle ground. It is not a head banging exercise intended to please Ozzy Osborne, rather it is a slight bending of the back and neck, as if you were leaning forward to inspect some medals pinned on your grandfather's chest. Age and status should be taken into account when planning the bow. Meeting the nation's president or your new boss necessitates a considerably deeper and longer motion than becoming acquainted with your teenage neighbor.

Like the rest of Asia, it's a good idea to forgo intimate displays of affection between the sexes in public. New acquaintances should not receive Euro style kisses. Hearty back slaps and bear hugs are probably not cool either. The same goes for touching people's heads—including the ruffling of children's hair. The head is important because traditionally it was seen as the house of the spirit, so unauthorized melon fondling is strictly forbidden.

Special rules apply to monks, nuns and temples. Place your hands together when you bow to a monk or nun and avoid positioning your body higher than them. Don't sit with your feet facing a religious statue or person and enter via the side door of a temple instead of the middle one. Never step on the door lintel when you enter a temple.

Women should avoid being alone with monks and refrain from touching them. When giving monks something, women should not hand it over directly, but instead place the object on a table or pass it via a man. Keep your voice down, dress respectfully and don't even think about sampling those delicious offerings.

Keep your cool. This is one area where foreigners consistently come unstuck. When you lose it on a Korean you also lose respect and any chance of a satisfactory resolution. It's perfectly ok to be unhappy, annoyed or all out angry, the trick is to express yourself in a controlled, culturally acceptable manner. Polite negotiation will always get you further than heated confrontation.

Part of the challenge in keeping your cool is the damned smiling. When Koreans are embarrassed, in the wrong, or don't have a clue, they smile to express such feelings. This can easily be misinterpreted, so it's important when you see that cheesy smile to remember that they're not laughing at you.

A good example is the all too common bicycle accident. A car door opens unexpectedly and halts your journey. You're left bleeding on the ground, surrounded by your damaged groceries. The adrenaline kicks in and you're angry as hell. The nimrod driver then picks up the crumpled remains of your bike and hands it to you with a stupid grin.

At this point you have a choice. You can rearrange the offending dental work or you can deal with it civilly. Please select B. Point out his error, get his license, call the police but do not scream, hit, bite or otherwise attack the moron. To do so will only result in you being charged with assault and him getting off scot free, as the police always side with the locals in cases of physical violence.

The same advice applies to employment issues. Freaking out on the boss in front of other staff members will not magically produce your late pay or cancel that new conversation class. Go in calmly and discuss it privately but don't do anything to cause a loss of face. Try to reach an agreement by pointing out your concerns and grievances but be ready to compromise.

In the end these kinds of working relationships aren't about winning or losing, they're about long term survival and happiness. Instead of getting indignant, it's sometimes better just to keep track of favors rendered and collect them when the time is right, because there will come a day when you want to borrow the school van or get a cash advance on your next pay check. It sounds strange to say, but people sometimes forget that they're living in a different culture and operating under a different set of rules.

With these things in mind you should be able to get through your first few months without alienating the people around you. Chances are you're still going to say or do something offensive, but keep in mind that Koreans are a pretty easygoing bunch. They'll cut you a fair bit of slack on account of you being an ignorant foreigner, just make sure you never make the unforgivable mistake of

CAN WE PET THE TEACHER NOW?

A wise person once noted that if at all possible, one should avoid working with animals and small children. Steering clear of wildlife in Korea isn't too hard, because essentially there isn't any left, but managing to evade Kindergarten duty may prove somewhat more of a challenge.

Unless you happen to obtain a contract that specifically states that you're to be kept at least 100 meters from children under the age of five, expect to do your share of munchkin minding. Even if you're lucky enough to enter a Kindie free zone, don't be shocked if three months down the road your boss decides to open some classes. You'll only become aware of your status as an 'Experienced Kindergarten Professor' when you see the school van drive past with your hideously enlarged passport photo surrounded by elves and dancing pandas.

The first thing you need to understand is that these kids are very young, in fact many have come to class straight from a warm boob. To complicate matters further, you may notice that the children appear tiny for their stated age. This is because Koreans are considered one year old when they're born. Yep that's right, even time spent in the womb is valid in a culture that places so much importance on age. So when the boss says that you'll be teaching four year olds, it really means you are going to be attempting to conduct a foreign language class with students who've only just stepped out of diapers.

On your first day be prepared for tears, trembling and general mental anguish, (expect similar reactions from the students). This emotional maelstrom isn't just the result of separation anxiety, though for many it will be the first time away from their mothers, it's also something much more powerful—primal fear and loathing. You have to remember that the vast majority of these kids have never before seen a face that isn't Korean. Every person that has passed before them in their admittedly short lives has had black hair, smooth skin and dark brown almond eyes.

You probably consider yourself to be a rather acceptable looking member of the human race, but to them you're a hideous monster. Just think of all the freakish genetic characteristics they've never seen; red hair, blond hair, curly hair, lifeless white skin, weird black skin, freckles, big round eyes, strange blue eyes, beaky sharp noses, beards on men, earrings on everybody, and women that weigh over one hundred pounds dry. Admit it, you're scary. You're a walking nightmare, all covered in body hair and jabbering away in some strange barbaric tongue—no wonder these kids are screaming for mama when you enter the classroom

So . . . . don't be too down on yourself at the end of day one, as a few kids will always wig out when they meet you. Smile, be patient, talk softly and they'll warm to you. Stickers, smiley stamps and the odd pocket full of candy can work wonders for your popularity during the first week or two. That said, unless you are beholden to shadowy figures in the dental underworld, try not to become overly dependant on the sugary treats.

The worst possible mistake you can make during the first few days is to believe that they will remain as they currently are; quiet, timid and reserved. You must remain vigilant and never let down your guard, for at any moment the transformation may occur. Do not let their tiny smiles and shy glances lull you into a false sense of security, for they are watching you, weighing up your every move, coolly appraising your abilities and instinctively gauging your mettle. Soon they'll realize that you are not some fiendish monster sent from hell to torment them, but just another stupid adult waiting to be twisted around their cute little thumbs.

When the change occurs, and it will, you must be a firm practitioner of tough love if you want them to actually learn anything. While it's true that they're only kids, you can't let them hijack the show. All it takes is a few gonzo classes to ruin your reputation.

If possible, have your assistant or another Korean teacher explain the ground rules in regards to classroom behavior. This will probably need to be done quite a few times during the first couple of weeks to drive the message home. Screaming, biting, hitting, drawing on the table, throwing pens, bringing toys and what ever else you think is out of line must be clearly and repeatedly explained as unacceptable. Give multiple warnings, three strikes or sad faces on the board so they can see what's coming but don't be afraid to be the 'mean' teacher. If you fail to follow up warnings with repercussions, your lessons will become nothing more than exotic daycare sessions.

One of the most effective treatments for a troublesome tot is to remove them from the room for a short period of time. This will not be an easy task as most will turn on the bilge pumps at the mere mention of banishment. Korea is the land of group activities, and even by this early age the thought of being separated from their peers is a terrible thing. For many the threat will be enough, but if they persist in their recalcitrant ways, you may have to help them help themselves. The little blighters will cry, beg and plead to be spared but you must harden your heart and walk over to the door.

If they do not heed your orders it will be time to get physical. Many of these children possess the strength of small demons and will attach their limbs to whatever provides some degree of security. Do not give in, even if it means carrying both child and chair across the threshold. Hand the little rascal over to the secretary or a passing Korean teacher and ask that they please explain to the child why they were removed from class. Return to your room and carry on the lesson. After a suitable amount of time has passed, go fetch the chastened student, smile and show them that all is forgiven.

A few expulsions to the secretarial gulag can have a marked effect on classroom discipline; just don't use it for every minor transgression. Try not to worry about the kids disliking you, as the crying child today won't hold it against you tomorrow as long as you're fair and consistent. You can also remind yourself that you're there to be the teacher and to do that job effectively you can't always be a friend.

Be flexible, patient and remember who you're dealing with. Their attention spans are only slightly longer than brain damaged hamsters, so try and keep things fresh, fun and short. You'll have better success repeating a short task three times over the span of a week than trying to keep them focused for fifty minutes on one thing. This of course doesn't apply to coloring in pictures or playing musical chairs, but the boss will wise up pretty quickly if you focus solely on those activities.

A good kindergarten class should be one where the line between playing and learning is hard to distinguish. Flashcards, mimes, songs, games, bingo, dances; all of these are part of the unique recipe that you'll perfect as time goes by. Your school will probably have a program in place and provide textbooks and other teaching supplies, but feel free to bring over your own gear, as it's up to you to keep the students happy and engaged.

Any type of game will be a winner but bear in mind that kids are insanely competitive. Ensure that when you have contests everyone feels valued, as prizes for just the winners are a sure way to get half the class crying. Children can also be quite cruel to their fellow team members if they mess up on a question, so it may be better to allow them to answer as a group or in twos. A popular reward for winning, or good behavior, is helping the teacher clean the board or being allowed to choose a friend and sing a song at the end of class.

Children in Korea under the age of five don't hear the word 'No' very often. Parents and grandparents tend to spoil them, especially the boys, because they understand that once they hit elementary school they'll be striving endlessly to meet near impossible expectations regarding study, work and responsibility for the rest of their lives. Bending to their every demand is viewed as inconsequential for family members but it spells trouble for teachers. You and your fellow Korean instructors will be responsible for bringing discipline, order and control to them for the very first time. Not surprisingly, they aren't too keen on the whole obedience program and more than a few teachers resort to bribery and intimidation.

The first month will be a traumatic period for all participants. Be firm but don't be too hard on the poor little buggers, as the shock can be highly traumatic. Paint will get spilled, tears will be shed, books will get ripped, pencils will be lost, crayons will be eaten, inky hands will ruin your pants, excited students will yell directly into your ears and one thousand other frustrating things will arise to test your patience. Take a deep breath and try to stay on top of things, but don't be embarrassed to seek Korean assistance if things get out of control, as it's much harder for the kids to ignore someone yelling in their own language.

Parents all over the world love to dress up their kids and Korea is no exception. You'll see everything from dyed hair and perms to earrings and cowboy boots. Cute is king and at times it can seem like you're hosting a Miss Punyverse competition. Try not to be too cynical, as it's just as bad back home. Instead sit back, enjoy the ride and take some pictures of your class, as once you're finished teaching it will all seem like some strange surrealist dream.

A variety of new experiences await the Kindergarten teacher, some good and others not. Unique to Korea is the Dong-chim or shit needle. This delightful little action is carried out on your unsuspecting anus. It usually occurs when you're bending over to pick up a pencil. As you expose your innocent posterior, an evil child will quickly assemble his instrument of humiliation by joining his palms and interlocking all the digits except the two index fingers, forming what appears to be a gun.

He'll then charge across the room and with pinpoint accuracy attempt to touch your tonsils via your large intestine. The only thing that will save you from a complete rectal probe will be the structural integrity of your undergarments. More than a few teachers have lost their cool after experiencing their first Dong-chim. Both male and female instructors are at an equal risk any time their backs are turned. Consider yourself warned.

Ladies can expect a few bum squeezes, titty twists and fanny pats, while hirsute gentlemen should be prepared for small fistfuls of fur to be ripped off their legs and arms at regular intervals. Both sexes can look forward to a variety of colds, flus and other respiratory infections after inadvertently being sneezed, spat and coughed upon. Other workplace hazards include partial hearing loss, ringworm and the odd bout of pink eye.

But that's not all, there's more.

Little bodies aren't exactly leak proof and sooner or later accidents will occur. If you hear a child plaintively repeating what sounds like "She, she, she!" be prepared to act immediately, as what they're actually saying is "Wee, pee, or I am in desperate need of emptying my bladder!" If you are fortunate and fleet of foot, you'll get to the toilet in time. If you fail, you will be carrying a soggy, sobbing child at arms length to the nearest Korean, usually the long suffering secretary or receptionist.

Many foreign teachers take these stoic workers for granted, and fail to give them the credit they deserve. They do everything from cleaning the bathrooms to collecting outstanding school fees with baseball bats. Considering the crap they take on a daily basis and the miserable wages they receive, all foreign staff should salute them. Flowers, chocolates and the odd iced coffee in summer won't go unappreciated by these noble creatures.

Most of the time the plumbing issue is only liquid in nature but once in a while the dreaded number two makes an appearance. A certain female teacher once entered her classroom to find one of the boys dancing vigorously on her table, much to the amusement of his fellow students. She yelled at him and a rather strange thing occurred.

Whether it was the shock of the teacher catching him or the effect of his vigorous gyrations is hard to say, but what was quite clear to all present was the firm little turd that shook loose from his pant leg and rolled across the table. After a second of shocked silence the whole room erupted into a pandemonium of screams and shouts. The rest of the lesson was futilely spent trying to get the amazed students to discuss anything other than the subject of disco poo.

Wise teachers ask before class if anyone needs to visit the restrooms, because they know that if a major bowel incident occurs there will be scant learning to be had. Far better to waste a few minutes waiting for little people to get back from the loo than running the risk of Code Brown.

It isn't all tales of woe, for there are lots of times when they're just adorable little monkeys. It can make you feel one hundred percent better when you wander into work after a weekend spent homesick and depressed, to have a class mob you at the door, squealing and pushing for the chance to hug you first.

If you live in a smaller town or city you will often see them out walking with their parents and receive a hearty scream of recognition, a frantic wave and a big smile. Sometimes at school they'll just quietly surprise you and hand over a drawing, a sticky candy or a much needed pat on the back.

There will be rare days, (God willing), when you may even get them to sit quietly on the floor and listen to a story. At times like these, your hairy arms can resemble a pair of oversized kittens, complete with attentive students calmly petting them. It is a strange thing indeed to have a couple of four year olds gently stroking your arms and softly discussing the comparative merits of animal versus teacher fur but it's certainly one to cherish.

During the long, muggy afternoons of summer, nothing beats surprising your class by announcing that you're very pleased with their behavior and you're all off to the corner shop for ice cream. An even cheaper treat for a good crew is to merely utter those well loved words, "No book today—game!" Twister, Hokey Pokey, musical chairs, flashcard races and bingo; you'll quickly learn which ones they prefer.

Western holidays such as Easter, Christmas and Halloween provide the perfect excuse for hour-long crayon binges, costume parties, mask making sessions and sing-along's. Bring a selection of Jello packets with you and make an edible rainbow or buy a cake to share with them on your birthday. Enjoy the little devils, for they can be more than just a source of migraines if you let them.

In a surprisingly short span of time the gang of hellions you took on at the start of term will begin to change, and before you know it they'll be reeling off the alphabet and counting backwards to zero. It can come as a shock to those who have never been around young children how quickly they absorb new information. Try to keep slang and profanities to a minimum, as the eager little sponges happily suck up the bad with the good and nobody wants to hear them stating that "these textbooks are shit!"

All too soon the year will draw to an end and nauseatingly cute graduation ceremonies, complete with robes and those funny little hats, will occur. Your last task will be to plan, choreograph and direct the students as they perform an endearing short play or skit. It won't be mentioned in your contract but that doesn't mean jack squat. Do it with grace and humility and you'll win the hearts of the parents and maybe even the thanks of your boss.

Kindergarten classes can be hell on wheels and more than a few teachers have brokered deals with the devil in order to avoid them. They are however a refreshing change from Soju breathing business men, so if you end up with a pack of pint sized pupils try to enjoy yourself. If nothing else they'll reinforce your thoughts concerning family planning.

SOME KIDS GOT NO TIME FOR PLAY TIME

For old Sherlock Holmes, the statement "It's elementary" meant that the case was closed, but when it comes to teaching English it's just the beginning. For many teachers, taking on elementary students ends up being the greatest challenge they ever face, and to succeed you need to be resourceful, patient and sharper than a sushi knife.

The situations that you'll encounter will be far more fiendish than anything Dr Moriarti ever imagined. For instance, just how do you simultaneously console a traumatized student who has just seen a mother hamster devour her own offspring, share one pack of crayons between a table of fighting children, and succinctly explain what two to two means on an analogue clock, all the while ignoring the obvious fact that you are being evaluated on your first day at work by a group of anxious housewives peering through the classroom window.

It won't be easy but then again what is? Elementary students are usually beyond the plumbing issues that plague kindergarten classes but that doesn't mean you're on easy street. It just means that the challenges, like the children, have grown a little bigger.

A bald Australian once sang that "some kids got no time for play time" and for most Korean children it's a pretty accurate description. The belief that English is the key to a successful future, combined with a strict Confucian outlook, has created a situation that's great in terms of employment opportunities, but terrible for the kids you'll be teaching.

The pressure on students to achieve high marks grows with every passing year, and the age limit for a carefree childhood keeps getting lower. In Korea, it's the parents who map their children's futures and all roads lead to Seoul University. The desire to keep up with the Kims and have their child attend 'The University' is intense. This means that more and more parents, (whether they can afford it or not) are enrolling their children in Hagwons at an earlier age in the belief that this will pay off scholastically. These educational academies provide after school instruction in everything from English to Art, though the majority of parents during the elementary years focus mainly on the ABCs.

If you are reading this book you're probably a card carrying member of the Hagwon fraternity or soon will be. The preceding information wasn't provided to induce feelings of guilt and self loathing over being directly involved in an industry that sucks the joy and innocence from small children. It was included so that you'll hopefully gain greater insight and understanding into the apathy, boredom and lack of appreciation your students will demonstrate during your lessons.

You can't really blame them for feeling this way, as according to all the natural laws known to man, young children at four p.m. on a balmy Tuesday afternoon in spring should be (a) roaring around on bicycles, (b) discussing the relative merits of certain toys/dolls/animals, (c) attempting to scale large trees or (d) being mindlessly enthralled with the latest computer game. What they shouldn't be is trapped in some airless concrete dungeon learning why "more beautifuller" isn't grammatically acceptable. They know that the situation is wrong. They naturally resent the injustice of being forced to learn some ridiculous language that their own parents can't speak from some foreign devil with coffee breath, all while the sun is shining and there are a thousand more interesting things to do outside.

That said, they and you have little choice in avoiding each other's company. Once you've accepted the status quo (and your first paycheck), you can move towards establishing a classroom that will teach them English and successfully deal with their educational funk at the same time.

Theoretically you could just teach dry, boring lessons straight from the text book and rely solely on your own vocal power and the threat of physical violence to ensure sullen compliance, but seeing as they get enough of that at their local public school, why not consider other possibilities. These alternatives offer sanity, pleasure, and even personal fulfillment but they do require a little extra effort on your part.

The cardinal rule to remember is that you take in and retain more information if the learning process itself is fun and meaningful. This isn't rocket science. Just look back on your own educational experiences. Which subjects fired your imagination, remained fresh and interest you to this day? Which ones made you secretly cringe and still cause an involuntary shudder to pass through your body? Teachers who create a sense of fear and anxiety cause far more damage than good, whereas those who set out to make their students feel positive and their lessons enjoyable are doing everybody a favor.

This doesn't have to mean countless hours in the staffroom writing an annotated version of Gilbert and Sullivan's Pirates of Penzance, complete with authentic period costumes, or forking over thousands of your own hard earned dollars on the latest educational games from some internet company based at Harvard. No, what it means is thinking smart.

Consider the age groups and interests of your students in order to help them connect with this thing called English. Do art lessons when you're learning about shapes and colors. Blindfold your students and have them identify different textures, scents and flavors. Turn things upside down and stimulate those little brains.

Do an amazing race around the school. Introduce written English into a math problem that incorporates a code leading to a prize hidden somewhere in the classroom. Have a show and tell session based on a different theme each week—toys, clothes, food, tools, etc. Role play the movements and actions of a different continent's animals or copy popular characters from TV.

Explore the sounds you might make if you felt sad or happy. Create a wall where you regularly add new words you've discovered together. Invite other teachers into the classroom to share their experiences. Bring in clippings from newspapers and magazines. Make collages. Visit the fire station. Get your local police force to send over some poor sucker to hone his English skills in front of the children. Teach them Western nursery rhymes or bastardize the classics. The only real secret is to be creative, because if you enjoy yourself they will too.

If you are having trouble in the beginning, don't feel ashamed to pick your fellow teachers' brains. If scheduling permits it, see if you can find a few confident teachers who will let you sit in on a class or two. While it isn't feasible or particularly desirable to copy them exactly, it can help to take in the general flow of a lesson and see how they keep their students engaged.

The internet has a host of sites that offer up an astounding variety of advice and information for all levels of learners. Just keep in mind that these are only ideas and opinions and that nothing is carved in stone. What works for someone else might not be the right approach for you. Be flexible, be persistent, and be yourself, and eventually you will become the teacher your students deserve.

While it's true that bored students are the root of all evil, there's still the possibility that a local Damien could turn up. Behavioral and compliance issues rear their ugly heads in even the most exciting, fun and stimulating classrooms, so it's a good idea to be aware of your school's policies on crime and punishment.

Do you have prior approval to indulge in tyranny? Is the next Guantanamo Bay only a classroom away? The important thing is to find out early on what the protocol is when it comes to trouble makers. Do you have to deal with them yourself, can you call in a Korean teacher, or are you allowed to send them off to see the Director? (The last one is unlikely, as more than a few Hagwon owners only want to see their students when they hand over the cash at the end of the month.)

One way to change the dynamic concerning punishment is to get the students directly involved before problems arise. Find a Korean co-worker who will help translate, and together with your students sit down and discuss what behaviors are acceptable and unacceptable in a classroom setting. Resist the urge to dictate and listen to what they already know, as most of the time they will be quite the sensible little scholars. Common suggestions will probably be no shouting, hands up when you want to ask a question, no name calling, etc. Once you've agreed upon the rules, bring up the issue of punishment and discuss what they feel to be suitable consequences for breaking them. (Here you may need to moderate, as they can get a little bloodthirsty!)

When you've reached a consensus, print them in both Korean and English on large posters and put them up in the classroom where they'll be plainly visible. This way everybody knows the rules and what happens when they're broken. Not only is this a fairer system, it's a better one because it moves away from the old equation of teacher equals trouble. It empowers students because it gives them a sense of ownership and equity in their own learning experiences.

Another tool that can help students to self moderate their behavior is the talking wheel. This is simply a large cardboard circle with a moveable hand on it that is located somewhere at the front of the room. The circle is divided into four equal sections. These are marked No Talking, Whispering, Class Voices and Outside Voices and the hand is shifted to match the current activity and desired volume. Of course this method isn't foolproof, and in the beginning it will require both patience and reinforcement on your part for it to be adopted, but after a while the students will become accustomed to using specific voices for different activities.

If you are coming from the US you may wish to follow in the footsteps of California and initiate your own version of the Three Strikes Policy. This can be done by making a large poster with numerous pockets, each marked with the name of a student. Cards that fit the pockets are then cut from yellow, orange and red paper and inserted in that order when undesirable actions arise. Yellow is a warning, orange means let's talk after class, and red is a call from a Korean teacher to the parents that evening. Red should, and probably will, scare the living sin out of them as it will undoubtedly result in a severe dressing down and at worst a cane across the backside, so make sure the class understands what it means to get the red card and only hand it out if it's truly warranted.

These various tools are designed to help students avoid getting into trouble, but even with the best of intentions, kids will still be kids and there will always be a time for retribution. Feel free to let your internal inquisitor run wild, but keep in mind that even in Korea there are limits.

The question is which way do you swing; will it be mental or physical punishment? The young body's ability to experience pain offers an almost limitless canvas to work upon, tempered only by the fact that while they have to go to public school and put up with the odd sadist, their parents can move them to another Hagwon and charge you with assault. This means that subtle acts of retribution and revenge are probably the smarter route. Why settle for a crass twist of the ear when you can forgo deodorant for a few days in summer or drink super strength espresso before every class?

Such worldly things are all well and good, but it's in the area of the mind and spirit where you can truly excel. Separate unruly friends. Interspace talkative boys with horrified girls and marvel at the decrease in idle chatter. Bring smart asses up to the front and give them their own personal desks within glaring distance. Play the shame game and send them out for a while to be seen by the rest of the school. Revoke game privileges. Hand out homework during the Soccer World Cup. Do whatever achieves results.

It should be noted here that Korean children are a little perverse, and some tasks that might be seen as punishments in the West are actually sought after rewards in South Korea. Think twice before threatening that the next child who shouts out will be cleaning the white board. The same applies to differences in age, for while teenagers will happily die excruciatingly painful deaths in order to avoid standing out from their peers, eager young beavers will beg for the chance to come up to the front of the class and strut their stuff.

Last, but certainly not least, is the dreaded art of confiscation. Ah, what would a teacher's desk be without a drawer full of childhood debris? Some things like dehydrated frogs and baby chicks are best returned promptly after class, whilst others like those nifty little laser pointers may never make it back to their owners, for rightfully to the teacher goes the spoils of war. It's quite amazing the junk you'll collect over time; all manner of model cars, dolls, spinning tops, balls, shiny stones, bells, whistles, jacks, electronic games and every other type of childhood ephemera.

The best thing about confiscation is that the student knows the object in question shouldn't have been out in the first place, and he or she will be quiet as a mouse when they recall your theatrical vow to throw all confiscated items in the river after class. No other action perpetrated by a teacher has the potential to cause so much heartache and regret. You are the judge. Will the sentence handed down to a repeat offender be confiscation for the week, the month or forever? It's up to you and your own sense of twisted justice, but a reasonably prompt return and a friendly warning will do more for the student-teacher relationship than burning the offending article and posting the video on YouTube.

As light balances darkness, so too does a healthy classroom require a system of rewards as well as punishments. These can be as simple as a smile and a sticker, or as expensive as a classroom trip to the corner store. It shouldn't be too hard to make them happy—just think child brain; a game of hangman at the end of a great class, a box of strawberries from the local market, a mini excursion to the park, or a whole lesson spent playing and having fun.

When it comes to games based on English your imagination is the limit. Most schools will have a motley collection of board games, including everything from Scrabble to Snakes and Ladders, but some of the best games are those where the whole class can actively participate. Flashcards offer a variety of options. One of the simplest is just dividing the class into two groups and seeing which team can answer correctly when a card is flashed. More elaborate versions consist of laying the cards all face up on a table and having representatives from the different teams come up and search for a word, bonus points being given for correct pronunciation.

Older students can be shown cards and asked to describe them to their teammates without naming or spelling the object in question. It probably goes without saying that if you suffer from migraines you shouldn't be in this job, let alone playing any of these games, as there's no way to keep them quiet once the competition begins.

You can have students draw a whispered word on the white board and the rest can guess and spell it. They can mime a mystery action, feeling or animal. You can play musical chairs, hold a spelling bee or do a round of 'eye spy with my little eye'. Try finding a word for every letter in the alphabet and attempt to remember them all as you go around the class. Grab a stuffed toy and pass it back and forth as you practice counting up and down.

Whisper silly sayings like 'seven soft shoes' or 'big bad babies bite broken bottles' down two lines of students and see which group mangles it the least. Teach them old fashioned tongue twisters like 'rubber baby buggy bumpers'. Play 'Simon says'. Create a disgusting menu for an imaginary restaurant and act out the different parts, such as the forgetful waiter, the irate customer and the completely crazy cook. There aren't any rights or wrongs when it comes to having fun, just make sure that there's some educational value involved in case the boss decides to check up on the ruckus.

How and when you decide to play your games is up to you. Many teachers prefer to have some type of system whereby well behaved classes are rewarded with a star, and after so many they earn a prize or game. This can help avoid the monotonous chorus of "Game, Teacher, game!" at the start of every lesson. Others like to hand points out to individual students for great behavior or exceptional work. These can then be redeemed for fake money, and once or twice a week the class as a whole gets to visit the teacher's 'toy store' where they can shop for small shiny things like balls, beads or other trinkets that twinkle in the harsh fluorescent light. The main thing to keep in mind with these kinds of systems is that the rewards must be real and tangible, as younger students will quickly lose interest in a prize that's months away.

Games and treats are great, but some of the best goodies you can dole out are praise and attention. Positive reinforcement and encouragement will often turn around troubled students and can make all the difference at report time. It's sometimes hard to do, but spending extra time with the children who appear to hate you can really change their feelings about English and give you greater insight into your own educational practice.

Teaching elementary class is a pain in the ass but it can also be some of the most fun you can have with small children. Yes, you could accept that job in Pusan teaching businessmen how to write resumes, but you'll never feel the urge to take them all for ice cream on a hot summer's day or enthrall them with your impersonation of a break dancing robot.

Sure, the odd kid may innocently ask why you're so fat, or where your hair went, but in the end these kids will probably be some of the best friends you'll make during your time in Korea. So play a few games, cut them some slack and thank God you didn't have to go to language school when you were their age.

ALL WORK AND NO PLAY MAKES FOR A DULL TEENAGE DAY

Gone is the sweetness and light, gone too are the smiles and cheerful greetings, replaced in turn by sullen glances and monosyllabic grunts. What has happened to the little ones? What demonic forces have transformed the charming children into these withdrawn, moody creatures whose only response when asked for an answer or opinion is to shrug their shoulders and stare blankly into space?

It isn't drugs, nor do they seem interested in human flesh, so you can strike zombies and opium off the list. The World Health Organization hasn't mentioned any new pandemics on their website, thus it isn't viral in nature. The elementary kids still dig your animal impersonations and the adult students continue to take you out for beer, therefore it's obvious you haven't suffered any critical loss of teaching mojo.

Thankfully the answer isn't quite so crazy or complex, they've just hit the teen years. What you're facing is only the local version of the puberty blues; excess hormones, social angst, and the crushing weight of school (not to mention unsightly acne and parents who "just don't understand"). It's been this way for a long time; chances are there were kids back in the Stone Age who wore their nose bones backwards and dreaded being seen in public skinning mammoths with their mothers.

They'll come to class bored, tired and distracted and you can't change this, because the causes are outside of your control. Teachers who don't remember their own adolescent years, or fail to comprehend the magnitude of schoolwork and familial pressure placed on these kids, can easily fall prey to an attitude that says "If you don't want to pay attention, I won't either". However this kind of logic is flawed due to the fact that you're getting paid to be there.

Admittedly it can be difficult to maintain an outlook tempered with empathy and care when all you see are yawns, bored smirks and covert text messaging, but you have to keep in mind what these kids are going through. Their school experience is far less free or exciting than anything you experienced. Imagine getting up six days a week and studying an hour before breakfast (yes it happens for the older ones), then going off to a school where uniforms are compulsory, hair length is monitored, jewelry and makeup are banned, and teachers can make their lives a living hell. On top of that, add the joys of attending another couple of hours of instruction in English, Math and Science at the local Hagwon and then heading straight home to study until midnight. These kids are not having the best times of their lives.

There's no cruising around with friends in cars or just watching TV, no gossiping on the phone for hours or hanging out at the mall, because time is too precious to be wasted. This is a place where the study motto "sleep five hours fail, sleep four hours pass" is accepted as a gospel truth. South Korea is pervaded by an atmosphere of pressure and competition. It's a society where students who get ninety three percent on a paper are afraid to go home and a country where doing poorly on one exam can mean the difference between attending a prestigious university in Seoul or spending the next four years at some community college in the rice fields.

These kids have every right to arrive burnt out and exhausted, so don't take their complete lack of energy and enthusiasm too personally. They don't owe you anything, and going hard ass won't improve class morale one damn bit! At the risk of sounding repetitive, the only thing you can really do to change the dynamic is get to know them and then tailor your classes so that what they're learning holds some relevance.

Brainstorm together topics that interest them. Encourage them to bring in articles from magazines and internet sites they read and frequent. Discuss technology and gaming. Do group projects on subjects that are meaningful to them. Examine marketing and how it focuses on their age group. Get them to plan, write and perform their own advertisements for products they would buy. Role play hypothetical situations from their own lives and let them act out different outcomes. Have an open question culture night. Try two truths and a lie and learn some surprising facts about each other's lives. Bring some photos of when you were a teenager and have a good laugh as you discuss fashion, fads and family.

Run a fake doctor's office and get them to prescribe all kinds of ridiculous treatments for ailments both common and absurd. Make posters for travel agents specializing in escape plans for weary students. Conduct debates between the sexes. Hold kangaroo courts to judge unfair parents and cruel teachers. Have a design competition for the perfect teenage bedroom. Discuss their short term goals and long term dreams. Take the time to reassure them that this stressful period in their lives will pass. Ask them to write something positive about each member of the class on a piece of paper and tell them to keep theirs to read when things get tough.

Not all of these things should be attempted during the first few weeks of class, but the sky is the limit once you accept them for who they are and attempt to teach them within the context of their lives. It will take a little time and effort to gain their trust and friendship, but it's a far better deal than bashing them repetitively over the head with a textbook for the next fifty two weeks.

Play some games. Give them the opportunity to enjoy themselves, to be young, to be silly, to laugh. At first they may try and send the message that they're too mature for this, but a little fun is exactly what they need and once you get them going they won't want to stop. All the tricks of the trade that work with the little kids will work here, you just have to fine tune the level of difficulty. They will play with a passion everything from Pictionary to team spelling bees. You can hold formal trivia nights with mystery prizes, play celebrity heads or speed test their reflexes with Simon Says. It really doesn't matter what you do as long as you're honing their English skills and helping them let off a little steam.

Having fun doesn't mean that you have to abandon the books or throw out the curriculum; it just means finding some time in between the drier lessons to relax. Anything from telling a bad joke to celebrating a birthday counts when it comes to keeping these students interested in attending your classes (besides which it makes it a hell of a lot less boring for you!) Some teachers will object, and state that it isn't their intention to become comedians, but when it's all said and done you've really only got two choices. You can either be a grumpy jailer five nights a week or a part-time entertainer. The choice is yours.

True teaching is a human endeavor and as such requires a light and living touch; people who can't laugh at themselves or see the value in a smile are going to burn out fast, and sadly, take their students down with them. If you don't think you're the right kind of person, then maybe you should think twice about teaching.

While you're considering that question, now might be the time to tell a few horror stories. Depending on your age and looks, they're either going to identify with you, fall in love with you, or see you as some kind of ancient life form left over from the Jurassic period.

If you're fresh faced and straight from college, you may encounter the problem of students viewing you more as a peer than an authority figure. This can be great in that they'll be more likely to open up and share their lives with you but it can also lead to discipline problems. Some students will resent being made to work by someone who doesn't appear much older than themselves, especially if you're female. If you think this is a likely scenario, it may be wise to start off a little firmer and ease into a less formal relationship once you have established yourself as boss.

Attractive women will find the teenage boys a frustrating lot to teach as they'll tend to blush, lose focus and stammer a lot, while handsome guys may find their female students doing everything from staring dreamily at the object of their infatuation to pestering them daily for their phone number and email. Whatever your sex or age, limit your contact information to a few close friends and colleagues, as nothing is more annoying than answering a phone at midnight to the sounds of distant giggling.

The older and uglier amongst you won't face these particular problems; however you'll still find your patience tested. Adolescence is a time of worry and change, and students that are uncomfortable with their own body image may experience the need to make themselves feel better by making someone else feel like shit. That means that if you are bald, hairy or overweight you can expect to hear some rather cruel comments whispered behind your back. When this kind of thing happens just cast your mind back to a time when you cursed your orthodontist and agonized over every zit, and hopefully you'll avoid saying something you'll regret.

Expect them to look at you in dull amazement if you dare to talk about when you were their age, and always keep in mind that anything you experienced couldn't possibly be similar to what they're going through. Age is relative, and while you might consider yourself a spring chicken, they will see you as a doddering old fool with one foot in the grave, regardless of the fact that you are only thirty two. Stay calm, breathe evenly and psyche them out by talking about how when you were in high school you only had half an hour of homework, owned your own car and lived down the street from a liquor store that happily sold booze to underage drinkers.

If things get crazy keep your cool and don't let them forget who's in charge. Korean teenagers are no different from the rest of the world when it comes to hassling teachers, however most will only fantasize about telling you to fuck off. The odd firebrand may have to be reprimanded, or at worst asked to leave the room but for the most part they're very well behaved compared to their Western counterparts.

Teaching teenagers will give you a thick skin and either prepare you for having a family or get you thinking seriously about sterilization. It will also remind you that while you sometimes might wish to be young again, you certainly wouldn't want that fantasy fulfilled in South Korea. Try to ignore their stupid comments and remember that your class might be the only time in their whole day where they can actually be themselves and have some fun.

ADULTS OVER THE EDGE

Though it sounds like a terribly sexist comment, it's true to say that the majority of adult students studying at private English institutes fall into two distinct groups, housewives in the morning and businessmen at night. While you may get the occasional feminine free spirit venturing into your evenings of male bonding, you're highly unlikely to find any lads joining the ladies during the day.

Each of the aforementioned groups offers unexpected problems, unique challenges, and all too frequent frustrations. They can be arrogant, rude, stubborn, late, lazy, and lack even a passing interest in the subject they're studying, though admittedly this list of adjectives applies mainly to the men.

Some new teachers may be hesitant to take on adults, fearing higher expectations, grammatical superiority and unrealistic demands. While this may accurately portray the odd student, the majority of the class will revere your inherent English abilities and never suspect that your Master's degree was earned in the field of invertebrate biology.

These lessons are generally quite interesting and provide a welcome change from teaching children. They offer you the chance to meet people your own age, gain a deeper understanding of the local culture, and exit the classroom with your hearing and sanity intact.

The average ladies English breakfast lesson is held anywhere from nine till noon; basically whenever hubby and offspring have left the nest and granny can be dragged out of bed and convinced to take the helm. These classes tend to be a more homogenous gathering of souls than the testosterone toned classes at night. They usually consist of bright young mothers and middle aged ladies who have sacrificed much on the alter of matrimonial bliss but still yearn for intellectual stimulus beyond improved Kimchi recipes and their children's homework.

They come for English lessons but also something more. They attend for the chance to have a moment to themselves, to pursue an interest that is theirs alone, to inhabit a space where they are not only mothers and wives but individuals with thoughts and opinions. This is a precious thing in a country that places so much pressure on women to meet the needs of their families before themselves.

Some genuinely wish to improve their English, whilst for others it's a chance to have intimate contact with the world outside. It is an opportunity for them to hear you speak about your life, and through you explore cities, countries and situations that they in all likelihood will never experience. It's as much a travel study course—'Western Geography and Culture 101', as it is a language lesson. They want to know what it's like to live in London with five flat mates or study drama in New York. How it feels to backpack solo around Australia or work on a ski hill in Banff.

Teaching these classes is fairly problem free, as your students are usually on time, keen to learn and happy to be there. In the beginning they may be a little shy and reluctant to speak up but after they become accustomed to your presence and comfortable with each other they'll become some of your best students.

They're also your portal to a parallel Korean universe. When they begin to relax and discuss their lives, you'll never see things the same way again. Through them you'll view the cozy Confucian household in a completely different light; coming to understand that those soldiers and riot police are someone's babies, that living with the in-laws isn't all free babysitting and that most of those late night drinkers chatting up bar girls have wives waiting for them at home.

The men that will attend your evening classes are more of a mixed bunch; arrogant business men, curious students, lonely bachelors, weary shopkeepers, bored bureaucrats and retired academics. A wide cross-section of the community, all present for various reasons and expecting you to put on one hell of a show.

They come to class for a variety of reasons. The young attend to increase their chances of scoring that elusive university position and the old wander in for stimulation. Some arrive out of curiosity and a desire to learn, whilst others are present simply because their bosses have decided that it will improve the company image. The former see the evening as a challenging opportunity, the latter as a cruel and unusual punishment.

A few come to flaunt their positions, dropping their business cards like alms to the poor. Others arrive to argue with a foreigner, regardless as to whether the conversation is about the Korean economy or your mother's favorite recipe. Some seek to relieve their loneliness and meet new friends. Many turn up for entertainment purposes; to see their fellow classmates make mistakes, to listen to the gossip, and more importantly, to watch you bounce about with your weird eyes and big nose as you recount your life's story for the hundredth time.

Teaching these classes can be a trial, especially on Friday nights, when one third of the students wander in late with an all too obvious mint in the mouth and a bad case of Soju poisoning. Ah, what joy. They enter the room hesitantly like naughty schoolboys late for class, faces flushed and sweaty. They fall asleep in their seats, stare blearily at the board and show off their favorite phrases to giggling companions at levels louder than required.

Before you swear or walk out, remember that these jokers are paying your wages and that while they're extremely annoying, they only make up part of the class. The rest of the students are excited to be there and probably just as sick of these drunken idiots as you are.

Teaching adults, whatever their gender, can be problematic, as they're more rigid when it comes to achieving educational satisfaction. They were programmed years, sometimes decades ago as to what constitutes effective teaching practice and this can be a difficult hurdle to overcome.

For the majority of adults, learning is teacher orientated. You are the font of knowledge, whose endlessly gushing orifice will eventually splash them with wisdom and perfect pronunciation. Convincing them otherwise; that learning is in fact most effective when it is student directed, will take a great deal of effort on your part.

What this means for you is plenty of frustration and angst, as they'll resist all the modern tactics and techniques you've so diligently adopted. They won't want to talk in pairs or in groups; they'll want to hear you lecture. They didn't fork out all that cash in order to listen to each other speak poorly; they paid up so they could bask beneath your faultless pronunciation, strange slang and questionable grammar. Most of them don't understand that it's only through their own hard work that they'll gain passage to the fabled land of fluency.

This is especially true of older students, who just can't accept that all of these seemingly pointless games and activities are of educational merit. They're quite convinced, due to their Confucian cultural bias, that true learning lies locked within the teacher and his books. They find it hard to grasp the benefits of wandering around the room with a post-it note stuck to their forehead, asking questions to see if they are Mickey Mouse or Lady Di. A Korean teaching axiom might be that the older the class the harder the teaching.

By all means persevere, as your long term goal is to improve their English, but remember that if they aren't happy with your style they'll eventually vote with their feet. As a new teacher you'll find that compromise is often necessary and that a few 'old school' lessons are sometimes required before you can assault them with the latest ESL activity.

With most adults, it's a good idea to spend the first night or two getting to know each other. That's why a photo album or PowerPoint presentation filled with images of your family, friends, home and community is something you should bring. You were so curious about Asia that you traveled half way around the world to live there, what makes you think they aren't just as interested to learn about your country?

These first classes are the time to find out what they hope to achieve and why they're attending. It's a great opportunity to discuss your own teaching style, methods and expectations. This is when you can explain your strong, almost religious beliefs regarding the necessity of students talking and not being afraid to make mistakes.

A good analogy for improving their English is learning how to ride a bike. Point out the obvious similarities; that to learn to ride takes both time and commitment, that it seems scary at first and that it often appears as if the learner is wobbling around in endless circles. Explain that while some people naturally have better balance than others, everybody falls off, loses some skin and makes a fool of themselves. The point being, that with perseverance everyone can eventually learn to ride, but to do so involves an element of risk taking and personal responsibility.

As the term progresses, don't forget to touch base with them to see how it's going. Are they enjoying themselves? Do they believe their English is improving? Are they happy with your teaching? Listen to their concerns, value their feedback, and don't be too proud to talk to colleagues if the news isn't good. Nobody is born the perfect teacher and part of the game is about assessing and modifying your own practice.

If your spider senses are tingling but they're reluctant to give feedback, you may have to employ a less confrontational method to gather information, as many Korean students won't feel comfortable saying that your lessons suck. Try an anonymous drop box, student survey or consider asking your boss to chat with them after class.

Many adults are convinced that all they need to become fluent is conversation time, but in reality they also need bookwork. A mix of both is best, especially when it comes to new students with low fluency levels. They find bookwork both safe and familiar, and in this non-threatening environment you can work towards building up their skills and confidence. More advanced students will unfortunately regard this as a waste of time, as many have had their fill of grammar lessons over the years and consider themselves above and beyond it. This may be true in some cases but for the most part a balanced diet is the most important element in terms of steady growth.

Keep in mind the old caveat that you can't please everyone all the time. Sometimes you won't even be able to please yourself, as many schools have their own set curriculum and won't allow you to teach whatever you wish. That said, there is always a certain amount of room to maneuver, as even the most anal employer understands that sometimes a page or lesson just won't work with a particular bunch of students.

When it comes to conducting conversation classes, student ability and your imagination are the only limiting factors. Hold debates. Stage mini soap operas. Get them to role play the opposite sex. Present them with hypothetical situations. Discuss politics, religion and extra marital affairs. Explore their views on Western life and culture. Learn about each other's superstitions and folklore. Share childhood memories. Vote on favorite flavors. Bring a blindfold to class and explore the world of scents and associations. Compare old wives' tales. Look at ink blot tests. Argue about extra terrestrials, conspiracy theories and paranormal activity.

Complete psychology tests. Pretend to be marriage counselors. Solve crossword puzzles. Have a murder mystery night. Run an advice hotline for computer addicts. Dictate recipes. Analyze English sayings. Listen to Western music. Transcribe lyrics. Play scrabble but use your word in a sentence. Go to a restaurant and order in English. Critique the menus. Go bowling. Work them alone. Work them in groups. Reassign seats. Roll dice or dip in a hat to choose topics. Do whatever it takes to keep them interested and having fun.

And remember to keep an eye on the flow, as it's easy for the more fluent students to dominate the class. This can happen easily and before you know it the rest of the group can feel neglected. Ensure in your most diplomatic manner that you occasionally sideline the gifted gabbers, and engineer lessons where the quieter students have the opportunity to engage you in conversation without the threat of a hostile takeover.

Another danger is OMS, otherwise known as Old Man Syndrome. This uniquely Confucian problem arises when some venerable old sage decides to join the class. Suddenly your mob of chatterboxes becomes ominously silent due to the fact that nobody wants to look smarter than grandfather, as respect for the elderly is one of the golden rules in South Korea. There isn't a lot you can do in these situations except encourage everyone to speak, and remove the handrails from the stairwell.

Teaching adults is far safer than kiddie classes but just because you are free from the threat of Pink Eye doesn't mean it's entirely without risk. Occasionally a sleazy businessman will fall in love with you, or the street fumigators will cause the windows to be slid shut in a hurry, but the real threat to your health lies in the form of the friendly invitation.

Not all are dangerous. The daytime ones are fairly safe and generally provide an interesting afternoon. Your students will, if you accept their generous offers, take you on lovely weekend picnics to explore beaches, museums, folk villages, national parks and temples. All of these are great ways to see the country, though admittedly it pays to find out exactly where you're going, as a second or third trip to the same attraction can be a little tedious.

It's the ones at night that you have to watch out for. The risk exists mainly for male teachers in the form of extended drinking sessions after school. There will always be at least one student in every class who wants to make you his new boozing buddy. In itself there's nothing wrong with this, it's just that each one thinks he's the first to have thought of it, so unless you are an alcoholic or come from hardy Russian peasant stock, it's best to accept weeknight invitations on a limited basis.

Whatever you do, think twice about handing out your phone number. Sure it is nice to be wanted, but the good feelings fade rapidly when the drunks start calling. The same goes for your address. If you don't mind lying in bed at three in the morning trying to ignore good natured pissheads banging on your door, then by all means invite students back to your apartment on a regular basis. If on the other hand you value your privacy and regard sleep as a sacred right, then you might want to consider maintaining a little emotional distance from your students during the first few months of teaching.

Before this begins to sound too depressing, there should be some mention of the lighter side of teaching adults. It can be a lot of fun, as unlike teaching children, there's time to let your guard down and have a laugh. The following are only some of the benefits.

You don't have to watch for biters. You can wear white. You can occasionally swear. You can turn your ass to the class without fear of violation (See 'Can we pet the teacher now'.) You can teach for forty five minutes without confiscating a toy. You can design a lesson not based around animals, magic or princesses. You can leave the flash cards in the cupboard. You can flirt. You can ask questions and not know the answers. You can sit back and relax. Best of all, you can be yourself.

When you take one of these classes, get ready for some weirdness and don't take any of the comments too personally. Expect unflattering comparisons to Bryan Adams, Meg Ryan or whoever else your most prominent facial features resemble.

Be prepared for unsolicited advice, as Koreans in general are pretty blunt. If you're a little heavy, look forward to being told you should join a gym. If you like the natural look, understand that make-up would "make you pretty". Warmly accept the observation that if you weren't bald you'd be quite handsome and don't get upset over the fact that "braces would make your smile attractive".

They don't mean to be offensive; they're just being Korean in a foreign language. If you are female, young, blonde and have all your teeth, you can expect to be told that "you are beautiful" on a regular basis. If this comes from a woman it's just a compliment, if it comes from a man it translates to "I find you sexually attractive in a strangely exotic way".

Another thing will be the questions. In the West, even amongst close friends, there are some topics that are generally avoided. Not so in Korea, as everything here is fair game. They really won't get the point if you stare at them and coolly state "I beg your pardon?", they'll just repeat the query loud enough for everyone to hear.

You'll be hit in the first week by all the big taboos. How much do you earn? Why aren't you married? Why haven't you had children by your age? How much do you weigh? How old are you? Just take it all in your stride and don't feel you have to answer just because they felt comfortable asking. Moments like these are a great time to discuss cultural differences and the reason why many foreigners think Koreans are a rude and insensitive people.

A lot of the time spent teaching adult students is hard and unrewarding work. You need to be prepared, awake and responsive to your students. They on the other hand, will often be late, lazy and disinterested to the point where you'll wonder why they bothered to attend. There will be times when you want to bash your head (or theirs) against the whiteboard in sheer frustration, when you'll question what you're doing and wonder whether anyone has learned a damned thing.

The good news is that this will only be some of the time, for there will be other days when your lessons get them talking, when the shy students put up their hands, and you'll exit the classroom feeling like you've made a difference. Most of them will enjoy your teaching and look forward to your classes. They'll buy you dinner, shout you drinks, and take you places you'd never have found on your own. Adults can be a lot of fun, just keep it all in perspective and remember that no matter what happens it'll be over in an hour.

THE FORBIDDEN PLEASURES OF EXPOSING YOUR PRIVATES TO ENGLISH

A moment if you please, and your fortune will be revealed. Some time soon, perhaps tomorrow, a short dark stranger will approach you in a crowded coffee shop and discreetly inquire if you are interested in conducting private English lessons. They may offer you large sums of money and free meals at their dumpling shack, however you must be on your guard, for danger lurks unseen within this attractive and seemingly innocent proposition. Think long and hard before you commit to any binding agreement, but feel free to let them pay for the cappuccino.

Teaching privately in Korea is one of the few times where crime actually does pay, but there are serious risks involved and numerous things to consider before you launch yourself into the shady underworld of secret lessons and backdoor dealings. This chapter will give you the inside scoop on both the dangers and benefits of this forbidden pastime, and a little advice on how to survive and prosper if you should choose to engage in a life of crime.

First things first, it's technically illegal, so you could be fined, jailed and deported with a criminal record should you be caught with sticky fingers in the private pie. The Korean Government has conducted previous purges on unethical idiots working with false degrees, so theoretically there is nothing stopping them from taking aim at foreigners not paying their fair share of tax.

All kinds of crazy rumors abound, from tales of elite government agents who work undercover to catch and expose 'private' teachers, to toll free hotlines where disgruntled neighbors or angry bosses can anonymously report suspicious educational behavior. While these are probably just the delusions of a few burned out individuals, it's wise to keep in mind that this is a country unlike no other, one where there is still a standing reward for turning in "persons involved in anti-state activities" (that's Orwellian speak for spies) and a possible death sentence for those "caught seducing government officials". Of course these laws obviously refer to matters relating to North Korea, but it's probably best to err on the side of caution when residing in a place with these levels of paranoia and suspicion.

Hagwon owners will tell you that if you're caught they may be fined or even have their business licenses revoked. This mantra is repeated to discourage you from freelancing, but it's worth considering that you could be putting more than just yourself in a precarious situation, as most schools employ a number of Korean teachers, cleaners and bus drivers; people who don't have the luxury of leaving the country and finding another job back home if things go cock-eyed.

Probably the wisest thing you can do for the first few months on the job is to follow Nancy Reagan's advice and just say "NO". Take your time and settle in, make some friends, shoulder the workload, get to know the schedule, discuss the private scene with other teachers and then, and only then, start to consider whether you really want to give up any of your valuable free time to teach a few lessons on the sly. Sure money is a wonderful thing to have but is it worth losing your job and your sanity over a few hundred dollars?

The answer to that question will probably depend on how much dough you owe various financial institutions, which by definition includes ma and pa. While a zealous student loans officer can be a real pain in the ass, at least they don't mention your outstanding debts at the dinner table. Private tuition can certainly make a difference when it comes to meeting these obligations but it isn't the bona fide cash cow that it's popularly made out to be.

A reasonable rate seems to be anywhere from 30 to 60 thousand won per hour, though some charge less and others a whole lot more. One way to find a balance between greed and charity is to teach a few lessons for free—some 'get to know you time' and from what you see and learn base your fees accordingly. A family that wants tuition for their children and whose sole income derives from market vending or rice farming no doubt merits a lower charge than one that owns two medical clinics and a string of pharmacies.

Others would argue that the risk is the same regardless of the families' financial situation and that the only thing up for consideration is how much money you require to put your ass on the line. It also depends on what's happening during these classes, as it takes a lot more work to prepare and teach formal grammar lessons than it does to chat about what you did on the weekend. There are no easy answers or simple formulas, it all comes down to what you feel comfortable charging for your time and effort, (not to mention your fear and loathing).

Even with the best intentions it can be difficult to avoid the siren's song, as a certain teacher in Seoul found out to her chagrin. She'd taught a family's three young boys for a period of about a year before deciding that she valued her weekends more than the 50 thousand won she'd been receiving for the two hour sessions she conducted every Saturday afternoon. She explained this to the parents, highlighting the fact that she wanted to travel and see more of their amazing country during her final year in Korea. They seemed to accept her reasoning and wished her well, even taking her out for a farewell dinner after her last night on the job.

She occasionally dropped by their car dealership to say hello, but each time she did, the father complained bitterly about how much the boys missed her and attempted to get her back through a potent combination of guilt and greed. She in turn protested that it was not about the money but rather her quality of life. By the time a few months had passed he'd upped the ante to 200 thousand won per lesson. She eventually caved in and decided that it was pointless to resist, for what sane individual would refuse that much money for time spent basically playing with three intelligent little boys.

Along with the money can come other benefits as well, depending on what businesses the families are involved in, and what you are willing to accept in lieu of payment. Teachers have been known to receive a wide variety of free services and products including dental work, health care, medicine, meals, new clothes, books, shoes, jewelry, haircuts, manicures, even bar tabs and questionable massages.

The students themselves vary almost as greatly. You may find yourself spending Sunday afternoons dressing up dolls with four year olds, or discussing impotent husbands with a bunch of angry housewives. Alternatively, you may while away your weeknights proofreading assignments for lazy university students, analyzing global events with well-spoken scholars or guzzling whisky with a gang of rowdy businessmen. The possibilities are endless, but most likely you'll find yourself sitting in a tiny bedroom, helping a few average 12 year olds improve their English skills one verb at a time.

When it comes to finding privates it probably isn't the best idea to accept offers from students at your place of work, as the boss will go ballistic if he suspects you're cheating on him. On the flip side however, you know they'll be happy with your teaching style and aren't likely to be ruthless government agents setting you up for a sting.

One of the best ways to get good privates is just to sit back and wait. Chances are there's a teacher you know who will be leaving soon or who just wants a break and will be happy to pass their students on to you. Alternatively, you can trust in fate or your ability to separate the sheep from the goats and go with one of the many strangers who will approach you. All you have to do in this case is answer one simple question—"Do I feel lucky?"

If you already have a few privates and they're happy with your performance, they'll more than likely mention you to their friends. This in itself can be quite disturbing, especially after you've repeatedly told them not to tell a soul about your secret relationship. Unfortunately Koreans, like the rest of humanity, enjoy the odd boast and many find it hard not to reveal that they have a Western teacher exclusively tutoring their children. While this talk may bring in a few more students, it's also one of the likeliest ways to get caught. Sadly there isn't much you can do about this except stress the risks to all parties and hope your Karmic balance is still in the black.

Once you've got clients, the next question is where you're going to meet them. Common sense says that a Korean person entering your apartment building is less noticeable than you going into theirs but sometimes it just isn't feasible. This may be because your place is next door to your school, the students are too young to travel alone, or the parents, for some odd reason, prefer to hold classes where they can keep their eyes on you and their teenage daughters.

Some teachers prefer adult conversation classes, with their lack of incriminating material and their ability to be conducted in plain sight. These kinds of lessons can be held over a cup of coffee or a cold beer and should you be questioned, you can always pass yourselves off as just some old friends catching up after work.

If you suffer from a tendency towards paranoia be careful, as teaching privates may send you over the edge. Was that neighbor staring at you out of curiosity or does she suspect? Have you seen that old guy on the train before? Is that ferret-faced businessman with the ill-fitting suit following you or does he just live nearby? Thoughts like these will gnaw at your sanity and rob you of your precious sleep if you aren't mentally prepared for the task.

That said, a cautious mind isn't such a bad thing, you just have to minimize your risks and strive for a balance. Forget the things you can't control and focus on those you can. Try to teach classes at odd hours or when it's dark. Keep a low profile. Approach the client's house via back streets. Wear a scarf and hat in winter. Drive over on a scooter and keep your helmet on until you're in the building. Come back in 10 minutes if nobody answers the door. Don't transit wearing your weirdest clothes. Exit in a different direction and for God's sake leave your teaching materials at their place, as ten pages of photocopied notes and a box of animal flashcards does look incriminating.

Try not to get too greedy or your illicit labors will become as consuming as your day job. A certain teacher once had a different private student for nearly every free hour of his weekends and thought himself ahead of the game. Admittedly he was raking in the cash, but he also drank like a fish in an attempt to deal with the stress of late minute cancellations, nosey neighbors and a non-existent social life. Trying to teach more than a couple of students can suck the joy out of the activity, as well as increase the odds that you'll be caught. Avoiding the eyes of the law is a numbers game, and with more paying customers comes an increased chance of slipping up.

The following are things that you should work out with your new benefactors before you start teaching any lessons. When will you be paid—weekly, fortnightly or monthly? Will you receive your anonymous white envelope before or after the classes have been taught? How often and for how long will you teach? Do they require you on weekends or weekdays? How can you contact each other if something comes up that dictates a change of schedule? Do you teach extra lessons if you cancel? Do you get the same pay that week if they're the ones who go AWOL? What's your cover story if either party is questioned? What do they actually want to learn? Are their expectations realistic considering the proposed timeframe? Who pays for materials like books, CDs and flashcards? Are they and their children aware of the risks to both parties if you are busted? Is the first month a trial period? Are pay rises linked to exam performances? Some of these may seem a little finicky but it's best to be on the same page when conducting what amounts to a felony offense.

Once settled into a rhythm and past the worst of your fears, you'll be ready to start enjoying some of the finer points of private teaching, one of which is the hospitality. Koreans like to make you feel at home and for the most part you'll be treated more like an honored guest than hired help. This usually means food, and plenty of it. What you're served will depend on when you're teaching. Evening and afternoon classes are usually complimented with a generous plate of fruit, some coffee and cookies, while those conducted before a major meal may include an invitation to dine with the family. Doggie bags are common and all kinds of home cooked delicacies will wend their way home with you.

As your relationship deepens you may find yourself invited on picnics by the river, outings to restaurants and the inevitable trips to climb mountains and explore old temples. Accept these offers when you can, as they come from the heart and you'll more than likely have a memorable time. Consider taking a camera on these outings, for your time in Korea will be over before you realize, and it's nice to have some decent pictures to show your family when you get home.

Whether it's Teacher's day, Christmas or your birthday, you can expect to receive a present as an expression of gratitude for your labor. Koreans don't usually open their gifts in front of the giver but if they urge you to do so, feel free. Regardless of whether it's a pair of pink socks or a freshly fermented batch of homemade Kimchi, be sure to express your thanks, and plan for extra luggage when you eventually leave Korea, as your privates will load you up with all kinds of farewell gifts.

Private teaching allows you to get to know Koreans outside of school. It offers you the opportunity to make lasting friendships as well as pocket money. At times you may feel a little guilty charging these people for your time, but as long as you are doing a good job and they're learning English, who's to say it's a crime. It isn't for everyone but if you're careful and your luck holds, it can be a rewarding alternative to sitting in the pub every night with a bunch of whining expats.

A TASTE OF HOME

There comes a time when even the most ardent Kimchi fan longs for the familiar tastes of home. Haunting dreamscapes of roast beef and gravy fill the night, while the daylight hours are consumed with visions of sticky date puddings and chocolate éclairs. When memories of cheeses past become more poignant than those of loved ones, and the Kindergarten students develop sinister yet admittedly appealing ham-like characteristics, it's time to stand up, say your name and admit that you have a problem.

Can glossy cook book porn truly satisfy? Will those Italian pesto patches stop the cravings? Is a return flight to the family kitchen your only route to salvation? Must you abandon all that you've achieved in order to satisfy your treacherous taste buds?

Luckily for you, the answer to all of these questions is "No". Depending on where you live and what you require, there shouldn't be any need to join epicures anonymous or run on home to Mommy. Korea has lots of delicious Western food that will get you through the dark days and hungry nights; you just have to know where to find it.

Seoul, and to a lesser degree cities like Pusan and Daegu, have a wide range of restaurants catering to those in need of something special. Indian, French, Chinese, Japanese, Turkish and other national cuisines have established themselves, and in general, offer good quality food and service. Internet sites, iPhone apps and newspapers all provide reviews and locations, but the best source of edible info is probably your fellow teacher.

The Hermit Kingdom, resistant to foreign influence for centuries, has proven sadly lacking in immunity when it comes to Western fast food. Hamburger, pizza and fried chicken franchises blight the land of the morning calm in biblical proportions. Everything from your instantly recognizable imports like McDonalds, Subway, Burger King, KFC and TGI Fridays, to countless local fat forming variations litter the landscape.

Lotteria is Korea's answer to McDonalds and its super sized L can be seen across the country. It holds the dubious honor of being the first fast food franchise to raise its head in Seoul. What started as a small experiment on Oct 25, 1979, turned out to be a winner, and by 1995 over 200 stores were feeding the public's insatiable demand for cholesterol. Strong branding, tasty fries and a continued ability to please discerning local tastes enabled it to do the unthinkable—out perform the Americans. By 2002 that figure had risen to over 800 local stores, and offshore they were popping up in countries like China, Japan, Thailand and Indonesia.

Lotteria's success, unlike other burger chains, actually lay in its products. Sensing a dissatisfaction with foreign flavors, Lotteria carefully developed a line of burgers that appealed to local palates. Patties crafted from bulgolgi, Kimchi, shrimp, teriyaki pork, and crab were added to the menu, and even an optional rice bun helped to win converts. Over time, many Westerners come to prefer Lotteria above traditional McProducts, though it takes a seasoned campaigner to appreciate a Kimchi burger bathed in extra mayonnaise after a long night of drinking.

A diet traditionally low in saturated fats has spawned a generation more than happy to pay for the privilege of hardened arteries and obesity. Restaurants compete to out cheese their competitors, and all kinds of dairy-based monstrosities exist to feed this addiction, from mozzarella and sausage crust pizzas to decadent deep fried cheddar sticks.

It's young people who are driving this culinary revolution; older people tend to be more conservative and most folks above 50 are definitely Kimchi and ricers. This growing infatuation with Western food will sadly result in the gradual disappearance of the spry old men you now see wandering the streets, replaced in time by pudgy slugs on motorized carts heading off to meet their cardiac specialists. God bless America.

A sweeter source of dietary kicks is your local European style bakery. These appear in most towns and cities and vary accordingly in scale and quality. Ma and pa operations compete with slick chains like Paris Baguette, selling a range of cakes, cookies, breads, and pastries. While not providing exact copies of your favorite baked goods (yes those are Maraschino cherries on your savory snack), these bakeries do offer a welcome respite from the rock hard persimmons and endless plates of Dok that count as the standard dessert offerings in South Korea. In house munching with a sweet cup of coffee is always a good way to kill some time between classes. If you should be so lucky as to possess an apartment with an oven, fresh baguettes and a little garlic butter can do wonders for a homesick soul.

Try to keep in mind when you do get some crazy combination that you're in Korea, and that few chefs or bakers have had the opportunity to study abroad. Their aim is to sell to the locals and your obsession with authenticity is of little concern. Peas on your pizza or cornflakes in your soup are no different than the creamy curries you get back home.

Unfortunately most Koreans labor under the assumption that all Western food must be prepared with extra sugar, and that the pinnacle of Western culinary achievement is the hamburger. Don't rage against the machine, seek to subvert it. Invite a few Korean friends over on the weekend and feed them something new. Tingle their taste buds with a pot of thick Irish stew or melt their minds in a bitter chocolate fondue. Even if you don't manage to impress them with the wonders of the West, you'll still provide yourself with the opportunity to cook something different.

The production of junk food is another arena where Koreans excel, dominating their Asian opponents like some kind of glucose enhanced gladiators, exporting their sickly sweet wares to every corner of the globe. The average convenience store, often strategically situated near an elementary school, bulges with all manner of artificially flavored food stuffs. Strangely named products like Jolly Pong and White-E gum compete for your dollar with a hundred other toxic treats.

Chocoholics face bewildering racks of cacao-based combinations, from indigenous choco-pies to all kinds of bars and double dipped biscuits. Ice creams in every imaginable shape and color await your seasonal weakness, while the refrigerators brim with mysterious wonders such as Pine juice, Aloe Vera cocktails and Liberation cola. Perhaps the strangest of all is Milkis, a sickly sweet carbonated beverage that tastes like fizzy ice cream, though the oddly named Pocari Sweat comes a close second.

Though many Koreans still shop in traditional markets and street stalls, there's a growing trend towards larger Western style supermarkets. Foreign owned chains such as Carrefour and Wal-Mart carry a large range of Western food, drinks and hard-to-source ingredients, and their local rivals like E-Mart and Kim's Club are also havens for the rice-weary soul.

One way to get your foreign food fix without too much work is to invite some people over for a potluck dinner. Sure, there will always be at least one lazy bugger who only brings buns and a bottle of Coke, but most people will rise to the occasion. It's a fun way to create a Kimchi free zone for an evening, and best of all the guests take the dirty dishes with them when they leave. Potlucks are about having fun. Go retro and stage a fifties style dinner rotation. Theme it up on a monthly basis with a Hawaiian Tiki night, or a Mexican fiesta complete with Mariachi music and Tequila shooters. Sure it sounds silly, but the trick to surviving Korea is being able to have a laugh with your co-workers.

The last, though admittedly more desperate source of succor, involves hinting to loved ones abroad that you're deeply depressed and that only through the timely dispatch of oversized care packages can self harm be avoided. A pack of Tim Tams, a box of Kraft Dinner or a jar of Marmite will help you soldier on and can be used to bend fellow foreigners to your will. Demand and scarcity combine to create value, and it's not inconceivable to trade off Kindergarten classes for such sought after delicacies.

No doubt other savory sources await discovery, but with all this choice, there's no reason why you shouldn't be able to last out your tour of duty. Bon appétit.

EVERY DAY'S A FEAST IN THE EAST

Rice is the solid foundation that supports every Korean meal. It is the rock upon which the national cuisine is built. It's a unique culinary core that exerts its own gastronomic gravity and a star around which all other dishes revolve. You might think you adore wheat, in fact you probably believe you're happily devoted to your bread and pasta, but when it comes to deep commitment, to true cereal monogamy, you just can't compete with the average Korean and their life long love affair with rice.

They need it at every meal and expect it on every table. They feel empty, both physically and spiritually, if they miss out on a dose of the fluffy stuff. Breakfast, lunch and dinner, it's rice that keeps the good citizens of South Korea on track. Sure, the kids dabble in the odd bowl of corn flakes and are beginning to turn to bread for their glycemic kicks, but it's rice that rocks their socks on a daily basis.

But not just any old grain will do, it has to be good Korean rice. You won't find any pitifully thin Basmati rubbish on the table, or that suspiciously feminine Jasmine junk waiting to come out of the cupboard. No, millions of Koreans rely on the short, sticky white grains of their native rice to nourish their bodies and feed their souls. Foreign rice is viewed with a great deal of suspicion and won't be encountered outside of Seoul's curry ghettos.

Rice is the blank canvas upon which you create every memorable mouthful. It is an endless procession of stainless steel containers borne to your table, and a thousand clouds of fragrant steam. It is the only ally a rebellious stomach will admit after a long night on the Soju, and a valuable source of succor when the fiery forces of Kimchi threaten to overwhelm you.

Rice is usually served in ceramic bowls or small stainless steel pots with lids. Each of these holds approximately one cup of cooked rice. The metal ones can be extremely hot, though they may appear deceptively cool in the steady grasp of your smiling waitress. Selective breeding over countless generations has produced women with asbestos coated palms, and care should be taken when receiving these rice pots lest you shriek like an injured child and dump the steaming contents on your lap.

A typical Korean meal consists of rice, Kimchi, a couple of meat dishes, and a seemingly endless array of small bowls brimming with delicious side dishes. Korean cuisine is definitely not bland, and those coming from less intense culinary traditions may find it a little overwhelming. Pepper, ginger, garlic and chili all feature prominently but in varying degrees of intensity, and after a little experimentation you'll find the dishes that best suit your gastric temperament.

Eating is rightly perceived as the main pleasure, so don't expect a lot of conversation during meals. Words may be lacking but sounds are not. Koreans suck and slurp their meals with extreme gusto. It's a way of conveying their appreciation, so don't be surprised if it sounds a little tribal at dinnertime. The smacking of lips and the odd belch are all within the polite boundaries of dining etiquette, but blowing your nose is strictly forbidden.

Smoking is still king in Korea, and there's little chance of finishing dinner in a restaurant without a nearby table of business men lighting up and contributing to your meal. The concept of smoke free restaurants is about as foreign as nipple piercing and just as unlikely to catch on. Your best evil glare will do little except to elicit a friendly offer of cigarettes. If you happen to be a smoker, light up and enjoy this last bastion of freedom and emphysema.

Cutlery consists of a spoon and chopsticks. Those who have chopstick experience need not feel overly confident. Korean chopsticks differ from the type you've probably used in that they are metal, thin and rectangular in profile. This means that once your hands get the Kimchi sweats or become oiled with a little Kalbi grease, the complexity of operating them grows exponentially. If substantial food restriction occurs, try to view it as a complimentary weight loss program and take to carrying a fork in your pocket at all times.

The price of dinner is eternal vigilance. What this means is that if you want to pay your way in Korea, you have to be quick and willing to fight. Splitting the bill is not acceptable, and the person who pays is usually the most dominant member of the group. It often ends up as a tug of war between the richest, oldest or most socially important people at the table.

The bill will not be brought to you; payment relies upon whoever gets to the cashier first. This may prove an economic boon or a personal trial depending on your morals and current bank balance. Koreans genuinely want to take care of you, but after a while it's acceptable to make a stand and fight for your turn to cough up the cash. After a prolonged period in Korea it actually becomes a time honored and enjoyable game. Real sadistic pleasure can be found in extending this culturally specific behavior to visiting friends and family.

Yoga experience is an asset when dining out as the majority of Korean restaurants do not have Western style tables and chairs. Instead you sit at a low table on the floor, with only a thin cushion to shield you from the concrete reality of Korean dining. Aching ankles, restless limbs and a tendency to fall over due to numb bum are all common complaints, but in time these symptoms decrease in severity.

To attempt to provide even a brief description of every Korean dish available would drastically alter the course of this book and rob you of some of the joys to be found in exploring Korean food. What follows is merely a little information to help guide your culinary journey of discovery.

Two dishes held in high regard by many visitors are Kimbab and Mandu. Kimbab is similar to a California sushi roll. It's basically rice and an assortment of ingredients rolled up in a sheet of dried seaweed. Many versions come without meat and it's often mentioned in the evening prayers of grateful vegetarians.

Mandu are dumplings of varying size, stuffed with mouth watering fillings. They come boiled, steamed or fried. All types are cheap and widely available at restaurants and on the street. They can also be purchased in larger quantities frozen at the local supermarket. Mandu are the traditional fast food of the region and make a great meal or snack for the road.

Other standbys for the Kimchi phobic include Omu Rice and Jajang Myun. The former is a linguistic corruption of omelet rice and is simply fried rice wrapped in an omelet and liberally doused in Ketchup. The latter is a Korean-Chinese dish in which noodles are buried beneath a thick blanket of mysterious black bean sauce containing trace amounts of meat and vegetables.

Bibimbab is another common dish. It consists of a generous serving of rice with Kimchi, ground beef, vegetables, hot sauce and a fried or raw egg laid on top. It often comes served in a hot stone bowl that continues to cook the dish (and your hands) as you eat it. With linguistic assistance, sign language or good luck, it can be ordered to suit your taste, sans egg, meat or hot sauce. If you happen to be visiting a restaurant up in the hills be sure to enquire if they offer mountain vegetable Bibimbab. It's basically the same dish except that the more generic vegetables have been replaced with various roots and shoots gathered from the surrounding slopes by roving grandmothers of goat-like persuasion. These fresh local additions give it a unique taste and texture.

Outside of monasteries, meat dishes are common and vegetarians may find their diet at times lacking in scope. Koreans are slaves to fried flesh, and fish, chicken, pork and beef are all consumed with a passion. The first three are cheaper and thus more commonly encountered, but it is in the realms of barbequed beef that Korean cuisine takes flight and soars to unimaginable heights.

Bulgogi—delicate strips of beef marinated in a special elixir of soy sauce, vinegar, sesame oil, green onions and seasonings, roasted on an iron platter. Kalbi—a Boy Scout's wet dream, delicious ribs sizzling to perfection on a miniature grill set into the table. A spicy chicken version, Dak Kalbi, is also available, though the chicken tends to be indiscriminately chopped up with a meat cleaver. The resulting bone fragments sadly require a slower rate of consumption.

Most of the barbeque grills are gas fired, but a few charcoal ones remain. These babies impart a fantastic flavor to the meat and shouldn't be missed if you come across them. Caution should be taken when sitting, as a knee accidentally pressed against the metal rim beneath these tables can result in a painful burn. More than a few Westerners have returned home with the scars of their infatuation plainly visible.

Amazing soups and stews abound and are certainly worth getting to know on a more personal basis. One of the most frequently encountered is Doenjang Jjigae. This soup possesses a pungent reputation and has been likened to a broth made from old gym socks. This description however is rank sensationalism, and though the smell is distinctive, it's certainly worth trying. Being the product of fermented soy paste, it is strong and salty. If you like Japanese Miso soup, you will probably enjoy it. Other popular stews include those made from Kimchi, tofu, potatoes and beef.

Seaweed soup is held to be a restorer of the body and is given to both pregnant women and people on their birthday. The broth is quite tasty, but the slimy hanks of drifting seaweed require both mental fortitude and a non existent gag reflex if you're planning on finishing a bowl. It's avoided by Korean students at exam times due to the traditional belief that its nasty texture will cause a slip up.

In summer, Korea offers the sweaty diner relief from the heat in the form of Naeng Myun. Fine buckwheat noodles lounging in a frigid bath of icy beef broth, it has often been a source of solace for the overheated teacher on their lunch break.

Last but not the least of these liquid delights is Samgaetang. This dish consists of an innocent young chicken violated post mortem with a Ginseng root. A glutinous stuffing made from rice, salt, garlic, Chinese dates and sections of Ginseng root is packed into the body cavity of a plump pullet. It's then simmered for a few hours until the flesh is just about falling off the bone. Koreans traditionally eat this in summer, but many Westerners find it just the ticket when colds begin to rear their ugly heads during the winter months.

Students and just about everyone else keep a supply of Ramyon close by. These instant noodles come in a bewildering variety of flavors and probably rate as the unofficial food of the nation, for at times it can seem like every second person is slurping from a steaming Styrofoam container. Students in particular are partial to the noodles, due to the fact that preparation and consumption pose little threat to their precious study time.

Korea is rich in seafood, it's just not always prepared in the way you're used to. Finding a grilled fish bigger than your hand takes work and most Koreans view it as a waste. Why dry it out like that when it could be turned into delicate slices of Hoe, the local version of Sashimi? Everything else goes into the pot to make Haemultang, a spicy stew comprising of clams, shrimp, crab and fish.

If you know what you're up to, a trip to the local seafood market or a nearby fishing village can be very rewarding. All manner of produce from crabs to sea cucumbers await your shopping pleasure. Be prepared to bargain, but keep in mind that a smile and a few Korean phrases are the key to good will and reasonable prices.

Those of you who choose to indulge in pies, pastries and cakes may find the pickings slim. Koreans traditionally aren't big dessert fans and the choices outside the local bakeries are few and far between.

Dok is one indigenous treat that will often be brought out after dinner. These sweet sticky rice cakes come in many different styles, and range from soft, honey filled, cinnamon scented balls of bliss, to thick wads of cardboard that would defy the jaws of a rabid cow.

Patbingsu is a summer dessert that enjoys enormous if somewhat mystifying popularity. It consists of shaved ice, red beans, fruit and condensed milk. Frozen legumes don't naturally appeal to most Westerners, but it can take the edge off a sweltering Sunday afternoon when there's no ice cream in sight.

A meal is never considered complete without a cup of coffee and a plate of fruit. The platter will reflect whatever is in season locally; apples, watermelon, strawberries and the mysterious persimmon are all likely candidates for the knife. Koreans for some reason tend to prefer their fruit on the hard side, so be prepared to smile graciously and gnaw like a starving beaver.

Eats from the street are no less varied and offer the added bonus of being easy on the pocket. Yachae Twigim is an indigenous tempura that turns boring vegetables into battered gold. Many of these street foods are sold from mobile carts. In winter, look for the pot bellied stove on wheels, as it's likely to be full of Goguma, sweet potatoes roasted to perfection.

Other wheels with meals dispense Pajon, a savory pancake that comes in a variety of flavors including onion, Kimchi, potato and seafood. Spot a cluster of yelling school students and you have probably located the Tteokbokgi stall. Kids go crazy for this simple snack of steamed rice cakes and boiled eggs soaked in a thick, spicy sauce.

Cavity inclined expatriates may find relief in the banana and walnut flavored breads that appear on the streets in winter, crudely modeled on their natural forms. That said, don't fear the fish-shaped ones, as they only contain tongue blistering doses of sweet bean paste. Occasionally they're found filled with chocolate pudding but these are rare aberrations best kept to yourself.

Wherever you choose to eat in Korea, you'll find something to suit your tastes. Kimchi isn't for everyone, but there exists enough variety that you shouldn't have to subsist on a diet of peanut butter and jam.

HOW MUCH IS THAT DOGGIE IN THE SOUP BOWL?

While some may suggest that this is a rather tasteless title for a chapter on Korea's more exotic dishes, others will hopefully view it as a delightful introduction into what the country has to offer the guerilla gourmand.

One of the most infamous dishes being dog soup. Let's not beat around the bush. It's true that some people in Korea eat dog meat, just like some people in the West choose to consume roast veal or those tasty tender chops made from fluffy wuffy little lambs. This world is large, and regardless of what the internet gurus say about an emerging global culture, there still (thankfully) remain a few differences between various nations. If this were not the case you probably wouldn't be interested in leaving home.

The majority of Koreans do not eat Boshintang. It is not being cooked right now in the school's soup pot, nor is your kind old neighbor fiendishly fattening his pug for Thanksgiving. You're free to eat any number of hotdogs without fear, and the guy out jogging with his pooch is not into lean meat. The vast majority of dogs consumed in Korea are a specific breed raised for slaughter, just like cows or pigs are in the West.

Dog soup is viewed as a virility enhancing dish and as such it is eaten largely by aging men who need to put back a little yang in their wang. It is consumed mainly in the summer months, especially on the Bok days, three specific dates during a period that lasts for a month from mid July to mid August. Boshintang literally translates to soup that builds up the body and many older Koreans believe that it has the capacity to restore stamina and vigor.

(The author at this point wishes to make it clear that he will resist the admittedly compelling urge to refer to 'doggy bags' during this chapter and hopes that his readers will follow his tasteful precedent and keep the Lassie jokes to themselves.)

No one is going to force you to eat dog soup, and chances are extremely low that you will unknowingly wander into a Boshintang restaurant and order a bowl, as the cute little puppy on the specials chalkboard would give it away. (That of course was a joke, as only adult dogs have enough meat to make a really good stew. Yes, that was another one. The author apologizes and will try to behave.)

What will probably happen is that a few of your more outspoken students will bring up the subject and invite you to give it a go. Their motives for the most part will border somewhere between curiosity and entertainment. A polite answer in either direction is all that's required. Regardless of your own culture-specific beliefs, a self righteous rant will not change anything, though it may go some way towards confirming their darker opinions regarding racism and how Westerners think they always know best.

If dog eating offends, it may help to remember that your own place of origin isn't exactly a shining utopia of animal husbandry. Think foie gras, veal pens, battery hens and industrially farmed pork before you get too high on a certain horse named righteous indignation.

Koreans have been eating dog meat for a long time, and as a sovereign nation it's their business whether they choose to allow this practice to continue. If Western visitors really wish to facilitate change, they would be advised to advocate for more humane and standardized methods of breeding and slaughter. Protests and demands for an immediate cessation have only resulted in driving the trade underground and out of the view of government scrutiny.

On a psychological note, those objecting should remember that labeling people barbarians seldom has the effect of bringing about positive change. Name calling and shame tactics only result in a more unified opposition and often entrenches the topic deep in the sticky soil of national pride.

A less contentious food source is the silkworm. In Korea it is known as Beondegi, literally "chrysalis". This time around, Western opposition is mainly about the smell. Who cares that millions of baby silkworms die to feed our appetite for fine fabrics and get callously gobbled up when their work is done. Certainly not most Westerners, as these little fellows tend to lack the deep brown eyes, glossy coat and innate ability to fetch that commands our love and respect.

These tiny snacks are a byproduct of the silk industry, which has a 4,000 year history in Korea. After the caterpillars have spun their soft cocoons around themselves, they are dipped alive in boiling water and the precious fiber is unwound. The boiled bugs themselves are bound for a less glamorous finale.

The plump brown bodies are packed with protein and in the old days they constituted a cheap and readily available source of nutrition for growing children. Hungry kids are no longer a problem in Korea, at least not in the south, but the bug remains to this day a common sight in markets across the country. They even come canned should you wish to take home something for the person who foolishly claims they've tasted everything.

Most Westerners don't end up trying them because they have one hell of a smell. Wandering through your local street market, you'll know where the Beondegi stall is long before you see it, due to its infamous wall of pong. It isn't easy to describe, it's a rich, cloying odor that's kind of like inhaling jungle compost steamed on old bricks. The taste actually isn't too bad, though it's more likely that the awesome odor has merely overridden the neurological zone responsible for processing flavors. They're a bit like a resinous raisin but probably one you won't be mixing in your muesli anytime soon.

If insects are too much to stomach then seafood might be just the thing. Koreans have long obtained much of their nutrition from the rich, cold waters that surround them and as expected, this category contains a few culinary surprises.

Raw octopus or Muno Hoe as it is known locally, is certainly one meal you won't forget. A live octopus is quickly cut up and a plate squirming with two inch sections is brought to your table, accompanied by a bowl of hot sauce. The texture is of course rather rubbery but what lends the meal its poignancy is the suction. People with fillings should exercise caution and those with dentures need not apply.

The parts in question are no more alive than a finger is when removed from the hand but this knowledge does not make the experience any less traumatic. The sensation is certainly stimulating and may well lead to an organic revolution in the field of dental hygiene. Octopus vulgaris Cuvier also appears in more conventionally prepared dishes and is quite delicious when fully cooked.

Another deep water dweller that features prominently in Korean cuisine is the squid. It appears in many forms, from savory packaged snacks to absolutely essential bar food. Koreans love squid and a sure sign of an old hand amongst Westerners is if they know the proper method of tearing it into strips. If you want to impress new friends, remember to always tear across the width of the body, never vertically.

As a newbie you'll more than likely be confronted with this delicious snack on your first night out drinking. A jug of beer will be ordered and you'll be busy shaking hands and meeting people when suddenly a platter laden with smoking hot squid and peanuts will be deposited on the table. Depending on the quality of the bar and the time of year, your squid may vary in texture from burnt shoe leather to very tender jerky, while the peanuts tend to be overlooked.

Like a lot of foreign food, the smell is what often discourages people from trying it. Many find it eerily reminiscent of scorched cat food but the taste is altogether more appealing. Warm dried squid dipped in a mixture of hot sauce and mayonnaise is positively scrumptious and you owe it to yourself as well as your hosts to give it a go. You may find, like many foreigners, that squid breath is a small price to pay for such a tasty addition to your dining repertoire.

Considering the number of squid eaten on any given night in Korea, it's reasonable to expect that a large industry must be at work to meet such heavy demand. A trip to the coast reveals the magnitude of the slaughter. Squid hang dangling from lines everywhere, strung up like a mad woman's laundry left flapping in the wind.

A war of epic proportions is waged every night at sea and the casualties are laid out to rest in the morning breeze. Perhaps someday a memorial will be built by PETA honoring these fallen aquatic heroes. A verse like this might do the job. (Apologies and deepest respect to Lieutenant Colonel John McCrae and his famous poem "In Flanders Fields".)

"On Korea's coast where cool winds blow,
Hang countless squid row by row,
For beer time snacks, they did die,
Dipped in sauce their destinies lie,
Bound for our stomachs, to rest below."

From ports around the county, boats head out each night to seek their catch. Squid have evolved over millions of years and the light of the moon is intimately tied to their breeding and feeding cycles. Fishermen have taken advantage of this knowledge for centuries and the modern fleets that ply Korea's coastline carry numerous lights the size of basketballs to lure their prey to the surface. The squid abandon their dark playgrounds and journey upwards in search of something brighter, only to find themselves scooped out of the sea and pinned to a clothesline, eventually finding their way to a bar near you.

The other seafood spectacle that you'll encounter is the large variety of salted and pickled fish and crustaceans that are part of most Korean meals. They'll be nestled in small bowls scattered amongst the mass of mouth watering side dishes that accompany any meal of substance.

The minuscule dried fish and shrimp certainly add flavor to the rice while the crunchy pickled baby crabs are more of an acquired taste. Kimchi oysters, salted mussels and other innovatively prepared shellfish also await your culinary pleasure, but they can occasionally be the source of a prolonged sojourn in the outhouse so caution is advised.

Korean food is fantastic and while many of the items in this chapter are not for the faint hearted, it could be said that by exploring the more extreme cuisine of other nations, you may come to more fully appreciate your own national dishes. Viva la sausage!

SAUERKRAUT ON CRACK

Kimchi, like Korea, is a unique combination of disparate elements that unite to form an unforgettable experience. Like accordion music or flannel sheets, Kimchi consumption is strictly a matter of personal taste and one that sharply divides Western visitors.

"Devils' cabbage", "that stinky stuff", "sauerkraut on crack" or "God's gift to taste buds", your concept of Kimchi will be colored by your reaction to it. Before you sample this Korean creation and label or libel it for yourself, perhaps a little information is in order.

Kimchi is basically vegetables fermented in a brine solution flavored with garlic, chili paste, and dried fish or shrimp, but like all great things, it's far more than the sum of its parts. Over one hundred and sixty different types of Kimchi are known to exist, and each one differs depending on the region and recipe.

The most commonly encountered Kimchi in Korea, found everywhere from formal dinner banquets to school picnics, is T'ongbaech'u Kimchi or Whole Cabbage Kimchi. Other popular varieties include Mul Kimchi or Water Kimchi, a perennial favorite among Westerners due to its sweet, refreshing taste and Kkaktugi or White Radish Kimchi, a textural extravaganza with its small cubes of crunchy radish basking in a sea of fire.

T'ongbaech'u Kimchi is traditionally prepared in late November and early December and continues to be a mainly female affair. As winter begins its relentless descent down the Korean peninsula the signs of Kimchi season abound. Countless blue trucks, piled dangerously high with Chinese cabbages and giant mutant radishes, whiz past farms and fields. Across the country, markets dedicated solely to providing Kimchi ingredients spring up overnight. These are some of the clues that it is the Kimjang, or Kimchi making period.

Like most Korean activities, preparing Kimchi is a social event, a time to reunite family and friends, to strengthen and reaffirm relationships. Daughters return home to join their mothers, and neighbors lend a hand to this most Korean of endeavors. Family recipes perfected over generations are used, and samples pass between friends like plates of cookies do at Christmas in the West.

In the past, a typical family of five would have processed over 100 cabbages, but now 20 or 30 is more the norm. This decrease in home Kimchi production is due to a number of factors, such as the modern availability of fresh vegetables in winter, the growth of commercially produced Kimchi, and increasingly urbanized lifestyles.

T'ongbaech'u Kimchi is made in the following manner. The cabbages are trimmed of any damaged leaves, split down the centre and soaked in a brine solution. When they have begun to soften slightly they are rinsed in cold fresh water and left to drain. Meanwhile, a fierce brew of thin radish strips mixed with hot pepper powder, salt, crushed garlic, sliced green onions and anchovy or shrimp paste is prepared. This mixture is then rubbed by hand between the leaves; it is from this physical action that the following Korean expression arises, "The taste of Kimchi is the taste of your mother's fingertips."

The halves are then packed into large ceramic jars, the top is layered with more salted cabbage leaves and it is covered and left to ferment. Two to three weeks is the usual amount of time for fermentation, at temperatures between 5-10°C—longer periods produce a sourer, softer Kimchi. Kimchi is best stored at around 5°C. This was traditionally accomplished over winter by storing the Kimchi in large earthenware containers buried partially in the ground and covering them with a straw mantle to limit temperature fluctuations. Nowadays, specially designed Kimchi refrigerators are available to keep one's Kimchi cool.

Asking any Korean about the health benefits of Kimchi is like conducting a survey to see if Russians believe in drinking Vodka. From lofty sources like the Kimchi museum and the Korean Food Research Institute down to your neighbor's grandmother, the answers will amaze and astound you, though at what point your skepticism kicks in is another matter. Everything from it being a major source of dietary fiber and B vitamins, to explaining the absence of SARS and Bird Flu in Korea will be expounded. It was even shipped out to Korean soldiers during the Vietnam War to boost morale, fight fatigue, and ward off depression.

Sadly no one mentions its highly addictive nature, and before you know it you'll be hooked. Tales of strung out Kimchi junkies begging for a taste from Korean tourists in Mongolia or ambushing porters in Nepal are becoming all too common, as more and more Western youths fall under its seductively spicy sway.

Kimchi began its long journey towards becoming a Korean staple when cabbage seeds migrated to China from India around 4,000 years ago. It was there that the humble cabbage and radish began to be preserved in salt, enabling people to have more vegetable matter during the long winters. Through the gradual flow of ideas and innovations, these vegetables and techniques eventually arrived in Korea, and the stage was set for its eventual transformation into the Kimchi we know today.

The earliest written records concerning Kimchi are from the Goryeo Dynasty (918-1392) and mention turnips preserved in brine or soy sauce. These are mere salty shadows, for it was not until Portuguese traders in the 17th century brought Columbus's burning bounty to the east that modern Kimchi was born. It is the chili pepper, in all its red hot glory that makes Kimchi so special. Kimchi derives its rich, red, stain seeking color, its invasive scent and tonsil toasting ability from this ultimate ingredient.

Though one bowl of Kimchi may look the same as another, it can be said that taste, not appearance, is what sets them apart. Some strike with the ferocity of a tiger cub stuffed up your sinuses, whilst others offer enchanting symphonies, each a nuanced masterpiece composed of delicate harmonies of ginger and chili, underscored by bass notes of rock salt and green onion.

Like wine making, multiple factors come into play in the creation of a truly memorable Kimchi. Soil, water, slope and sunlight all contribute to the cabbage's development just as they do for the fruit of the vine. In the production of good Kimchi, quality ingredients are as essential as the skills of the maker. If all goes according to recipe a miracle sometimes occurs, and if you're really lucky you may get to try some of the good stuff. Like fine wine it's to be treasured, though sadly the prospects of cellaring are poor.

Kimchi is present at every meal and is often an integral part of the main dish itself, as in the case of Kimchi stew and Kimchi fried rice. You could say that Kimchi is to Koreans as our salt and pepper shakers are to us, but that would be a gross understatement. Kimchi occupies an almost sacred place in the hearts and minds of most Koreans and woe betide any filthy foreigners who dare to impugn its honor.

Japan recently learned this and is still licking its wounds after suffering a resounding defeat in the Great Kimchi War that ended in 2001. This battle came to a head in 1996 when Japan had the gall to propose its counterfeit Kimchi as an official Atlanta Olympic food. This slight to national pride, along with the loss of export earnings due to Japan's rapidly growing Kimchi industry, sent Korea on the offensive.

It went straight to the top and took its case directly to the Codex Alimentarius, a commission created by the United Nations Food and Agriculture Organization to protect the health of consumers and ensure fair trade practices. Tempers grew hotter than their respective products and a war of words ensued, as each group sought to demonstrate the logic of their cause. Korean producers likened Japanese Kimchi to mere cabbage sprinkled with artificial flavors, while the Japanese patiently explained that Mexicans no longer owned the rights to the Taco.

After a long and bitter struggle a decision was reached and a standard was established for Kimchi products. Those products made without traditional ingredients and fermentation are not legally permitted to be sold using the name Kimchi. Like the French with Champagne, Korea had managed to stop foreign powers from hijacking a source of national identity and in the process gave an old enemy a firm kick in the pants.

As long as you live in Korea, Kimchi will be an intimate part of your life. The sooner you surrender to it the better. Its bold odor will invade the privacy of your apartment, and countless agents will surreptitiously add it to your food. Resistance is useless. Just accept the inevitable, allow yourself to be enriched, and let a new oral fixation take hold.

SOJU FLOWERS BLOSSOM AFTER DARK

Scratch a Frenchman and he'll bleed Burgundy or perhaps a fine Pinot Noir, stab the average Korean and what you'll find is Soju, a distilled alcoholic beverage traditionally made from rice. It's a clear, colorless spirit and ranges in strength from 20 to 45 percent ethanol. After Kimchi it undoubtedly comes a close second in the battle for Korean hearts and minds.

Most Soju tastes like cheap vodka distilled under dubious management in the Ukraine. A handful of change is enough to get you a bottle and a nasty hangover, but if you want something that doesn't taste like rubbing alcohol, you need to spend a few more won.

Most types of Soju are now commercially produced in large factories from sweet potatoes, but some family-run distilleries continue to produce their own liquid gold the old-fashioned way. These smaller businesses make distinctive drops but for the most part, a lot of the Soju on the market today would be better utilized treating swimmer's ear or cleaning whiteboards. If in doubt, try comparing Andong Soju with the muck for a buck sold in the little green bottles.

Soju has been made in Korea for over 900 years and plays an intrinsic part in family festivities and ceremonial occasions. It seals wedding vows and appeases the souls of departed ancestors, as well as performing other, less glamorous roles.

It's an essential component in the germination of the mysterious Soju flower, the poetic description for the piles of Kimchi-laced vomit that decorate the sidewalks on Saturday mornings. Soju also ensures that much needed trace elements and minerals are nightly administered to lawns, flower displays and public parks; for all Korean men are keenly aware of the poor soils that plague the country and patriotically choose to urinate in public if the chance should arise.

Soju is available everywhere. You can order it in restaurants, bars and clubs. Koreans usually drink it neat in small shots. If straight fire water is a bit too much, you can always order Lemon Soju. This innocent tasting combination of lemon cordial, ice and Soju packs a mean punch, and has been responsible for more than a few nasty incidents, (biblically, physically and socially speaking) so caution is advised.

Soju can also be purchased at convenience stores and supermarkets, which may come as a surprise to those from more regulated societies. In fact, depending on your relationship with the corner store proprietor, you may even end up drinking it there.

Soju and picnics go together like peaches and cream, in fact, at times it can seem like there's more green glass than grass at some of the really scenic locations. Chances are that in a few thousand years, the mutated inhabitants of a post apocalyptic Korea will grunt their praise to the vitreous bounty left by the ancestors.

Summer nights often reveal laughing groups of students and businessmen sitting in parks and on cool riverbanks enjoying an impromptu Soju session. The smell of grilled meat from tiny disposable barbeques fills the air and little paper cups pass freely. Koreans are born to share, and if you pass by you'll likely be offered a drink. A poorly chosen route at this time of year can prove quite intoxicating.

During the warmer months it may appear as if the circus has come to town, due to masses of orange and white tents springing up in certain areas of the city. These are Soju tents, and they offer both alcohol and a range of grilled food and other traditional snacks. The prices are low and the food is tasty, though things can get a little rowdy by the wee hours of the morning.

Soju may be the most common route to oblivion but it's not the only way to fill a cup. For a less potent though equally memorable excursion into la-la land try Makgeolli, an unfiltered rice wine, made by fermenting steamed rice. Makgeolli comes in large white plastic containers reminiscent of bleach bottles and is sold everywhere, but for the authentic experience you need to locate a Makgeolli house. These range from small traditional shacks on the edge of the city to whole floors of converted down town office space. Regardless of location they all have wood and adobe walls, tattered traditional windows, a smattering of antiques and a laid back 'Ye olde' feel. They offer a refreshing alternative to the standard pink neon pubs decorated with fake palms and plaster busts of Caesar.

The liquid in question arrives in a large ceramic pot with a ladle and is drunk not from glasses but from overly generous bowls. At first glance it appears to be nothing more than an unimpressive cloudy fluid, basically a yeast infection gone right. The opening gulps have all the charm of watery bad milk with a hint of funky citrus.

The sour flavor isn't one to really savor, so you're probably going to knock it back quickly and hope it ends there. Luckily you're in Korea, and no one is going to listen when you politely attempt to decline a second bowl. By the third, its rough character and brute charm begin to have an effect. A couple more and you may find it's you who's ordering another cauldron of this infernal brew, much to the chagrin of your captive left brain.

Dong Dong Ju, the rural cousin of Makgeolli, is often found in simple stalls at the base of trails leading up to famous peaks and temples. It tastes similar to Makgeolli and can be a nice way to celebrate the end of a long hike. A little time spent in the company of a big Dong Dong Ju pot can greatly ease the pain of a five hour vertical stroll in the hills.

Something a little more familiar to your taste buds might be Bok Bunja. This little number is made from blackberry juice and is unforgettable served chilled on a hot summer's night. It's a sweet luscious syrup, so deep a purple that it seems black. Baby Jesus in a velvet jumpsuit couldn't be smoother.

There are over 600 traditional types of alcoholic beverages, many of which are regarded more as health tonics than party juice. Bek Se Ju is one such popular drink, whose name implies that by regular consumption, a person will live to see one hundred years. It contains, along with alcohol, ten herbal ingredients, including ginseng, licorice and cinnamon. Recovering after a hard night on this stuff can make you question the point of living another hour, let alone a century, but in limited doses it makes for a pleasant change.

During your stay, you may be asked if you'd like to sample some homemade wine. This has nothing to do with grapes whatsoever, as the term wine means basically anything not beer. Homemade wine in Korea is prepared by mixing a few bottles of Soju, a pound of sugar and various herbs or fruit in a large jar and leaving it to soak for a few months. The resulting fluids can vary from quite tasty to downright foul. The fruit flavors, especially plum, tend to be more popular amongst Westerners.

Koreans love more than just our language, they've also developed an unhealthy appetite for our alcohol. You don't have to limit your consumption to homegrown varieties, as whiskey, beer and many other Western spirits can be found wherever Koreans feel the need to drink, (which is just about everywhere).

Most corner stores sell beer and badly cloned whiskey, and any decent sized town will have a few bars catering to those with a hankering for a gin and tonic. Premium Irish and Scottish whiskeys are always on hand for those with too much money and too little sense, and a number of local companies produce decent beer. It can be ordered in bottles or by the pitcher. In the last few years some bars have begun to offer a wide range of international ales and lagers.

Those in need of a Cosmopolitan or Margarita may have to visit the big smoke for cocktail hour, though most rural bartenders are quite happy for you to demonstrate the correct procedure if they have the required ingredients. A few will even order in your favorite tipple if you ask nicely, keeping it stored safely on the shelf with its own little name tag.

When ordering the first round of drinks in a bar or hof, you will be expected by the management to order Anju, a side dish. The choices vary, but the usual suspects include squid jerky, tofu and Kimchi or a fruit platter. In nightclubs, your mandatory entrance fee buys you a table, Anju and a round of beers.

Koreans are a resourceful lot and one of their greatest inventions must be the table beeper. This little device resembles the launch button for a missile designed by 007 drag queens. When depressed, small red lights flash at its base and within seconds a waitress magically appears to take your order. Resist the temptation to order Mr. Bond killed, as you'll only confuse her.

In Seoul, the Lotte department store, and some specialty shops in Itaewon and the nearby embassy area offer a range of hard to source wines, spirits and stinky cheeses. A thick wad of cash or a heat resistant credit card is necessary to avoid heartbreak. Try to remember that you are an informal ambassador for your country; nothing appears more degrading than a pack of feral English teachers fighting over the last wedge of Edam or a bottle of Baileys. Even if inside you possess about as much control as a pervert in a porn store, resist the urge to drool, and take home only what you can comfortably carry.

Now you know what your choices are and where to get your poison, you'd think that this would be the end of the chapter. Wrong. What you now need to learn is how to drink it. In Korea that means something more than just pouring liquids down the orifice with teeth and playing the air guitar. Korea has its own formal drinking culture, so learning a few basic rules will help you avoid offending the boss at your welcoming party.

First things first, you never pour your own drink, as it reflects poorly on your host. This sounds like it may negatively affect your rate of consumption but nothing could be further from the truth. The glass will keep being filled as long as you empty it; if you want to avoid total inebriation just leave an inch or so in the bottom and it will remain at that level. Just as the Bible admonishes us to do unto others as we would have them do unto us, when you see someone else's glass dry, jump in and fill it up.

Remember that Korean culture is a hierarchy based on age, so it's always the job of the youngest at the table to keep the glasses full. If your boss or a senior colleague pours you a drink, hold your glass in both hands. Likewise when pouring for them, hold your left hand, palm up and open, under and against your right wrist or sleeve as a mark of respect.

Those of a germ phobic persuasion may find this next custom a little hard to swallow, for as a way to foster close ties and signify friendship you may be offered a drink from a Korean's glass after they have just drained it. Refusing will likely offend, but then hepatitis and herpes aren't for everyone. If you choose to accept a backwashed beer, drink it completely and return it refilled to the person who offered it in the same manner.

Korea is a group drinking culture, and those who don't like to get drunk on a regular basis may find it a little oppressive. Girls should be ok, but guys would be well advised to formulate a cover story for why they refuse to drink—religious or medical reasons seem to be the most easily accepted. Consistency is crucial, for if you give in just one time and have a glass to appease the crowd, you'll be marked for future indoctrination.

People here love to have fun, and drinking is all about having a good time. Alcohol and the accompanying songs, toasts and general friendly banter all serve as a release from the hectic life of the average Korean. Being willing to drink with the boys will help you make friends quicker than anything else, just don't count on your liver being grateful.

WHEN EVEN THE DOGS KNOW MORE THAN YOU

It's ironic that one of the first things you'll realize when you arrive to teach English is how difficult it is to learn a new language yourself. Those who have never attempted to do so often find themselves at a loss, for acquiring language as an adult is a very different scenario compared to just soaking it up as a baby.

It can feel like some Herculean task, especially when it seems that even the dogs know more than you, but it's definitely worth the trouble. Learning to speak the local language is the key to getting the most out of your time in Korea. It will unlock the hearts and minds of the locals, helping to bridge the gap between you and your new home.

During your first few weeks it may seem unlikely that you'll ever grasp the language. People will open their mouths and out will pour streams of foreign syllables, flowing so swiftly that you won't know where the spaces between words lie. Your Western co-workers will murmur encouraging words of support whilst carrying on fluent conversations in Korean and you'll struggle to recall the difference between hello and goodbye.

In desperation you may find yourself regressing to elementary school tactics like writing reminders on inconspicuous body parts, or smuggling postage stamp sized language primers to the dinner table. Don't be surprised if you catch yourself laughing hysterically at the fact that you once thought high school French was "so difficult".

Don't be too hard on yourself. Latin wasn't learnt in a day and neither was Korean. The amazing news is that anybody can learn to read and write in a weekend. Yes, you read that correctly. If you can dedicate two full days to studying Hangul, the Korean alphabet, you'll have taken the first steps towards fluency. Admittedly, reading and writing aren't speaking, but they do go hand in hand. Just as importantly, they'll give you the confidence to carry on making a fool of yourself until someone understands just what the hell it is you are trying to say!

This alphabetic ease did not arise by chance, but came about through the vision of one man. It was the fourth king of the Joseon dynasty, King Sejong the Great, who gave the Korean people the script they use today. Next time you're handling a ₩10,000 note, stop to look upon the man and give him some respect.

King Sejong recognized that the use of Hanja, or Chinese characters, was instrumental in maintaining the high rates of illiteracy throughout his kingdom. This situation was due to the fact that only the Yangban, the aristocratic elite, had the time, money and privilege to educate their sons in the traditional Chinese script. Hanja is ideographic not phonetic, meaning that students had to memorize many thousands of characters over a long period of study in order to become literate.

King Sejong was one of those most rare of creatures, a practical dreamer. When he realized that Korean culture needed to change, he promptly assembled a select group of researchers and scholars for the sole purpose of creating an alternative to Hanja. Under his guidance they developed a new alphabet in late 1443 or early 1444 and published the results in 1446. Hangul Day on October the ninth commemorates this important event.

Hangul means "Korean script", but was known at the time of publication as Hunmin Jeongeum, "Correct sounds for the education of the people". Many of the Yangban feared the consequences of educating the poor and were openly disparaging, often referring to it as the women's or children's script. It retained this reputation until around the turn of the century when patriots adopted it as a symbol of unity and national identity.

In its present form it consists of twenty four letters; fourteen consonants and ten vowels. Originally there were four other letters but these have become obsolete over time. The letters themselves are very simple and easy to recognize, comprising of mainly vertical and horizontal lines. This combined with the fact that there are no upper and lower cases, makes it easy for kids (and you) to learn, unless of course you're dyslexic, whereupon it will literally become the script from hell.

Good old Sejong would be pleased to know that Korea now has a literacy rate of 98%, one of the highest in the world. It is read from left to right but can also be written from top to bottom. It sometimes appears in calligraphic form, which tends to render it rather inscrutable, but with a little effort even this can be deciphered by the foreign layman.

It'll make you feel pretty good, when after a quiet weekend spent playing around with homemade flashcards, you can actually sound out the beer label in front of you. Of course it won't really mean that much, because you'll only have the vocabulary of an alcoholic parrot, but it's a start.

Deciphering menus and shop signs can be fun because they often contain English words spelt phonetically. Ah, the eureka moment when you sound out "Be-de-oh shaw-pu" or "Hey-su-na-tu caw-pee" and know what it actually means. (Don't worry if you didn't catch that on the first attempt, it was actually video shop and hazelnut coffee.)

Being an English teacher is advantageous in that you'll learn to be more forgiving of your own glacial progress after explaining a seemingly simple grammar point for the seventh time in class. It also tends to help with your vocabulary, as students often repeat the Korean equivalent of the new English word they've learned.

One of the more frustrating things about learning the language is that Koreans have never heard other people butchering their mother tongue. This occasionally results in the odd condescending smirk, but far more depressing is the fact that no one ever seems to be able to guess what you're trying to say.

They just can't mentally process the hideous accents and many seem to blank out when faced with a foreigner trying to communicate in Korean. The elderly in particular can't fathom why it's so damn difficult for you to speak a simple sentence, when even their two year old granddaughters can politely ask a question ending in the appropriate honorific. Living in Korea for any length of time will forever change the way you feel towards tongue tied immigrants back home.

Expect to find yourself in bizarre situations like the following. You are in a bar or restaurant and wish to order a glass of water. You signal to the waitress and when she comes over you say clearly in Korean, "Water please." She stares blankly. You repeat yourself slowly, carefully enunciating the four syllables contained in the two word sentence. Nothing. You decide to ditch the formalities and pare down your request to a one syllable sentence. "Water." Again no response, at least not one that indicates you're speaking the same language.

After eight or more increasingly frustrated attempts to gain access to H2O, that include pointing to the empty water pitcher, miming a particularly fierce rainstorm and grasping your parched throat, your Korean friend intercedes and says what suspiciously sounds like what you originally said. At which point, the waitress replies in perfect English, "Why didn't he just say so?" and fills up your glass.

Another impediment to becoming fluent is that everyone wants to speak English with you. This shouldn't come as any great surprise, because it's why you're being paid to live there, but it can be a major handicap once you decide to learn Korean. One way to get them to cooperate is to explain that by learning Korean you'll come to understand their culture better. A more dishonest yet successful route is to specifically target their pride and vanity by telling them how you've recently learnt that Korean is regarded as the most logical language on the planet and that you're interested in learning something that's superior to English.

If informal street classes aren't floating your boat, it's easy enough to set up a language swap with one of your students. Books, CDs, DVDs and internet sites are also widely available to help you master the basics, and in larger cities there are even official language programs sponsored by the government.

Learning to speak another language is reputedly beneficial for the brain, but more importantly it's good for your personal wellbeing. A lot of Westerners come over and make no attempt to learn Korean beyond the basics: hi, goodbye, beer please and so on. Koreans genuinely feel flattered by visitors who take an active interest in speaking their language and they'll go out of their way to help you if you put in the effort.

Once you start feeling comfortable speaking Korean, all kinds of adventures will present themselves. Admittedly along with the successes will come a few embarrassing incidents but that's just par for the course.

A certain teacher who will remain nameless once visited a remote mountain temple. When asked if she'd like a drink, she misunderstood the question and thought they'd asked her where she'd come from. She replied Young Ju, the town where she lived. When they looked at her strangely she assumed they hadn't heard her and repeated the answer more forcefully. Her awful accent, combined with their question, led the nuns to believe she'd demanded Yang ju, whiskey. It took a few moments for the puzzled teacher to realize what had gone wrong and even longer to put the appalled nuns at ease.

Depending on the situation, things can also turn out favorably, as in the case of a drunken teacher who was once asked by a pretty Korean girl what he did for a living. He meant to say he was a Hagwon (private school) teacher, but ended up mixing his nouns and told her he was Yogwan (cheap hotel) instructor. She found his reply intriguing and requested a trial lesson later that night.

With equal amounts of discipline and curiosity you should be able to yak to the corner store lady, sweet talk your boss and get a taxi to take you home in less than half a year. That doesn't mean you'll be discussing Kant's Critique of Pure Reason anytime soon, but you'll be better off than if you hadn't made the effort. Knowing Korean will help you make friends, soften the occasional bout of homesickness and give you the confidence to get out and explore this truly amazing country, so consider putting down the game controller and picking up a dictionary instead.

INJECTIONS FOR ALL

Those who fear the needle had better not get sick in Korea. It doesn't really matter what ails the body, you'll be up for a shot in the ass if you visit the doctor. Sore throat—injection, feeling lethargic—injection, spot of heartburn—injection, there's probably even an injection for dandruff and chapped lips. Only hypochondriacs with masochistic tendencies will thrive in the land of the jab jockeys.

Like it has with many other Western concepts, Korea has wholeheartedly embraced our conventional medical system and doctors minister to their patients with unquestioned authority. This situation differs greatly to that which you might be familiar with at home. Most Western medical practitioners have come to recognize the wisdom of second opinions, alternative therapies, and the provision of information to allow patients to make their own decisions. This is not the case in Korea, as doctor always knows best and his word is final. This is an unfortunate symptom of Confucian culture and its inherently inflexible hierarchy. Just as the student accepts the words of the scholar, so too should the sick unflinchingly obey the directions of their physician.

In general they don't like to explain things beyond telling you what's wrong, and definitely get a little testy if you fail to meekly submit to their counsel. Expect more than indignation if you should be so foolish as to refuse a course of treatment or request a second opinion. Try to seek medical advice through a clinic that has previously had the misfortune of dealing with pesky Westerners, as its staff will be better prepared for your stubborn and perplexing ways.

Stand firm, ask questions and make your own decisions, as treatment tends to be a little over the top, as in the case of one teacher who visited a local clinic after returning from a short holiday in Cambodia. He had some infected mosquito bites on his ankle and was concerned that they weren't healing properly. It should be noted that while they were not exactly attractive, neither were they gangrenous ulcers of the flesh eating variety.

He didn't feel comfortable with the recommended course of treatment but felt uneasy arguing with a qualified health professional. His reticence cost him dearly; treatment being the complete dermal abrasion of the sores, a series of lengthy ass injections, a plaster cast and a pair of crutches, when all he really needed was the antibiotic tablets that came at the end of his ordeal.

If you somehow manage to avoid the needle, you'll still be sent to the nearest pharmacy to get your pills. Lots and lots and lots of pills. The miraculous power of antibiotics, first witnessed during the Korean conflict, has become deeply embedded in the Korean psyche and they're often viewed as an all round panacea. Many patients expect antibiotics to be prescribed whatever the diagnosis, and a large proportion of doctors yield to these demands, even when the problem is viral. This is regrettably leading to an increase in bacterial drug resistance, though this is by no means an isolated phenomenon unique to Korea.

After a few minutes' wait, the script you hand over will return, magically transformed into a long scroll of perforated paper pouches containing a bright assortment of pills in various shapes and sizes. If you're expecting your prescription to be accompanied by a printout in English listing all the possible side effects, ingredients and contraindications, you are going to be sadly disappointed.

If you're lucky, the pharmacist will speak English or at least write down on the packet when and how the medication should be taken. Don't be surprised if for just a head cold your pills total more than fifteen a day. Prices though are very cheap, and doctors aren't particularly hesitant to prescribe tranquilizers if you feel the need to visit zombie land for the weekend.

If you are not happy with the treatment you're receiving, your embassy should be able to recommend a list of medical facilities they consider safe and reputable, but for the most part your local doctor will suffice.

In Seoul, the Samsung Medical Centre comes highly recommended; it's known for being high tech, friendly, and efficient. Besides a vast horde of general physicians and services, it has over thirty eight specialists catering to both English and Japanese patients. Ladies may wish to make the journey as it has female doctors providing gynecological check ups, something hard to find out in the male dominated provinces.

While it may not indicate superior medical service, it should be noted that mounted on the ceiling of some areas of the hospital are sets of tracks along which small robotic carriages travel. What they are carrying is anyone's guess, but they provide some small measure of entertainment after you've grown tired of leafing through Korean gossip rags and trying to guess which of your fellow foreigners is present due to venereal disease.

Thankfully Korea didn't throw out all the babies with the bathwater and traditional Chinese style medicine is alive and well. Most Koreans tend to use Western style medicine for serious problems and traditional medicine for everything else.

These clinics don't look any different from the injection centers mentioned previously. If you're expecting incense and long wispy beards you're in the wrong century. The décor runs more along the lines of framed medical degrees, vinyl couches and spotless white lab coats.

Bring a Korean friend along as you'll be asked to describe your symptoms and give your medical history. Your pulse will be taken and your eyes checked, after which you'll be prescribed a course of treatment, usually a herbal infusion made on site or at your local pharmacy. These aren't known for their good taste but many foreigners have reported positive results.

You may also be asked if you wish to consider acupuncture or other traditional treatments such as heat cupping. This is a process that leaves your body covered in suction bruises that look like your love interest from ninth grade has returned for a final round of love bites.

Many pharmacies produce traditional medicines along with dispensing Western style pharmaceuticals. The dried ingredients are stored in the hundreds of wooden drawers that usually line the walls of these establishments. Inside are all manner of natural products, from lizard skins and cicada casings to cinnamon bark and powdered ginger.

To prepare these prescriptions, the various ingredients are mixed in specific proportions according to ancient recipes and placed inside large industrial pressure steamers. These modern pieces of equipment quickly and efficiently produce sterile infusions intended for oral consumption. The liquid is then sealed in standardized plastic pouches for easy transportation and storage.

The smell of a Korean pharmacy depends on which particular type of medicine is being brewed. Some really stink, while others can be an intriguing blend of aromas. There's one containing ginger, pumpkin and native dates that smells so incredibly wonderful it makes you want to be sick just to get a taste.

Suffering from too sweet a tooth? Relax and visit your local dentist. All procedures are carried out under hygienic and sterile conditions and are somewhat cheaper than home. If you are lucky enough to teach a dentist or their children, be sure to cultivate the friendship. Quite a few teachers have traded nouns for crowns and returned home with the smiles to prove it.

Medical coverage for most teachers is provided by a public insurer under the supervision of the Korean Ministry of Health and Welfare. After getting your E-2 visa and your Alien Registration Card your employer should register you. Fifty percent of the contributions come from your wage and the other part is paid by the employer. You are looking at handing over about four percent of your monthly income.

Many schools don't register their employees and instead adopt the hope scheme—hope you don't get hurt and hope it doesn't cost too much! If you are registered you will be given a small card that should be shown at hospitals and pharmacies. This card proves you are insured and reduces the cost of treatment and medicine by up to seventy percent.

Korea is a pretty safe country. The landmines are all north of Seoul and very few of the children actually bite. If you exercise the same caution here as you do at home, your biggest medical concern should only be the common cold and the associated ass injections.

THOU SHALT NOT WEAR OLD CLOTHES

All cultures have their own unique, unwritten rules. These regulations aren't usually discussed in glossy guidebooks or embassy pamphlets, but they become obvious once you arrive and start living in your new surroundings. Aussie men must drink copious amounts beer and discuss sports, Brits can't resist moaning about the weather, Americans are duty bound to hang flags from every projecting surface and in Korea no one is permitted to wear old clothes.

Koreans can be pretty anal about clothes and grooming, as the following story illustrates. A certain teacher once lived in Sydney. One of his best friends was born in Korea but had grown up in Australia. This chap was more Aussie than Paul Hogan eating a meat pie. He had long hair, loved watching cricket, wore flannel shirts and greasy jeans, enjoyed his beer, rolled his own cigarettes and played lead guitar in a rock band while studying at university. He was the quintessential poster child for Australian youth in the nineties.

When his friends suffered bouts of excruciating munchies, they would sometimes manage to convince him that it would be a good idea to visit the parental home, located oddly enough, above their Korean restaurant. The arrival of these decidedly messy, long haired boys would cause the mother to alternate between two highly polarized modes of behavior.

She would begin by muttering in Korean, shaking her head and circling the boys like a hungry shark. Next she would move in for the kill, kicking at the scuffed boots, yanking pony tails and twisting earrings, all the while moaning in her own language. She'd pepper this incomprehensible foreign monologue with English phrases like "girl's hair", "no good" and "dirty shoe" for the benefit of the Caucasian youths who'd led her boy astray.

After a suitable amount of melodramatic hand wringing had occurred and her offspring was visibly shamed, she would suddenly pat them on the back, smile manically and bring them mounds of mouth-watering Korean food. She'd encourage them to eat like gluttons, exclaiming how glad she was to see such healthy appetites.

It was only when that certain teacher went to Korea that it all made sense. His friend's mom wasn't crazy, weird or even eccentric; she was just a completely normal Korean mother, albeit one removed from her traditional habitat and struggling to deal with a poorly dressed son.

Koreans are conservative and the following rules are non-negotiable. Shorts are for boys, pants are for men, earrings are for girls, and frayed and torn clothing belongs on the wandering homeless. If you insist on not conforming, on wearing cutoff jeans, faded tie-dyed shirts and grimy sandals, you can expect to receive more negative attention than a tattooed pig at a Bar Mitzvah.

Most Koreans over the age of fifty lived through years of poverty and hardship and their children grew up hearing about it. The oldest were born during the Japanese colonial period and had to survive the occupation years, the Second World War, the Korean War, and the hard times that followed.

The majority of people during these periods were extremely poor and finding enough money for food was a scramble, let alone for luxuries like fancy new clothes. Many sacrifices were made, and one thing older people remember was that even if you didn't have much in the line of a wardrobe, you kept yourself clean and presentable.

This explains why most Koreans cannot begin to fathom why someone from a wealthy Western country would want to dress in rags. They won't appreciate your favorite shirt that you bought six years ago during your first year in college or that comfortable pair of fishermen's pants that you picked up in Phuket. All they'll see are some frayed old rags that look like they were swiped from a Salvation Army charity bin.

Don't even consider arriving with dreadlocks or multiple facial piercings unless you really dig intense scrutiny and wish to develop a heightened sense of paranoia—because everybody will be talking about you. You are coming to be a teacher, and that position in the minds of Koreans is one of respectability, maturity and conservatism.

The intensity of attention will naturally be reflected by your location. Flamboyant individuals with visible tattoos, shaved heads and a lip ring will find large cities like Seoul a little more accommodating than bucolic backwaters. Small country towns are definitely not for those unwilling to compromise. There you'll really feel under the microscope and everything you wear will be noted. In Korea you'll never be just another face in the crowd, you will always be what the crowd turns to face.

You will not change Korea. You will always be a *weigook*—a foreigner. Korea has been a homogenous racial culture for thousands of years and there are still plenty of people who have never seen a foreigner in the flesh. The sooner you accept these facts, the sooner you'll have a chance of being happy.

Image is very important in Korea. If you want to make friends, get along with your boss and enjoy your time there, you'll find the task much easier if you try to look the part. There's no need for drastic action like borrowing your grandfather's suit or shopping for dresses at the Amish outlet mall unless you are planning to teach at a university or Christian college. All you need to do is wear nice, new clothes, basically what you might slip on if you learned that Grandma was coming for dinner.

Being a Westerner gives you a little slack, but there will always be certain expectations. Pants and shirts should be stain free and never ripped, hair neat and clean, faces shaved and shoes shined. These might seem like infringements on your personal style but they're really a small price to pay for a well paid job and the chance to live overseas.

Breaking these most holy of Korean commandments won't see you dragged off to be stoned to death on some dusty soccer field, but neither will it endear you to your boss when you need a favor. Just keep the faith, put some effort into your appearance and good things will be a lot more likely to come your way.

PRIDE AND PREJUDICE

If Jane Austin had gotten out of the house more often, she might have realized that the English weren't the only folks in the nineteenth century to hold the twin traditions of pride and prejudice in high regard. Though Korea is no longer the hermetically sealed kingdom it once was, old paradigms linger on and continue to influence how the nation views itself and the rest of the world.

Should you ever wish to anger a local during the course of your stay, the simplest method is to say something disparaging about the country, for Koreans are a proud and fiercely patriotic bunch. They'll happily argue amongst themselves over which town, county or province is the best, but watch them unite if anyone dares attack their sense of national identity. Koreans love their country and can compete with anyone when it comes to heartfelt displays of national devotion.

This kind of patriotic fervor is easily enough understood if seen in the fading light of past glories, for it seems logical, if somewhat old fashioned, that certain nations should be inordinately proud of their earlier military, colonial and commercial achievements. Two thousand years later the Italians still rest upon their Roman laurels and the Dutch and English nostalgically recall the vast territories they once controlled.

Other nations prefer to point out the cultural achievements of their ancestors. The Greeks bestowed upon the world their sublime arts, the Egyptians their colossal pyramids, the Iraqis the first written laws, the Mayans their knowledge of the stars, the Cambodians their architecture and the Scots their bagpipes—though technically speaking the last example may count more as a strike than a home run.

This isn't by any means a final or definitive list of cultural highlights but they're all no brainers when it comes to national pride. Anyone who is able trace their ancestry back to these kinds of seminal discoveries and developments is likely to feel a bit superior. You don't have to possess a combined doctorate in the fields of rocket propulsion and neurosurgery to grasp why certain citizens of the world think they're pretty hot stuff.

Which of course begs a certain question. Why does a nation that most people couldn't find on a map before the cold war, (and quite a few still can't) consider itself to be the most amazing place on the planet? How does a country famed for cheap electrical goods, small to mid-sized hatchbacks and fermented cabbage come to regard itself as a cultural superpower? To answer this question, you need to consider Korea in terms of geography and invasion.

Korea was, and still is, a tiny nation compared to the might of China. Resting on the flanks of a hungry tiger, Korea suffered frequent maulings but always managed to somehow avoid getting eaten. This was because Koreans recognized that those nations that fought China for complete independence eventually became her next meal. They wisely decided that a little ass kissing wasn't such a terrible price to pay for autonomy and promptly puckered up. This meant paying tribute, which they did in both word and deed. Admittedly saying "uncle" hurt their pride, but along with humble pie came repeated servings of culture and technology.

The neighbors across the waters to the east also liked to play the intimidation game, though their specialty was invasion. Prior to the twentieth century it was more of a smash and grab routine, but then they got greedy and decided to stick around, all of which contributed heavily to the national psyche. Scratch a spot once and it bleeds, pick at it over a long enough period of time and what you end up with is a scar, otherwise known as proud flesh. It ain't pretty but it's tough, hairless, and a constant reminder of the past injuries.

Sandwiched between two bullies and assaulted on a regular basis, Koreans came to develop a strong and unified sense of self. They weren't Chinese, though they shared certain cultural traits, and they damn well weren't Japanese. They were Korean, with their own unique language, culture and physical characteristics, and to this day they remain a little prickly when it comes to anyone making comparisons.

This sense of difference, of being unique and separate from their neighbors intensified during the Joson dynasty, when for over five hundred years Korea closed its borders to the outside world. It was this period of self imposed isolation that gave rise to the name the Hermit Kingdom. Korea turned away from any cultural or commercial interactions with other nations, viewing exposure to foreign influences as a potential source of cultural contamination, racial pollution and social disturbance. Only the most critical diplomatic and commercial ties were permitted, all others were severed, and in a relatively short space of time Korea sank into a deep parochial slumber.

With the borders sealed, trade in both ideas and products was limited and generations of Koreans lived, worked and died in the same small villages where they'd been born. Within this closed and static environment family ties and personal reputations grew to be of the utmost importance. Families kept records of their descent, marking down the birth of children, the success of sons, and the honor brought through the careful arrangement of marriages.

To come from a taboo social group, a disgraced family or to be born illegitimate meant that a person would remain forever at the bottom of the pile. To be the child of a prostitute was to be condemned to a life of hardship and poverty. There was no chance of inheritance, no right to the father's family name and no ancestors to call one's own. In a society that prized filial loyalty, legitimacy and honor above all other things, the little bastards of the period were right out of luck.

These ancient attitudes and antiquated worldviews continue to exert a strong influence today, a good example being Korean views on adoption and marriage. Though there are lots of children in orphanages, it's extremely hard for these organizations to find Korean families willing to adopt, as most people find the concept of taking an unknown child into the family unsettling. Who knows the child's descent? What's their history? God forbid, it's possible that seven generations ago the child's mother might have been a concubine. These concerns may seem inconsequential to the Western mind, but in Asia a stain endures through generations.

To this day the national preoccupation with ancestry continues and similar concerns apply to marriage. Does the groom belong to a good family? When were they first mentioned in the history books? Where are her parents from? What's her family tree like? What social class are they descended from? All of these queries must be answered satisfactorily if parental blessings are to be given. Of course things are beginning to change in this respect, but the majority of Koreans still consider these matters to be of some importance when selecting a mate.

With this kind of scrutiny and concern, it comes as no surprise that Korea has a thriving professional matchmaking industry working hard to ensure that suitable singles from suitable families are introduced in the hopes of securing a suitable union for a suitable fee. Korean parents spend countless hours agonizing over their offspring's choice of a mate. More than a few relationships have died on the disco floor once the relevant parties have sobered up and probed each other's backgrounds.

This concern with blood and family is hard to take seriously when most Westerners don't even know the names of their great grandparents, but it's an important part of the national psyche and one that explains a lot about how Koreans interact with each other. Mix in a dash of Confucian snobbery concerning schools, jobs and hometowns, and you'll start to understand why Koreans are so interested in each other's business. Their culture demands that they learn as much as they can about the people around them, so that they understand where they stand in relation to each other. This explains why they ask what seem to be highly personal and irrelevant questions when they first meet you. They aren't trying to be nosy or offensive, they're simply attempting to place you in a social hierarchy that doesn't traditionally have a slot for foreigners.

Unfortunately, this history of isolation has also influenced their views on race. If the national belief system posits that Koreans are an ethnically pure people, then by illogical conclusion all other folks must be somehow a little inferior. This rubbish about pure Korean blood means that while Koreans are comfortable with the idea of you teaching their children, they definitely don't want you becoming a citizen, buying the house next door or marrying into the local population.

While it takes a pretty brave Korean to bring home a foreigner for dinner, it requires a suicidal one if the love interest happens to be a little dark of complexion. Sadly, many Koreans buy into the lie, and while white isn't right, brown is even further down on the totem pole. If you come from an ethnic group which has noticeably darker skin you can almost certainly expect to hear your fair share of racist remarks during your visit. These may range from naïve questions in the classroom to drunken insults hurled across the street. Neither should you be shocked to come across offensive cartoons in the mainstream media, or overhear ignorant comments from your otherwise educated Korean co-workers. That said, it emanates more from ignorance than genuine hostility.

By extension, not being Korean means that you'll be viewed by some members of the population as potentially dirty, diseased, degenerate, ill mannered, unattractive, uncouth and uncultured. It ain't right but this is what you're up against if you decide to live and work there, though of course most Koreans will be far too polite to come out and actually say what they're thinking.

The same discrimination applies to anything else that sits outside the great mass of what's deemed normal or acceptable. If you're homosexual, deaf, wheelchair bound, dyslexic, or epileptic, you'll find that Koreans are still quite conservative, and hold views that back home wouldn't have been deemed progressive during the early years of the great depression. This isn't to say you can't attain a position, but be prepared for the request of a photo in your job application and all kinds of highly personal questions during your interview should they learn you're not a member of the Brady Bunch.

It's depressing, but many employers still believe that there's a correlation between appearances and the ability to teach English as a second language. How a birthmark or a missing limb affects one's aptitude to succinctly explain the difference between a homonym and a heteronym is a mystery, but it's sadly one that you'll have to overcome if you're perceived to be different.

A similar bias extends beyond genes to culture itself. This will become especially apparent should you try to discuss the comparative strengths and weaknesses of different countries. Whilst it won't be difficult to elicit responses as to why the rest of the world is a screwed up mess, don't expect your students to be candid in regards to their own cultural shortcomings. By now you should have learned that Korea is basically a perfect place, a happy utopia where the problems that afflict the rest of the world are miraculously absent. Any attempts to point out the numerous inconsistencies between this fantasy and Korean society at large will be taken as a personal insult.

This inability to look objectively at themselves is no doubt a psychological reaction to the trauma inflicted by centuries of war, abuse and occupation. Anyone who comprehends the enormous suffering the Korean people have endured can understand how this cult of superiority has evolved over the centuries in order to protect them from the grim reality that they were considered nothing more than useful pawns by the great powers that surrounded them. While the injustices of history in no way excuse this kind of thinking, they do allow you to step back from the emotional edge and realize that a lot of what gets said isn't really about you at all. It's about a nation still coming to terms with itself, the world it tried to ignore, and the far reaching consequences of that fateful disengagement.

While this chapter doesn't paint the rosiest of pictures, it hopefully offers you a little insight into why things are the way they are. Your goal, should you choose to accept this mission, is to take it all in your stride and do your job to the best of your abilities. If, when it's all over, a few Koreans have changed their minds about how they perceive themselves and the world around them, then you can honestly state that your time there was an educational success.

SEX, DRUGS AND ROCK'N'ROLL

It is an undeniable fact that you're going to have plenty of sex in Korea. Unfortunately, the vast majority of it will be with yourself. While it's possible that a drunken colleague may show a passing interest, the locals won't be lining up for the experience. Korea is not the spot to visit if all you're after is a low budget bonk fest. Virginity is still a valued commodity and though things are changing rapidly, the sexual revolution that swept through the West forty years ago has only just begun to gather strength down in the hermit kingdom.

Of course, as in any country, it all depends on whether you are a guy or a girl. If you are a foreign female with a heartbeat, chances are someone will find you attractive and attempt to engage you in the horizontal polka. On the other hand, overweight gentlemen with questionable hygiene and underdeveloped social graces may find the offers few and far between. This isn't the Philippines or Thailand. Korea ceased to be an impoverished agricultural backwater decades ago, and young women no longer throw themselves at unappealing white guys in the hope of finding a better life.

Combine Confucian concepts of sexual morality with a heavy dose of pride and prejudice and you'll begin to see why this is not the land of the one night stand. It isn't that Koreans don't enjoy sex, you only have to pass through the hallway of any cheap hotel to dispel that notion, it's just that as a foreigner the stars are not favorably aligned in your direction.

There are lots of reasons why this is so. One is that from a young age Koreans are fed the line that the nation is one happy homogeneous entity, safe from the associated perils that haunt the mongrel nations of the West. Families can trace their lineage back hundreds of years and take great pride in maintaining the family tree. Understandably they aren't thrilled about the thought of Joe Blow being grafted to a bough of honorable ancestors.

Quite a few older Koreans openly denigrate 'mixed relationships', condemning them as pollution of the nation's blood. Most won't come out and say it, but the majority of elderly people are of the opinion that the East is best, the West is less, and never the twain should mix.

It's a weird inverted racism, kind of like visiting Alabama on acid. You can almost hear them thinking "White folks is good people, I like them, but God help my daughter if she ever brings one home." Those with more melanin needn't feel special, as it ain't just the paleskins that are held in contempt.

Most Westerners couldn't give a rat's ass about what their grandparents think when it comes to dating, but over here the views of the elderly command respect. Young people might not agree with their reasoning but neither are they likely to go against it. Just knowing that Grandpa could blow a valve and rotate in his burial mound for eternity discourages more than a few Koreans from taking things further than a friendly chat.

Another factor in the equation is that most Koreans don't find Westerners all that attractive. For some strange reason beer guts and bald spots aren't all that alluring for the ladies, likewise you don't find the fellahs going ga-ga over thighs that can crush watermelons. It can be frustrating to accept, but on this particular course you're starting out with a handicap. If your main purpose in coming was to get lucky with the natives, you're probably in the wrong place.

Unlike the West, which has always placed a certain mysterious value on the exotic oriental, Koreans don't traditionally associate foreigners with any particular notions of beauty or sexual prowess. For most guys, about the only thing running in your favor is the mistaken belief that foreign men are hung like donkeys. Unfortunately, this fallacy will be revealed as a lie the moment you drop your pants, so unless you're a part time porn star on vacation, it's probably not in your best interests to raise that particular myth.

You'll occasionally receive compliments that favorably liken you to some well known movie star or singer. Don't fall into the trap of thinking that because a female student says you look like Brad Pitt it means she finds you sexy, as these observations are made on the most superficial grounds. For most Koreans, comparing you to a famous person is like a farmer pointing out that one of his mares resembles Naomi Campbell. She may indeed have long legs and glossy black hair but that doesn't mean he's planning to bring her back to the barn for a sleepover.

The smart thing to do is smile, nod and accept these compliments with a shaker full of salt. They're ok for the occasional ego boost, but you'd be wise to resist reading too much into them. More than a few foreigners have made themselves look like idiots by professing their love, only to find that the feeling was in no way reciprocated. Before you say anything you'll regret, ask yourself if you really want to be involved with a woman who thinks you have the jaw of Bruce Willis or the forehead of Nicholas Cage.

It's all very well to meet for a few drinks after class or hang out together in the singing room, but for most Korean girls to take it any further is a serious matter. The hand of hypocrisy lies heavy on the land and it's the women who carry the burden, while the men are free to have sex with prostitutes, coffee girls and anyone else they can talk into bed. This of kind of promiscuous sexual activity has been traditionally viewed as a man's prerogative, and even today it's considered to be acceptable, if somewhat risky behavior. Good girls however, are expected to refrain from any form of naughty business and save themselves for Mr. Right, even if he's been banging away like a toy drum at Christmas time.

Attitudes are changing, but it's still the case that a girl intimately involved with a Westerner is likely to receive her fair share of public censure and abuse. The severity correlates to where she lives and how traditional the community is. The possibilities range from sly comments in the street to her parents threatening to disown her. This means that for a lot of young women, dating you just isn't worth the hassle.

The majority of those willing to brave your love assume that the relationship is heading towards the only acceptable conclusion they can conceive of, that being marriage. Hooking up, getting freaky, and seeing how things turn out doesn't sit comfortably within the confines of the existing social structure. Casual sex is a definite risk, in that if you get bored and move on, she'll be left to carry the label of monkey slut around town.

The point of this isn't to discourage you from dating Korean girls, it's to try and drive home the message that the situation here is a little different. Think long and hard about whether you really like someone or whether this is just a case of love at first erection, because your actions can have long and potentially damaging repercussions. If you do choose to play the field, have the decency to be clear about what you're after and how things will be in the morning. That said, there are more than a few girls who just wanna have fun, so a year in Korea doesn't have to spell solitary confinement for Mr. Happy every weekend.

Western women face a rather less complicated scenario when it comes to finding romance or a decent facsimile. You'll meet plenty of interested parties, but most of them will be more excited about what's inside your jeans than the contents of your mind. The chances for true love are slim, as most Korean men will view it as nothing more than an opportunity to carve an exotic notch in the bed board, but what else is new? If all you're after is a little loving then you won't starve, though foreplay and cuddles may not figure prominently on the menu.

When it comes to avoiding pregnancy, STDs and all the other joys of sex, it's probably a good idea to come prepared (no pun intended). AIDS, herpes and nine pound babies can seriously cramp your lifestyle, so be smart and play it safe. The only 100% effective method for avoiding these complications is to join a strict monastic order and avoid the opposite sex like the plague. A less dramatic option is to employ a little rubber during intercourse. Some men may complain that condoms negatively affect intimacy, but they probably haven't had to tell their partner why they have syphilis either.

Condoms are easily enough purchased in Korea, but girls had best fill their prescriptions before they depart. Explaining to an old male doctor in broken Korean why you need another year's supply of the contraceptive pill is never going to be fun, so do yourself a favor and get more than you need before you leave home. This way you'll know exactly what you're taking, when to take it and how it works.

If this all sounds a bit too daunting you can always fall back on the time-honored tradition of masturbation. There is absolutely nothing wrong with a quick wank and it's always cheaper than buying dinner for two. Again it's probably a good idea to bring over what you need, whether that be an item of hardware or a selection of 'reading' material.

Korean censorship requires that certain anatomical features be blacked out, which may come as a surprise to those used to more liberal standards of photography. Of course, there is always the remote possibility of being stopped at the airport by customs officers looking for 'objectionable material', so you could just move with the times and ask your boss to include high speed internet in your contract.

At this point in the book the topic of gay and lesbian sex must be calmly addressed. According to Koreans, there are absolutely no homosexuals there, and you should all be ashamed for even thinking about bringing your filthy habits with you. Everybody knows that it's a dirty, perverted lifestyle choice that can only lead to a lonely existence filled with polyester clothing, Persian cats and an unhealthy obsession with Broadway musicals.

If you insist on importing your wicked ways to the land of purity and righteousness, there are probably a few things you should note. Kissing in public is out. That means everything from a peck on the cheek to tonsil hockey. On the flip side, Koreans are ok with members of the same sex being relatively physically intimate. This means that an arm around each other in the pub is perfectly fine.

Two words spell how to get by without too much grief—be discreet. In a perfect world no one should have to hide who they are but this is, after all, Korea. The neighbors won't bat an eyelid if a friend sleeps over on the weekend, but they will take notice if you insist on running a conga line of oiled muscle boys down the hallway every night.

Lesbians have the advantage of being able to fly under the radar, as Koreans think of homosexuality as mostly a male affair. This means you can hold hands everywhere, hug with abandon and never feel like you're flouting local customs. Again discretion is advised. The locals will put down your lack of male company to an admirably sheltered upbringing, whereas hosting a 'dykes on bikes' chapter meeting may blow your cover.

Like real estate, think location, location, location. If an openly gay or lesbian lifestyle is important to you, one where you can express your sexual orientation and live freely without fear or censure, consider staying at home. If this isn't an option, then living in a big city like Seoul will make things a little simpler. Here you'll find bars, clubs and saunas run by queer folk. Your best source for up to date information on parties, people and happenings is the internet. While it's true that Seoul doesn't shine a light on San Francisco, it's a hell of a lot more fun and forgiving than your average small town out in the rice fields.

Now for some good news. Unlike the corrupt moral cesspools of the West, South Korea is a law abiding, drug free society. This means you no longer have to worry about menacing strangers forcing you to inhale that nasty Marijuana smoke. In fact, you could probably live here for the rest of your life and never get high again.

No more Charley induced yarn sessions down at the local pub. No more midnight runs to the all night gas station for a tub of triple fudge ice cream and extra rolling papers. No more disco biscuit dance frenzies where the love of your fellow man takes on a whole new meaning. No, you're quite safe here, and all that unfortunate drug business is behind you.

That's not to say that there are absolutely no drugs to be had. After all, even Koreans are human, and getting bent behind the garden shed is one of mankind's oldest tricks. A wide variety of gear is probably out there, but then again so are the cops and nosey neighbors just waiting to catch a foreigner with their hands in the cookie jar. The risks involved are many, and the government seems more than willing to make an example of foreigners who refuse to follow the rules.

If you do get caught with drugs it won't be a pleasant experience. The lucky ones busted with a joint might get away with a hefty fine, a short stint behind bars and a deportation order. Those found in possession of hard drugs, or unfortunate enough to be dealt a zealous prosecutor, can look forward to the possibility of spending some serious time behind bars. Korean jails aren't in the same league as the Bangkok Hilton, but neither are they the coolest of places to waste away your precious youth.

Of course the author categorically denies any attempts to link him with suggestions that this book encourages illicit drug use, and firmly recommends that whilst in Korea people keep their heads down and noses clean. However, if certain readers insist on placing themselves in harm's way, the following information may be of some interest.

As per earlier advice regarding deviant sexual practices, the key here is not drawing attention to yourself. In Korea you can't blend into the background, because out in public there will always be someone watching you. Take care in any attempts to gain access to psychotropic substances and keep bloody quiet if you should actually get hold of them. Loose lips sink ships, so think twice about who you tell. Though nobody likes a tightass, it's probably safest if you keep your stash to yourself or share it with only a few discreet friends.

On the sin-o-meter, most Koreans rank recreational drug use somewhere between human sacrifice and devil worship, thus it's a wise idea to keep a low profile when consuming the goods. Sparking up a joint at two a.m. on an empty rooftop is a better choice than fumigating the apartment on Sunday morning to the sounds of Cypress Hill. The same goes for party pills. Getting wasted in a noisy nightclub in Seoul with a hundred other freaks is much less conspicuous than groping each other in the park at lunchtime. Koreans will put a lot of strange behavior down to being foreign but they aren't stupid. Red eyes might well be the result of allergies, but giggling in your underpants on the subway is a dead giveaway.

Scoring drugs from random strangers in poorly lit areas is never a good idea. At best it results in shoddy merchandise, at worst it's a recipe for disaster involving police with false moustaches. If you're so desperate that you can't resist trawling the bars in the hopes of meeting Mr. Goodstuff, it would be (hint hint) beneficial to do so in large port cities with significant Nigerian, Turkish and Russian communities.

A smarter move would be to get out a little on the weekends and meet some people, because in any expat community, there are always those that do and those that don't. Be cool, exercise a little patience and sooner or later the topic will come up. If you nod affirmatively, salivate at the right point in the conversation and seem to know what you're talking about, someone will probably take pity on you.

As in all things, this will come down to how you conduct yourself on a day to day basis. If you're known as a self righteous prick who never lends a hand or shares his Oreos, you can forget it. On the other hand, those who are willing to cover the occasional Kindie class or help a co-worker move house have a much better chance of being invited back for a secret session.

After examining these first two rather dreary topics, it comes as something of a relief to discuss Korea's exciting music scene. While it's true that there are some great Korean rock bands out there, they unfortunately lie buried beneath massive piles of steaming Asian pop. The same applies to less mainstream music. Classical compositions performed on traditional instruments can be quite beautiful, and there are a number of unique solo artists in the musical wastelands, the problem is finding them. The few radio stations that aren't pumping out saccharine sweet bubble pop seem to be solely focused on indigenous Trot and Bonjak, the sonic equivalent of crooner rock played double time through a cheap 80's synthesizer.

Asian boy and girl bands are painfully abysmal and make groups like The Backstreet Boys and The Spice Girls sound like creative geniuses. The only real pleasure they offer is in the field of anthropology. The music industry's annual spawning of bleach headed dance drones grooving in identical tight white suits is one of Korea's most captivating sights and not to be missed. Most newcomers consider the matching costumes and highly choreographed dance routines to be the best part of late night TV, whilst true connoisseurs tend to focus more on the stylized facial expressions, dyed hair and the absolute lack of original lyrics.

As mentioned earlier, the masochistically inclined may wish to investigate the mystery that is Bongjak and Trot. These genres require a fairly detached intellectual attitude towards music if any enjoyment is to be had. There's absolutely nothing like it back home, and most newbies find it extremely difficult to appreciate. Listening to it is like being force fed amphetamine-laced cheese through a broken speaker, whilst simultaneously having a tooth pulled and your feet tickled. It is pretty crazy stuff, and once you've heard it you'll never look at elderly Koreans in quite the same light.

Aficionados of dodgy love ballads are also in for a treat. Korea excels in the production of whey faced anorexic idiots moping after their childhood loves, and it seems that every second song concerns some distant summer night and a kiss that might have been. Your typical music video is filmed in black and white, and features air brushed androgynous she-men clenching their fists in the pouring rain, or melancholy waifs in long dresses penning anguished entries in secret diaries as the lonely wind stirs the falling leaves outside.

This kind of pap is all well and good if you're only after a bit of mindless ear candy, but if you're looking for original music with depth, you'll need to go way beyond anything the local music industry deems marketable. As is the case with most consumer products, the stuff that gets the big advertising push tends to look great but lacks in terms of enduring quality. It doesn't matter if an artist is talented or innovative, all that seems to count is whether they can dance in formation and endure regular bouts of cosmetic surgery.

The best way to track down tunes is to start talking music with people who've been in Korea for a couple of years, as most folks are happy to share their nuggets of audio gold. Another option is the internet, which has the added benefit of you being able to listen to and download tracks if you find something that piques your interest.

The other major source of information will be your students. Again, think demographics if you want the good stuff. You can basically write off any students under the age of twenty one and over thirty five. Those in between will have had exposure to recent Western musical influences and the time to discover local bands that aren't completely at the mercy of recording executives and hair stylists.

In summary, if you want to get laid, get high and get by, then get out of the apartment on Saturday night and head down to your local watering hole. There is a pretty good chance that with equal amounts of luck and liquor you can have all your filthy desires met in one location. As for the rest of you law-abiding moral Mennonites, feel free to stay home, sing a psalm and pray for these wayward sheep.

WELCOME TO THE LOVE SHACK

The accommodation spectrum in Korea goes from classy international hotels with wine bars in the basement, to surreal love motels complete with mirrors above every bed and sex toy vending machines in the halls. Somewhere in between these two extremes lie hostels, home stays, traditional inns and camp grounds.

Hotels are rated by the Korean tourism board through the following categories: super deluxe, deluxe, first, second and third class. Super deluxe translates to five star, and they have all the top notch services and luxury you would expect and a correspondingly stratospheric price. A basic room will cost at least ₩300,000 and the fancy suites worthy of a president require a second mortgage and the promise of your first born child.

As you work your way down the hotel ladder the price drops and so too does the quality. Many of the lower class hotels aren't really worth the money, though they tend to have at least one person on hand who can speak English. Beware of extra taxes and service charges, as these can add up if you are staying for more than few days.

The best deals in town are the Yeogwans. These don't really seem to be any different from the third class hotels except in their lower prices. They are easily spotted by the large red symbol on the roof or above the entrance; it's a stylized bathtub with steam rising from it. This symbol is also used by public bathhouses, so if you ask for a room with cable TV and are instead escorted to a sauna full of naked men, chances are you're in the wrong establishment.

Rooms come in two flavors, those with Western beds, and rooms with Korean-style floor mattresses. Many of the beds are so solid you might think that the floor option would be the same, but the key here lies not in hardness but in heat. Korean rooms are heated by the Ondol system. Traditionally this was achieved by burning charcoal in an oven at one end of the foundation and the resulting smoke and heat was then channeled through a mazelike configuration under the floor until it exited from the opposite side of the building. Nowadays an oil or gas furnace takes care of the combustion process and pipes carry hot water through the concrete floors, a much more efficient heating system that also avoids the danger of carbon monoxide poisoning.

Some Westerners like sleeping on the cozy Ondol floors in winter, but the downside is that most hotel rooms do not have individual temperature controls, and your average Korean tends to like it hot. This can result in sweaty, nightmarish sleep and a predisposition to crotch rot. Western beds don't cool the room down but they get you at least a foot off the molten linoleum.

If you do choose to sleep on the floor, ask for some extra Yos (Korean mattresses) early in the night, because getting the front desk to round up more at 1:00a.m. can be a difficult operation, especially if you are conducting it as a sleep deprived pantomime. Be aware that these mattresses are basically anorexic futons, or to be more precise, thick padded cotton quilts. It can take quite a mound to usher the skinny hipped into the land of nod.

Yeogwan rooms can be noisy, as they're often located near train or bus stations. Depending on the price and check-in time, you might not have a lot of space, but you will usually have a private bathroom. Beds often lack sheets, leaving you to sleep on the slippery satin bed covers. Depending on the temperature of the room you may not need the large psychedelic quilts that are on hand. TVs are standard issue in most Yeogwans, though if you don't know much Korean you'll end up watching a lot of CNN.

Décor usually includes a few framed oriental watercolors, a faded photograph of a mountain, last year's beer calendar featuring well endowed models and a box of Kleenex. Furniture routinely consists of pre-Ikea veneer dressers and a large mirror. Wallpaper and linoleum are almost always the standard pink or pastel lime. Rooms tend to be hot in winter and summer, though all come with fans, and air conditioned rooms are available for only a little extra.

Yeogwan employees tend to speak little English and the prices are almost always non-negotiable. What makes them a good deal is that they are fairly cheap, ranging from ₩35-60,000, and they're found just about everywhere.

The Yeogwan evolved from the Yeoinsuk. These are leaner operations, often with shared bathrooms, fewer frills and are family run. The rooms can be very small and simple, but the price is cheaper, from ₩25-50,000. Remember to ask to see the room before you pay, as some can be a little on the medieval side—think monks' cells without the uplifting frescoes.

If you want to meet real locals, perhaps you should consider staying at a Minbak. These are Korean homes that have a room available for rent, either by the night or for longer periods. They are generally cheaper than Yeogwans and are sometimes the only thing available if you hit a resort town during holiday periods.

The quality of accommodation varies from family to family, but there are some great gems out there, especially in some of the coastal fishing villages and mountain areas. If you run a search on the internet using the words 'homestay' and 'Korea' you should be able to find something that appeals, though half the fun can be going with the flow and seeing where the grinning old lady at the bus station takes you.

Another interesting option is the motel or love shack. From the outside they don't look unlike your average Yeogwan, but that's because it's what goes on inside that counts. The standard rooms come with lots of large mirrors (some in interesting places), twenty four hour soft porn on the TV, red mood lighting and condom vending machines. The fancier ones can have funky shaped beds, erotic murals, glass walled bathrooms, and come decorated in what art historians would probably call Mutant Rococo-Boudoir.

A short drive outside of larger cities finds them in business catering to monkey business. Hidden down quiet country lanes, these pleasure palaces have all the standard bells and whistles, plus car parks with plastic drapes that hide the license plates, and vending machines that dispense room keys with guaranteed discretion. Some suites even come equipped with sex chairs, accompanied by laminated diagrams illustrating the fifteen possible positions for those who lack imagination. They might not be your first choice but they're certainly an option worth considering if nothing else is vacant or you're lost, it's raining and your traveling partner has gone ominously quiet.

Korea has quite a few hostels but they tend to not always be situated in the most convenient of locations. They're clean, have friendly staff and are very well appointed. Korean hostels have great facilities, and the prices for dorm rooms start at a reasonable ₩10,000 and go as high as ₩25,000. More expensive private rooms are also available. Hostels aren't always that cheap but they offer you the chance to meet other travelers. Their staff are used to helping English speaking customers, and many come with additional perks such as cheap tours or Korean culture and language lessons.

Camping can be great in Korea, just make sure you have the right equipment, especially during the rainy summer months. A certain teacher and his girlfriend once set out to circumnavigate the country by motorbike. They left in June and planned to keep costs down by camping. The problem was they were a little too frugal during the preparation period and bought a cheap tent. (Never buy a cheap tent in a monsoonal area!) They suffered from no shortage of beautiful campsites on their journey, but they did find that their tent leaked like a sieve and steamed up like a Turkish bath. They spent three quarters of the trip sleeping in Yeogwans and love motels, as it poured nearly every night of their journey.

Most camp sites are free, and where you do pay a fee, it is usually between ₩5,000 and ₩10,000. For this you get a touch of luxury like hot showers and flush toilets. Many have raised wooden platforms on which you can pitch your tent, greatly reducing the chance of waking up wet. Campsites often have a small store attached to the office, selling basic Korean essentials like Ramyen, beer and butane canisters for gas stoves.

In the mountains, the National Park Service also operates huts and shelters for hikers. These are found along trails in many of the larger parks and they provide an alternative to pitching a tent. They aren't anything fancy; just water, a squatter, and a place to lay your weary head. There isn't a standard operating season outside of summer, so it would be a wise idea to contact the relevant authorities before setting out on an overnight hike without a tent in late autumn or early spring.

Where you stay in Korea when you aren't working is up to you, your budget, and the kind of crazy stories you want to tell friends when you get home. A year should give you enough time to sample all the dishes on the accommodation buffet. Some are admittedly a bit rich, but a varied diet is the key to a healthy life. Bon appétit.

RUB A DUB DUB—HAIRY MEN IN A TUB

Koreans think you're dirty. Not so much the mind, (they don't know the half of it) but the body. Sure, the majority of you shower at least once a day and occasionally floss, but in their opinion that just isn't good enough. To really "cleanse the skins", as a wise man once said, you have to visit your local Mogyoktang and get down to some serious scrubbing.

Your first visit to the public baths can be an uncomfortable experience on many levels. Raised in a cultural framework that teaches people from a young age to regard their bodies as shameful, or at the very least extremely private, communal nudity can be a threatening concept. Mix in the lovely work done by the mass media concerning acceptable body images and you may find it hard to just drop that tiny towel and relax.

If you're a Western man you're probably already hairy compared to the average Korean. Those who lie towards the Robin Williams end of the scale should prepare themselves for some unwanted notoriety, as the zoning laws for Korean body hair tend to be a tad more restrictive. If you happen to be a freckly red head with pubic hair like rusty steel wool, try to ignore the incredulous stares and remember that in Ireland you'd be considered a handsome devil.

It all begins by cramming your gear into a locker and taking a hand towel, (well, nothing more than a woven fig leaf really,) from the pile near the door. Next, you are expected to sit beneath showers on tiny plastic stools designed by dwarves and wash yourself clean. At this stage you may feel a little embarrassed but not yet ready to bolt for the door. Now is the time to think about an exit strategy, because things are about to get painful.

Meet the "ITALY TOWEL". True, it doesn't sound that scary, in fact it often conjures up images of soft white cotton glowing in the warm Tuscan sunshine, but the name sadly has no relation to the object in question. Instead, imagine prickly green fiberglass woven into a cloth the size of a magazine or a torture glove designed by Michael Jackson. It is with one of these two varieties that you must remove the truly tenacious grime that clings to your body.

Whatever you do, don't accept any enthusiastic offers to help scrub your back using the Italy Towel. The danger lies not in unwanted homosexual encounters but in blood loss. Exfoliation may be the name of the game, but for those unaccustomed to its rasp-like qualities, the Italy Towel can feel like a cheese grater slowly rubbing the flesh from your bones.

Once the pain threshold has been reached and your Korean hygiene inspector is convinced you're clean, you may move on to your reward. Each facility is different and will, along with the standard hot and cold pools, offer a vast array of spray chambers, saunas, and massage machines.

Amongst the various tools and pools, you may see what appears to be a large orbital sander mounted on a wall. This is just another variation on the towel of terror. Watch the local patrons as they rub their backs against it, glazed eyes rolling like buffalos scratching on some lonesome prairie rock.

The big tubs vary in temperature from scalding hot to downright freezing. The trick is to slip between pools like a bi-polar seal, whereby a sensation similar to the sauna and snow routine is produced, a kind of ecstatic body buzz. The heat in some of these tubs may convince you of their sterilizing capacity but forty million Koreans can't be wrong.

People will stare, the odd monkey comment may be bandied about, but in general, Koreans are happy to see Westerners getting a little culture. The real trial comes in the form of sooner or later meeting a student and having him or her stare in fascination at your naked body. You just have to relax and accept that by tomorrow the whole school will know you have a hairy back or that "Miss Brown have yellow fur!"

Those ladies who summon the courage to try the tubs are up for an even more intimate encounter—if they so desire. After your scrub and soak, you'll be led off for your own personal spa package. A massage followed by a yogurt body wrap or other herbal treatments are just some of the things you may receive at a fraction of what they'd cost back home.

Expect some extra attention if the carpet doesn't match the curtains, or if you're carrying a few intimate piercings. Laughter, comparisons, and the odd nudge are part of the show, but it's all good natured, so don't take offense if the ladies looking after you seem compelled to point out your Brazilian wax job more than once to your fellow customers.

The only area where trouble may arise is tattoos. We in the West seem for the most part to have moved past regarding them as having any negative connotations, but in Korea, as in many parts of Asia, they are still associated with gang membership and criminal activity. You may be asked to leave, but a more likely scenario is that you'll find it hard to get a scrubbing partner.

Saunas also differ in that they're usually dry heated instead of the more familiar steam variety. A few minutes inside can feel like your nostril membranes are being brazed with a butane torch. This is admittedly an uncomfortable sensation, but the dry sauna can also prove to be a handy location to escape overzealous spectators.

A certain teacher, who can't be named for reasons that will become apparent, once took refuge there from the amorous attentions of a mentally challenged admirer. He graciously permitted his pelt-like chest to be touched, and nodded in uncomfortable agreement when it was compared to the majesty of the nearby mountains. However, when the rather awestruck local was inclined to go lower in his explorations of the exotic Western body and began rising to attention, it became clear that it was time for that teacher to abandon any thoughts of cultural sensitivity and retreat at full speed.

Half an hour in the dry sauna kept his horny new acquaintance at bay, though it nearly mummified the teacher, leaving him with a Ramses-like complexion, an unquenchable thirst, and a firm resolution never to enter another sauna in his life. It should be noted that this was his first visit to the Mogyoktang and it left him quite shaken, much to the amusement of his so called friend who took him there. That said, he was eventually coaxed back for another visit and enjoyed many subsequent trips over his time in Korea.

This particular anecdote was of course a rather extreme introduction to the world of Korean Baths and unlikely to be repeated. A lot of visitors avoid the baths out of ignorance or fear, but in the opinion of the author, it's worth the pain and shame to know you're as clean as the rest of them.

BLEEDING EARS AND COLD BEERS

Sweeping generalizations in works of non-fiction usually reflect the ignorance of the author, but in this particular instance it's a well documented fact that there are only two types of people in this world, those who like to sing and those who don't. You, as the average Westerner, probably fall into the latter category, while most Koreans between the ages of 2 and 79 are definitely in the former.

The Noribang, otherwise known as a singing room, is a sacred institution and its worshippers meet on a regular basis. These holy places vary in both size and shape, from teenage karaoke cubes the size of phone booths to gilded baroque monstrosities complete with smiling hostesses. You can even spot them on the highways, in the form of wildly rocking buses, which come decked out with Dolby speakers and a light show that wouldn't look out of place in Ibiza.

Koreans love to sing. If there's one thing that unites them more than football or instant noodles it's getting together for a good old croon fest. It doesn't matter whether they're politicians, policemen or kindergarten kids, if there's a chance to belt out some tunes they'll leap at the opportunity. People feel comfortable doing it just about anywhere but it's at the singing room that they really shine.

There's every likelihood that within a week of arriving you'll find yourself standing awkwardly before a cheering mob of Koreans with a mike grasped between your sweaty hands, so take a leaf from the boy scouts handbook and be prepared. The following chapter attempts to offer some insight and advice on this most Korean of pastimes.

If you go out for a meal with your new co-workers and wish to avoid singing you'll have to act decisively. Once the coffee arrives, consider faking a heart attack, because if you don't manage to escape in the next few minutes your fate will be sealed. Koreans are very predictable, and if you haven't come up with a good exit strategy there's a good chance you'll be escorted to the nearest Noribang before you can say Neil Diamond.

Should you be so foolish as to consume seven pints of beer and a round of shooters at your welcome party, you may find it extremely difficult, if not impossible, to muster the immense personal willpower needed to resist a group of drunken Koreans bent on hearing you yodel. They absolutely love to sing and will put it down to admirable humbleness when you claim to have a voice like Golem.

As with many decadent Eastern pleasures, the singing habit is highly addictive, but the first dose can be a painful experience. If you find yourself trapped with no rescue in sight, it's advisable to consume copious amounts of alcohol as quickly as possible. This won't improve your performance, but it will go some way towards helping you enjoy it.

So go ahead and accept those free drinks. Dilute your inhibitions. Wash away your self consciousness. Drown your better judgment in a swirling sea of Soju as you search for a way to let go of that prickly Western pride.

Allow yourself to recall how once upon a time you loved to sing nursery rhymes. Reach back through the years and find the kid who drove her parents barking mad by mindlessly chanting Baa Baa Black Sheep, because if you're to truly find pleasure in the night's entertainment it's essential that you reconnect with your demented inner child.

Singing rooms for some arcane reason never seem to be on the ground floor, they're either up three flights of incredibly steep stairs or lie buried deep beneath the earth. A typical establishment consists of a main lobby, kitchen, tiny bathroom, and anywhere from 2 to 20 singing rooms.

Most rooms consist of a long table surrounded by booth style seating that will comfortably sit up to eight people. They are often kitted out in pastel pink vinyl that wouldn't look out of place in a Barbie themed brothel. Opposite this ode to upholstery is a bank of nine TVs, or a massive single screen, endlessly repeating images of waterfalls, birds and occasionally the ever popular 1989 Girls of Hawaiian Swimwear.

Hooked into a complex machine at the base of the wonder wall are two microphones, each with enough surplus cord to strangle an elephant. This generous amount enables the singers to move freely around the room, drinking, dancing and performing for the cheering crowd. Tambourines are provided to allow onlookers to engage in the Dionysian frenzy.

You won't encounter a lot of modern tunes in the English section of the music menu. The Beatles and Elton John rule supreme, supported by a select cast of easy listening gods from the sixties, seventies and eighties. Occasionally the odd heavy hit manages to get past the censors but they're few and far between.

Try not to fret about the limited selection and how cheesy you'll sound singing these ancient anthems. Instead throw back another beer, grab a mike and worry about your musical reputation in the morning. Expose your secret Cher fetish to the world or if you're really old school, tell them how you did it "Your Way", because the only shameful act is choosing not to participate.

The joy of drinking is that it works on so many levels to ease the pain; it dissolves your sense of self, numbs aching eardrums and anesthetizes vocal cords worn out by repeated Bohemian Rhapsody renditions. Amazing ethanol can even convince you that singing Scarborough Fair with a bunch of trashed businessmen is a good idea. (A certain author retains an audio recording of that dubious night and guards it with his life, for should it fall into the wrong hands his credibility would be seriously compromised.)

Alcohol is the revealer of secrets and the unveiler of wonders. Sit back and watch the school bus driver pose like a backup dancer in an early Madonna video. Appreciate the dark and terrible beauty that is your best mate impersonating Whitney Houston. Behold the forbidden love that blooms between your wasted receptionist and the boss. Everything is possible and nothing is prohibited within the confines of the Noribang.

Be sure to take note of your surroundings on the way to the toilet, as it's easy to get lost on the return trip. The rooms all look identical from the outside and bursting in on the wrong one can result in a half hour delay that may involve a bottle of whiskey and an impromptu Elvis impersonation.

Other than liver damage, lung cancer and Tintinitus, the only real danger posed by a night out at the Noribang is the threat of suicide once you sober up and recall the embarrassing events of the night before. Dancing the Can-can, snogging fellow teachers and punching out your Hagwon manager are all distinct possibilities. Luckily the rule is that what happens in the singing room stays in the singing room.

A real treat at the Noribang are the hilariously bad translations that appear on screen. Highly recommended comes the Chubby Checker classic, "Let's twist again". You might not know the exact lyrics but anyone can tell you that the following version is way off target!

> "Let's twist again like we did last sun up,
> Let's twist again like we did last years,
> Let's twist again like we did last sunup'
> Let's twist again like we did last beer.
> Cause we go brown an brown an brown again you know"

Karaoke sets in Korea are designed so that at the end of a song you receive a score out of a hundred. Unfortunately the tone deaf bastards that program them obviously value volume over style. The desire to smash the machines can be intense, especially when you witness someone receive a perfect score for yelling out unintelligible gibberish at a 120 decibels. Forget rhythm or sophistication, if you want high points just scream your head off for the duration of the song.

The night will roll on and in no time you'll be transformed from a shame-faced croaker to a hip thrashing rock god. Cases of beer will be consumed in quick succession and hot snacks gobbled with wild abandon. The cruel reality of teaching a kindergarten class in three hours will only become apparent when you face the harsh light of dawn. Your retinas will burn like some cheap wino vampire, and you'll swear to never sing again as you stumble back to the temporary shelter of your bedroom.

For Koreans there is no rhyme or reason for a trip to the Noribang. Good day, bad day, it doesn't really matter, it's all about coming together, getting drunk and having fun. From an anthropological standpoint, you probably couldn't find a more authentic Korean activity that's open for you to be an active participant.

Most foreigners find three sessions per week a little too much but the odd one can do wonders for your mental health. A big night out at the Noribang helps to remove the stains of daily living from the fabric of your soul. It's also a great excuse to drink yourself silly—if being an English teacher isn't good enough.

BULLS AND BALLS

Koreans love their sports. Be it an impromptu game of badminton in the park or a World Cup qualifying match, you can always count on two things; a keenly fought battle and a fun-filled atmosphere of good natured rivalry. Korean sports can be broken down into two basic categories; homegrown varieties that don't need balls and foreign ones that do. Indigenous sports like Tae Kwan Do, archery and wrestling have been enjoyed by Koreans for centuries, while popular imports like baseball, table tennis and golf are all relatively recent arrivals.

The earliest of these exotic ball sports; baseball, basketball and soccer, came with the bible thumpers as part of their educational curriculum. The missionaries were strong advocates of "Mens sana in corpore sano"—a healthy mind in a healthy body. They believed that by developing the physical condition of their charges they could keep them focused on more spiritual matters, though it's obvious to anyone who has ever spent time in a high school locker room that physical activity in itself has no redeeming effects on the average teenage mind.

Of those three early imports, it could be said that soccer is now the unofficial sport of South Korea. This love affair with the black and white ball began at the end of the nineteenth century. Many believe it was first introduced through an informal friendly played on the docks of Incheon, but the first reliable sightings of the beautiful game occurred on the grounds of missionary schools in Seoul during the mid 1880s.

Soccer was enthusiastically adopted by the Korean people, and during the colonial period it was a source of solidarity and hope, allowing them to do the unthinkable—kick the Japanese occupiers in the nuts and get away with it. After the war, in 1948, the Korean Football Association was established, though of course the Korean conflict and the cold war that followed caused some disruption to game scheduling. Korea joined FIFA the same year and became a member of the Asian Football Confederation in 1954.

The official nod of recognition came in 1996 when South Korea and Japan were chosen to be the official joint hosts of the 2002 FIFA World Cup. Just to be selected as hosts was a great honor, as the games had never been held in Asia before, but for most Koreans there burned an unspoken dream, they wanted to win the Cup.

South Korea entered the rankings that year below the top thirty, and anyone who wasn't Korean saw their chances of winning on par with a London curry house being awarded three Michelin stars for fine dining. International soccer fans laughed at the thought of them even reaching the semi-finals, and most Koreans quietly admitted that they'd be quite happy with the national team just beating the Japanese.

What actually occurred was something much more miraculous. Fundamentalist Christians believe it was proof of God's benign love for the underdog, while a few spoilsports continue to mutter about match fixing and corruption. Whatever the case, Korea went on to beat football giants like Italy and Spain and made it to the semi finals.

By that point things had gotten a little crazy. Millions of people were assembling in Seoul's parks and public spaces to cheer on the team at every game. The nation ran out of the red dye required to produce the team colors. Spontaneous street parties erupted with every win. Notoriously xenophobic politicians pushed for the Dutch coach to be naturalized, and the local Catholics lobbied the Holy Father for the purposes of canonization. For a short while it seemed that the Red Devils might actually do the unthinkable and win the Cup.

Alas Korea was eventually beaten by Germany and lost its third place bout with Turkey in a respectable 3:2 defeat. Koreans mourned the death of their collective dream but were buoyed by just how far they'd come. It was a testament to how good natured Korean sports fans are that when that fateful game drew to an end the crowds stood and cheered. There were no ugly scenes, no rioting fans or hurled projectiles, only the applause of a people who had been lucky enough to witness a piece of Korean history in the making. (The author was present and can verify that even for a non sports fan, attending a game like that was one hell of a rush.)

Soccer remains an extremely popular sport and even in the smallest village you'll find a set of goals. If you want to make friends, ask if you can join in a game, as nothing bonds Koreans like a quick kick of the ball and a few shots of soju afterwards. In fact, if you end up at a Hagwon you'll probably play a few games with your students, as it's a popular option when it comes to taking a break from the books.

Another biblical import that has prospered is baseball. Brought by those fun loving American missionaries, it was being played in schools by the beginning of the twentieth century, but it didn't really become popular until American soldiers started driving home runs over their camp perimeters during the war. Interest built over the following decades and with an improved economic climate came the money to sponsor big league games. In 1982, the Korean Baseball Organization was established for the purpose of conducting and promoting the sport. Millions of Koreans now follow eight professional teams, and the organization has begun to produce some world class players. It might not be in the same league as the World Series, but if you want to catch a fun filled event with dedicated players and fiercely loyal fans you shouldn't pass up the opportunity to attend a game.

There aren't a lot of spare diamonds in South Korea but there are still quite a few amateur leagues and informal games to be found. Just ask around and someone will know someone who plays. Koreans are pretty hospitable, and if you make it known that you're interested, an invitation will be extended.

The third game of God is basketball, but again it wasn't until a few black soldiers shot some hoops that it began to be played in earnest. Basketball blossomed in the '80s and '90s, when it seemed as if the younger generation of every nation wanted to be like Mike. By 1997 enough interest had been generated to form the Korean Basketball League.

High school and university students will, for the most part, be your teammates but there are amateur leagues in some of the larger towns and cities. If you decide to play you'll probably have a height advantage, but don't count on breezing through the defense just because you're taller than the competition. The only thing to keep in check is your attitude, as most Koreans see basketball as a game of skill as opposed to a full contact sport that requires dental insurance.

Table tennis came with another group of unwelcome visitors bent on changing the world—the Japanese. Nobody will discuss this unfortunate sporting link, due to the fact that it is forbidden to say anything good about the imperialist sons of bitches. If anyone is caught in the act of acknowledging that the despised colonizers did anything beneficial for the nation they'd be ostracized for life by their family, friends and the neighborhood dog.

Any town large enough to support a bar and a grocery store will have a table tennis club tucked away somewhere. Being such a hospitable nation, all you have to do is find the front door and you'll be invited in to play a few games. The cost will be low, and it's quite entertaining to watch the local spin masters throw down their wicked serves with pinpoint accuracy. Please remember that although for most Westerners it's just a bit of childish fun, in Korea, table tennis is a serious sport. If you don't want a shameful ass whupping with that little red paddle it's best not to refer to it as ping pong!

Ten pin bowling came with another occupying force and has remained far more popular than the US soldiers who brought it. Rules, balls and lanes are the same but there's something uniquely Korean about it all. Maybe it's those expensive-looking wrist guards, the restrained high fives or the snappy bowling attire that sets it apart from a game back home.

Whatever it is they sure take the game seriously, in fact they even managed to convince the IOC that it should be included as a demonstration sport at the 1988 Seoul Olympics. Bowling never made it to the podium but Koreans can take pride in the fact that it shares a place in Olympic history with such illustrious sports as water skiing, Australian Rules football and roller hockey. If you should feel the need to throw heavy balls at immobile objects, just scan the night sky and somewhere in that neon jungle you'll spot a gigantic bowling pin flashing in the distance.

Tennis is another sporting activity enjoyed by many Koreans, though its popularity does tend to diminish during the winter months. If you don't mind a bit of frostbite, you can walk onto an empty court any time after November, though even in summer you won't wait too long for a game, as most municipalities have installed public facilities for sports like tennis, soccer and basketball.

The worlds fastest racket sport is also popular, with many badminton nets set up in parks and other recreational areas. It might look easy, but at speeds of up to 260 kilometers per hour, you'll need to pay attention if you want to win. Watch out for kids and pensioners. They may look like pushovers but they'll feed you a generous serving of humble pie should you drop your concentration for just a moment.

Golf arrived one starry night with snobbish appeal and remains to this day an overt display of wealth, authority and prestige. A lack of wide, open spaces, a tangible association with power, and a mildly challenging game have all contributed to its enormous popularity and success. During the post-war period it was the domain of rich businessmen, influential army personnel and corrupt politicians. Admittedly some things have changed, with three out of every ten golfers being female, but the questionable love triangle between golf, money and authority continues to exercise its influence over the nation.

Four million Koreans admit to chasing the little white ball, and pay big biscuits for the honor of doing so, that is if they can actually gain membership to one of the elite clubs that infrequently dot the landscape. Most mortals have to make do with impotently swinging away at the local driving range and dreaming of a day when all golf courses will be open to the public.

Of course these are just some of the more common Western sports. Those out for a little more adrenalin can go scuba diving, mountain biking, paragliding, skiing, snowboarding and white water rafting, whilst individuals seeking less risky stimulation can swim at the local pool, throw some darts around the pub or go ice skating after a shopping spree in Seoul. Pretty well every sport imaginable, from cricket to croquet, is being played somewhere on the peninsula, you just have to track it down.

On the surface it would appear that the imports have eclipsed the locals, however there continues to be a huge following for traditional sports. The most popular one, the martial art of Tae Kwon Do, is the nation's official sport, and after plasma TVs and sporty hatchbacks it's probably the most famous export.

The name Tae Kwon Do, when translated directly, means the art of kicking and punching. In the Korean language, tae is to kick with the foot; kwon is to hit with the hand and do means the art of. Like many traditional martial arts, it was developed for the purposes of unarmed self defense. Tae Kwon Do is much more than randomly attacking innocent pieces of wood or learning how to beat up your older brother, it's about developing in an individual the positive attributes of discipline, confidence and control through rigorous and responsible training.

Beginners start by learning different stances, blocks, punches, kicks, strikes and thrusts. These are eventually incorporated into a number of Pumsae or movement routines, which allow these skills to be practiced in an ordered and logical manner. Belts are awarded when students master these routines. A black belt is achieved when a student knows all the Pumsae and can demonstrate these skills in combat with another student. The origins of Tae Kwon Do stretch back over two thousand years to the Koguryo and Silla Kingdoms of Korea. Tomb paintings originating from those periods display scenes in which figures appear to be engaged in Tae Kwon Do. Later, during the Yi dynasty, it began its transformation from a mainly military activity practiced by the nobles into a recreational sport enjoyed by the masses.

During the occupation years it was banned by the Japanese, which naturally enough made it an extremely popular if somewhat dangerous sport to practise. To this day in Korea it holds firm associations with notions of independence, culture and identity. Woe betide the fool who espouses the theory that Tae Kwon Do is nothing more than a dumbed down version of Karate.

In the 1960s the Korean Tae Kwon Do Association was formed with the intention of regulating and improving the sport. It was at this time that Korean instructors began to travel and teach around the world. By the '70s there were competitors from over twenty countries arriving for further study. It was demonstrated during the 1988 Seoul Olympics and became an official sport at the Sydney Games in 2000. Today, if defined by the number of people currently training, it is the world's most popular martial art.

If you decide to take up the challenge, be aware that when it comes to black belt testing time you may have to operate under conditions of extreme pressure.

A certain teacher once studied Tae Kwon Do diligently until his master decided that he was ready for his examination. Though nervous about being the only foreign candidate, he felt somewhat relieved by the fact that the tests were always conducted according to age, which meant that his examination would occur at the end of the day, by which time most of the spectators would be absent.

Imagine his horror when the judges announced at the start of the day how proud they were to have a foreign candidate and that in light of this special occasion they had taken the unusual step of rearranging the schedule so that all 2,000 black belt applicants and their families could have the pleasure of watching the foreigner go first.

The teacher in question somehow managed to quell his terror and scraped through his movement routines, though whether his mistakes had cost him a pass was unclear. When it came time to spar with a partner he remembered that scoring high points here could make up for a few nervous fumbles in the previous section.

The poor Korean teenager who was selected to spar with him didn't have a chance. Not only was he thrown off by facing a hairy, overweight foreigner but he got one who was determined never to go through this kind of torture again.

Theoretically each candidate is supposed to give the other a chance to demonstrate their skills, but that's not the way it went. The foreigner attacked from the moment the judges gave the nod, and if eye witness accounts are to be believed, there was not a single moment during the encounter when his feet, fists or elbows were not in play. Due to this vigorous and extremely enthusiastic sparring match, the judges overlooked the earlier mistakes and awarded him his black belt. (What happened to the Korean kid is unknown, but chances are he's out there somewhere nursing a healthy phobia towards hairy men in white.)

Archery is another traditional sport whose roots stretch far into the distant past. First utilized to feed the family, it quickly became a weapon of war. Nobody knows for sure when Koreans started to shoot arrows at each other, but by the time men were declaring themselves king there were archers present to back them up. Throughout recorded history official documents have noted the importance of archery in the defense of the various kingdoms that existed on the peninsula, and it remained a mandatory component in military exams up until 1894.

Archery was also an important social activity for men, a way to unwind during peacetime whilst maintaining their martial skills. It received a boost at the end of the 19th century when it was sponsored and standardized by the royal family. Though obsolete in terms of modern weaponry, this patronage ensured that it remained a fashionable pastime amongst the middle and upper classes.

Today archery has a strong following and is practiced by both men and women across the country. Koreans dominate the field at an international level and are justly famed for their dedication and accuracy, holding twice as many Olympic gold medals than any other nation.

Archery clubs are found everywhere, and like other sports you'll find a friendly welcome if you show a passing interest. That said, archery is viewed as a serious sport, and if you want to get involved you'll have to commit yourself to regular practice and following the rules. There's no room on the range for Robin Hood and it'll take a while before you're even allowed to fire an arrow on your own.

In Korea the sport is known as Goong Do, or "the way of the bow". Though some people compete with Western recurve bows, the majority of Koreans prefer to use traditional bows. These are highly reflexed composite bows, similar to what Genghis Khan and the boys carried with them on their world tours.

Today's traditional bows are crafted in exactly the same way as they were a thousand years ago, using a combination of laminated buffalo horn, sinew, birch bark, fish glue, bamboo, oak, and mulberry wood. These bows take many hours to produce and consequently cost a lot of money. Due to the nature of the materials used in their construction they require a great deal of care and maintenance.

Most people choose to buy cheaper bows that contain modern materials. These appear remarkably similar, and only differ in that they contain carbon fiber and synthetic glues. The advantage is that they cost a third of the price, are more easily strung, and aren't affected by humidity. The arrows come in two types. For wet weather events carbon fiber arrows are used. If it's sunny, or the competition is operating under old school rules, then traditional bamboo arrows come into play.

Archery grounds usually have a pavilion which is called a Jung, upon which hangs a sign with the Chinese characters "Jung Gahn" written upon it. This translates roughly to "Righteous Room" and its message applies to both your actions and thoughts. It is customary upon arrival to bow in the direction of the Jung Gahn as a mark of humility and respect.

The range is 145 meters long and the targets are about 2.7 meters high by 2 meters wide. They are made from plywood covered by rubber and are tilted back on an angle. These may sound like pretty big targets to hit but they shrink dramatically when you're standing at the other end with a bow in your hand.

Each Jung's set up is a little different. Some may have three targets being shot at by 8 competitors, others may only have two targets and five shooting squares. Regardless of how they're arranged you'll be closely supervised, so there's no need to worry about standing in the wrong spot.

The scoring is fairly simple. During an individual competition a round of three ends consisting of five arrows per end is shot. The winner is the person with the most hits. In the case of a team event, five archers per team shoot five arrows each in an elimination style match until one team emerges victorious. If a draw occurs it is naturally settled by a shoot out. Hits count only if the arrow strikes the target and stays there.

Just as in Tae Kwon Do, there's a ranking system and participants are graded at special competitions. Dan status is awarded according to a person's ability to hit the target in a given number of shots. Dan achievement is signified not by belts, but through different colored bow covers. As in all Asian martial arts, great store is set on correct etiquette and the demonstration of respect.

While there isn't exactly a uniform, the standard Korean dress rules apply. On practice days, neat tidy clothes should be worn, as sloppy dressing signifies a sloppy mind. At competitions, white shoes, socks, pants and shirts are donned by all competitors, the color denoting purity and peace of mind.

Wrestling or Sirum is probably the least popular traditional sport, yet ironically it is believed to be the oldest. Ancient tomb paintings and Chinese historical documents record its existence long before Tae Kwon Do or archery gets a mention. Sirum evolved naturally from tussles and fights to become a grappling and wrestling activity that was practiced both as a sport by the general public and as a fighting technique in the military.

Traditionally, competitions were held on agricultural and Buddhist holidays, with most falling at the end of autumn to celebrate the successful harvest. The champion received an ox, which represented both strength and wealth to the peasant lucky enough to win.

The sport itself is very simple. Two competitors meet in a 7 meter ring of sand and attempt to force any part of their opponent's body above the knee to touch the ground. The bout begins with both people bowing, kneeling and grasping their opponent's belt, known as a Satba, which is tied around the waist and right thigh. A win is achieved by pushing, pulling or dropping the opponent to the ground whilst maintaining a grip on the belt. If a competitor leaves the circle a restart is required. A match consists of three rounds and the contest is presided over by three judges and four referees.

Sirum remains a popular folk sport but at a professional level it is slowly losing ground to more brutal forms of competitive fighting. A martial art with no punches, kicks or chokeholds is admittedly hard to market to a generation of jaded teenagers raised on violent video games. However, because of this lack of danger, Sirum is probably the perfect sport to try out as a foreigner, as you are unlikely to lose any teeth during your first training session.

But enough with the health and safety concerns. The real reason you've continued to read this chapter is to hear about the bullfighting—isn't it?

Well, for you bloodthirsty freaks it may be something of a disappointment to learn that in Korea bullfighting doesn't actually come with red capes and three feet of cold Spanish steel. Here the fight is between the bulls, and while it may not be completely painless, no deaths are required to declare a winner.

Korean bullfighting is basically reproductive urges harnessed for a bit of entertainment. The bulls naturally aren't too keen on rivals, and instinctively act to establish dominance by pushing and shoving each other until one says "uncle".

Traditionally this was an agricultural celebration of the bull and by extension, his master's strength and virility, but recently the sport has gained a wider following amongst both domestic and international tourists. Whilst in the past fights were staged locally between villages, today there's a vibrant bullfighting circuit with more than a dozen towns hosting weekend events. One of the largest is held in Chongdo, which sees over half a million visitors arrive annually to eat, drink and gamble as they watch the big beef clash for the cash.

The rules are pretty simple, which is probably just as well considering that the competitors aren't particularly bright. Two bulls are led into a sandy ring by their owners. Once they've seen each other and are suitably worked up (pawing the ground and snorting like a pair of Columbian drug lords) the ropes attached to their nose rings are released. The bulls then lock horns, pushing and prodding each other in an attempt to find out who's the strongest. The loser is the first bull to give up and turn tail.

The aim of the sport isn't death and destruction; it's all about paying homage to the strength and vitality of the living. Nobody in the audience wants to see a dead bull, and while injuries do happen they are extremely rare occurrences. The worst you'll probably witness is a little blood around the horns.

And there you have it, everything you need to know about Korean sport in one handy chapter. While archery and bullfighting are certainly unique, there are plenty of other options to choose from where the equipment isn't quite as expensive or the smell so pungent. Getting involved in a sport will not only allow you to meet new friends, it'll help keep the dreaded beer belly at bay. So don't be a blob, get off your butt and get stuck into a sport.

DIAL M FOR MOUNTAINS

A conquistador, when questioned about the difference between Spain and his newly conquered lands, answered by taking a sheet of flat paper and crumpling it, thus demonstrating its mountainous virtues. Pizarro and his dogs of war never set foot in Korea, but if they had, they would have found a landscape somewhat familiar in its narrow valleys and endless stony ridges.

If Holland is the flat chested teen of Europe, then well endowed South Korea surely ranks up there with the best of Asia's buxom beauties. No peaks of Himalayan grandeur dominate the peninsula but in terms of sheer numbers, Korea is in a class of its own. Unless you happen to face the sea, your view will probably include a generous serving of mountains. (And forget everything you saw on M*A*S*H—it was all filmed on some dude ranch in Southern California.)

Korea is not a huge country, barely bigger than Portugal or if you prefer about 1/100th of continental USA, but it weighs in at over 70% pure peaks. Take away the cities, rivers, and loose rocks and you're left with only about 17% arable land.

The big boys obsessed with Everest might convince you otherwise but when it comes to mountains, height isn't everything. Korea's tallest mountain lies off the mainland on Cheju Island. At a respectable 1950 meters, the volcanic cone of Mount Halla towers over the blue sea and will definitely give you the firm calves you've always dreamt of, but it's on the mainland where the real alpine action is.

Asian art buffs will feel like they've magically wandered into a scroll painting, surrounded by steep cliffs, hidden waterfalls and scraggly twisted pines. The beauty here isn't to be found in Himalayan grandeur, but in the multitude of hidden details; a heap of boulders shrouded in mist, a clear stream littered with autumn's gaudy remnants, the brief flash of a wild cat's eyes deep within a bamboo thicket.

Koreans are justly proud of their natural heritage and will whisk you up a peak quicker than you can say Kimchi. Many Koreans believe that it's good luck to greet the new year on top of old Smokey, but climbing a boulder strewn trail in freezing conditions, with a shared flashlight the size of a peanut and your nose jammed in a co-worker's butt isn't for everyone.

Hiking in the mountains is popular throughout the year, but summer and autumn are when they're at their most beautiful. In July and August the valleys are swathed in vibrant greens and the peaks dusted in wildflowers, while in autumn the hills and mountains are saturated in a rich palette of red, orange and gold. Wandering alone or with a couple of friends gives you the chance to appreciate the silence and beauty of the high country, but a group outing with a gang of Koreans hell bent on reaching the peak is an experience not to be missed.

For Koreans preparation is paramount, even if the expedition is only heading out for a three hour loop with wheel chair access. Knee high socks, ultra chunky boots, fleece vests, GORE-TEX coats, wide brimmed hats, brilliant bandanas, collapsible water bladders, shiny compasses, beeping GPS units and backpacks crammed with snacks are just some of the subtle signs that Koreans take their hiking seriously. Try not to smile too much as you wander past families that look like they're about to tackle the north face of Annapurna; it's all just part of the way things are done there.

Although hiking gear is popular, not everyone wears the standard uniform. Don't be surprised to see fashionable matrons tottering up the rocky slopes in black dresses and high heels. Hold your tongue in check when you stroll past wizened old ladies laboring up the path, for chances are in another ten minutes they'll inch by laughing as you sprawl in a sweaty, gasping heap halfway up the mountain.

Off to the side of the path, you may notice areas where countless stones have been stacked to create little towers that bring to mind the works of Gaudi. These aren't the work of architecturally inspired gnomes but rather fellow hikers, who have erected miniature stone stupas. In Buddhism, the stupa symbolizes compassion, peace and the noble qualities of the Buddha. The reason you see so many of them is the belief that if a person makes enough of them in a single lifetime, he or she will acquire karmic merit, thus avoiding reincarnation as an English teacher in the next one.

A less charming phenomenon is the litter you'll encounter along the trails. Korean municipalities often lack garbage bins but employ fantastic sanitation crews that clear up the mess long before the sun has a chance to hit the sidewalk. This has led to a mindset that feels comfortable littering, because there is always someone around to clean up the mess. However, this logic fails to take into consideration the fact that street cleaners rarely climb mountains at night. The bright side is that should you ever become lost, you can always follow the paper cups and candy wrappers home like some Alpine Hansel or Gretel.

On some of the more famous hikes, it can seem like you've abandoned the city only to hang out with the entire population on the mountain. Long lines often form at the base of stairs and you may see more corduroy than scenery on the approach to some peaks. That said, Koreans take it all in their stride, chatting amiably amongst themselves, passing around snacks and cigarettes, as they patiently await their moment at the top. This can easily be avoided if you visit the more famous national parks like Seoraksan or Jirisan during the week. Seriously consider taking a few Valium on the sly if you are unfortunate enough to be escorted to either of these parks during a Government holiday in autumn.

This love of all things vertical isn't just about getting out of town for the weekend. Like many cultures, Koreans revere mountains, traditionally seeing them and other aspects of nature as possessing an independent spirit.

This animistic world view continues to this day and can be seen clearly when you visit any of the thousands of Buddhist temples that lie nestled deep within Korea's national parks. The main temples pay homage to the Buddha, but often to the side are three small buildings dedicated to the indigenous deities that have survived countless centuries of Confucian and Buddhist control. They are: San-sin (the mountain spirit), Deok-seong (the lonely saint), and Ch'il-seong (the seven star spirits).

Inside the one dedicated to San-sin you'll find a small alter for offerings and a painting of the nature spirit personified. This is usually an elderly immortal man with a flowing beard and wispy eyebrows down to his cheeks, trusty staff in hand, reclining on a funky tiger beneath a gnarled pine tree. The tiger is his messenger and vehicle, while the tree symbolizes endurance and venerable old age. San-sin, when properly petitioned, is believed to have the capacity to grant protection, heal illnesses, provide children and offer spiritual enlightenment.

Much of the mountains are exposed granite immodestly draped in pines. These trees merit special mention due to their fantastic forms. If there exists a single upright pine in the whole country, it's undoubtedly a state secret. They say nature abhors a straight line and here she followed through on her word. Twisted brown trunks resemble groups of old men bent deep in conversation or ancient dancers frozen in motion. They are beautiful to behold and highly photogenic but probably a major pain in the ass for the lumber industry.

Korea has plenty of national and provincial parks to keep you busy. Some, like Bukhansan in the northern suburbs of Seoul, are literally only a subway ride away, while others require a more protracted journey. It should be noted that it's not all steep crags and gorges; some like Dadohae Haesang are marine parks comprising of hundreds of islands scattered in the cold clear water off the southern coast.

All of these parks are very well maintained considering the inundation of hikers they receive. Jirisan alone gets over 700,000 visitors a year. The parks have excellent visitor centers, and most offer designated campsites with toilet and cooking facilities. Even if you aren't a big hiking fan you should visit the odd one, as they contain some of the most beautiful scenery Korea has to offer.

Though great for tigers, monks and hermits, this warren of mountains proved to be a major challenge for engineers and the economy. Limited farmland and slow transportation meant that Korea remained for a long time a poor and relatively underdeveloped country. The past 40 years have brought great wealth and with it great change.

Along with improved standards of living has come a pretty impressive network of highways, roads and train tracks. Where once a tour of the country involved a drawn out journey of highs and lows, it's now a smooth ride across massive concrete bridges that span whole valleys and along vast tunnels that bore straight through the sides of mountains.

If speed is your only concern, then these new motorways are your best choice, but for those with wheels of their own and some free time, nothing beats exploring the countless small roads that meander through the hills. Sure you may end up losing your way, but you usually discover something of greater value: an abandoned farm house showered in plum blossoms, a lonely monk offering you tea, or a small village floating in a sea of emerald rice paddies.

Whether you end up in the concrete barrios of Seoul or some bucolic backwater, you're never far from the mountains. On any given Saturday, all you have to do is turn off CNN, extract yourself from beneath the sheets and get out to enjoy what many consider to be Korea's finest attractions.

LAND OF THE SUPER HIGHWAYS

The last three decades have dramatically transformed Korea, and nowhere is this more evident than in the proliferation of privately owned vehicles. Originally the status symbols of army bigwigs, politicians and powerful tycoons, they have become the object of the everyman. Where once they were coveted luxury imports from lands impossibly distant, automobiles are now locally produced and exported in their millions.

Koreans love their shiny new cars and the government has done a fine job in providing additional pavement. In preparation for the World Cup Soccer Tournament in 2002, they literally rebuilt the entire highway system. If Koreans have a weakness, it has to be national pride. The government wisely exploited this and spent billions on infrastructure projects by raising the specter of disappointed foreign visitors. An engineering orgy ensued as six lane highways, massive bridges, and tunnels worthy of Tolkien's dwarves were built to replace the old system of roads, lanes and goat tracks that snaked over the hills and mountains.

Once upon a time, the train was the fastest way to travel between most cities, but now buses do it more frequently, in less time and for fewer won. However they also lack the smiling attendant and her little trolley loaded with cold beer and cookies, so make sure you jump the rails at least once during your stay.

Most of the time a road is just a road, be it in Korea or at home, but occasionally one sees things that will remind you that you're not in Kansas anymore. It could be a gas station with an adjoining private zoo containing lions, monkeys and Saint Bernards (not in the same cage fortunately), giant mutant fiberglass vegetables proclaiming the region's agricultural expertise or the combination road-airstrip in Kyung San Buk Do province.

It runs straight for more than ten kilometers and is at least six lanes wide. It isn't there for the driving convenience of the local ginseng farmers, it's there in case of war. At each end of this covert runway is a dedicated area for the loading and fueling of planes in case more conventional airstrips are disabled in a surprise attack by those sneaky chaps from the North.

Every autumn it sees action of sorts, though it's probably not what the military planners had in mind. It seems the farmers in the area have taken the bible to heart, and instead of hammering swords into ploughshares, they've turned the hot black airstrip into one long rice dryer.

Other cute military touches include massive concrete blocks suspended above the main roads near the demilitarized zone (DMZ), which can be dropped to block the passage of enemy vehicles, and road tunnels through strategic mountain passes that are wired with explosives so they can be blown up to impede the enemy. Then there's the odd military checkpoint manned by bored army conscripts absentmindedly cradling their machine guns.

When it comes to bathroom breaks the facilities on smaller country roads can be a little archaic, but on the highways managed by the Korean Highway Corporation they're civilized with a capital C. These large modern rest areas provide everything from fuel and free internet to cafeterias and tourist information. Classical music and pleasant scents drift from shining, spotless bathrooms while smiling employees in immaculate uniforms wait to assist you.

One thing that can seem a little strange is how smaller private gas stations only sell petrol and other associated motoring products. No newspapers, drinks, chips, candy bars, or other superfluous items are on display to tempt the weary driver. This seems a little odd considering how good Koreans are at filling economic niches but it's just one of those things that can't be explained, so if you're hankering for a treat keep cruising till you spy a convenience store.

When it comes to buying cars, Koreans are prone to a little bias. Hyundai, Kia, Samsung, and Daewoo all produce cars for local consumption and reap the rewards of a loyal market. These new cars can be bought for less than five thousand dollars and motorbikes for as little as a thousand. Cheap prices combined with an effective "Buy Korea" campaign that ran during the International Monetary Fund (IMF) period have made the concept of buying a foreign car all but taboo. It's a fantastic tribute to national solidarity but it makes for rather bland auto scenery. Forget about the game where you get to be a thug and give your friend's arm a slug when you spot a VW bug, cause it ain't gonna happen on these homogenous highways.

If vehicle uniformity wasn't bad enough, consider color. A few days on the road will lead you to suspect that old father Ford was actually an undercover Korean, because here his quote still holds true when it comes to choosing any color as long as it's black. To be fair, it must be said that in recent years many of the smaller micro cars have been turning up in all kinds of crazy colors like red, green and yes, even gold, but when it comes to large status vehicles, black remains the number one choice. Other creatures of the road include the occasional 4WD vehicle (black of course and never muddy), blue farmers' trucks packed with produce, and around town, multitudes of small motorbikes and scooters.

These come in two different flavors; manic pizza teen and prim dairy lady. The first is responsible for getting your delicious dinner to you hot, and is usually seen speeding at night over sidewalks with a delivery box in one hand and a cigarette in the other. The second style calmly follows a set route during the day, delivering vital milk and yogurt supplies. The latter is much less of a threat to life and limb than the former, but both pose a danger when transiting back alleys and narrow sidewalks.

The curious observer may note that at times it appears these riders are wearing oversized boxing gloves. These aren't worn to protect the delicate knuckles of the milk ladies or to avoid bruising errant housewives who've fallen behind in their monthly payments to the dairy mafia. They're merely giant hand warmers attached to the handlebars. These oversized foam and vinyl oven mitts are large enough to contain the handle, brake, clutch and throttle. Though not super stylish, this smart setup allows the rider to keep his or her hands warm without losing sensitivity or coordination during the winter months.

Charges of racism may be leveled at the author by those residing outside the country but it doesn't take a genius to realize that Koreans aren't the world's best drivers. The fact that there are hardly any old cars on the road, yet almost all of them are dented, scraped or scratched, gives some indication as to how the locals perform under pressure. Anyone living here who's ground their teeth down to raw stumps sitting in the back seat of a van attempting to overtake uphill on a blind corner in the mountains at night during a monsoonal rainstorm will agree that there's room for improvement.

When questioned about the fact that their country has one of the highest rates of fatal crashes in the world, (five Latin American nations narrowly beat them for first place), Koreans will often respond that it's because they've modernized so rapidly that the driving skills required to ensure safety are not yet being passed down from father to son.

The strange thing is that in terms of testing and driver's education the standards are very high; no one can honestly say that it's a license in the cereal box scenario. Getting your ticket in Korea is prohibitively expensive, and the long mandatory training periods are conducted at special schools with their own driving tracks and vehicles. The fact that they never actually drive on the road to gain practical 'real world' experience until after they get their licenses may have something to do with it.

In general, the problem isn't really dangerous or reckless driving, it's more just a lack of common sense. The usual suspects like changing lanes without shoulder checking, entering one way roads from the wrong direction, and attempting to simultaneously text and shave on the way to work all add to the mayhem.

Oddly enough, high speed isn't one of the big contributing factors in vehicle related mortality. What kills most people is the rapid deceleration when the car they're traveling in attempts to sodomize a stationary tractor. Be careful, as these little bundles of bucolic joy are often left on the edges of country roads at night for unwary drivers to discover. They usually lack reflectors and are too small for conventional radar to detect. Unless you wish to replace your hips with a crumpled four cylinder engine, it's wise to err on the side of caution when cruising rural areas after dusk.

Apart from the new highways, most roads have a maximum speed of only sixty or eighty kilometers per hour and most Koreans are more than happy to stick to the limits. This can turn a short journey into a day's outing, but when you begin to stamp your right foot on the imaginary accelerator, pause to consider the carnage if the natives were speed freaks.

Parking is another area where Koreans are more relaxed. Cars get dumped just about anywhere and on every conceivable angle. It would seem to the casual observer that parallel parking was just a concept invented by anal Westerners with too much time on their hands. Vehicles come to rest wherever their occupants decide to exit. No-stopping signs, safety crossings, and sidewalks, are all immaterial to the driver if the place they wish to visit lacks available parking spaces. People in wheelchairs will quickly get used to playing in heavy traffic as the sidewalks are almost always blocked by cars or trucks.

Buses, taxis and student chauffeurs all have their merits, but nothing will give you the freedom to explore like your own set of wheels. Most of the country's most famous attractions can easily be reached by public transport, but it's up in the hills where you'll experience another Korea. There you'll find life isn't about the coolest computer game, the highest TOEIC mark or the latest mobile phone ring tone. It's a completely different place, and one that usually sends you back to work feeling refreshed and ready to face another day of screaming kids.

The new highways have taken a lot of traffic off the old network and this makes these smaller roads a safer and more relaxed touring option. Weekend getaways are a great way to relieve stress and touch base with this scenic landscape. All you need to do is get out into the countryside and start following a small road. It will always take you somewhere, and in Korea that's usually someplace worth seeing.

Beautiful old villages of clay, wood and tile, quiet gardens bordered in peach and bamboo, massive stone walls draped in vines and tiny patches of rice so narrow that they're still ploughed by ox and harvested by hand. Friendly old grandmothers who offer you lunch and old farmers whose guarded faces crack open into wide gummy grins if you stop to say hello. These are just some of the things you'll discover in the course of your auto explorations.

Sadly, getting your own vehicle isn't the easiest thing to organize. One option is to buy a car or motorbike and register it with your boss, but this requires a great deal of trust on both sides. The other is to register and insure it under your own name. If you're going to go down this route it's best to bring a Korean friend along to help with the bureaucratic boogie that will undoubtedly ensue.

If you're only after wheels for a short period of time, for example when family comes calling, you can always just pony up the cash and rent a car. A compact car will currently set you back anywhere from 80-60,000 won per day. As with rentals everywhere read the fine print, think carefully about insurance and make sure you possess a valid international driver's license.

The roads and highways of Korea hold many surprises for the independent motorist. Stay alert, drive defensively and you'll have a blast. If on the other hand you're a passenger in a Korean car; pray regularly, take up meditation, and consider leaving something to your favorite animal charity.

THE KINDNESS OF STRANGERS

Since time immemorial, loved ones left behind have offered up their prayers to heaven, while those traveling abroad have relied upon the kindness of strangers. Either the telepathic residue from countless worried mothers has mysteriously condensed over the land of the morning calm like some inverted Bermuda triangle, or Koreans are just an extremely nice bunch of people. Of course they'll humbly deny it, but the facts persistently prove otherwise.

Media hyped fears, and an increasingly insular suburban existence have eroded the Western sense of hospitality to the point where taking a stranger into the home reeks of latent suicidal tendencies. Koreans haven't yet reached that point, and if you find yourself in a spot of trouble, they will literally bend over backwards to give you a helping hand.

The following events happened to a couple who were visiting friends in Korea, and through a linguistic mix-up they found themselves in that delightful situation of being in the wrong city, late at night, with little money and no capacity to communicate.

As they stood in the bus terminal, staring hopelessly at cryptic timetables that made about as much sense as a Finnish iPod manual, an elderly gentleman approached them. He'd finished his work for the evening and had noticed that they seemed to be in some sort of predicament. Through broken English and the international sign language of the lost, he informed them that the last bus had gone, the ATM was out of order, the nearby hotels were only suitable for the purposes of prostitution and that they'd be better off spending the night with him and his wife.

Remembering advice given to them regarding Koreans and hospitality, they ignored everything their over protective mothers had ever taught them about stranger danger and cautiously followed the man into the night. As they wandered deeper and deeper into a labyrinth of alleyways and side streets, they prayed that their faith was not about to be tested by an ironic exception to the rule.

They later said it was like visiting Grandma's house as a child trapped in an adult's body. They were patted on the back, stuffed full of food and tucked into bed before they knew what had happened.

Waking early due to bladder issues, they opened the bedroom door onto a scene that astounded them. Their hosts lay sleeping in the middle of the living room floor, having put their guests in the only bed they possessed. This was when it really sank in, that for Koreans hospitality is about making sure the guest is being taken care of. Most people back home in the same position would have directed them to the nearest Salvation Army depot and boasted of their bottomless humanity over coffee the following morning.

But this lesson in kindness didn't end there. After breakfast they were led back to the bus terminal, had their tickets bought for them and got a bag of apples thrust into their hands. All of this done by complete strangers without any expectation of reward or future repayment.

Koreans are also extremely honest. During your time there you'll no doubt lose wallets, cameras and a whole host of other personal possessions under the evil influence of Soju. All you need to do is remember which watering hole you were frequenting and chances are they'll be waiting for you safely tucked behind the bar.

It's refreshing to live in a place where everyone isn't viewed as a potential criminal. Corner stores lack the ubiquitous electronic eyes so prevalent in the West, and those a few bucks short for the bill are usually trusted to pay it back next time they visit. It can be a little unnerving in the beginning but you quickly grow to appreciate this atmosphere of honesty and trust.

You're certainly safer stumbling blind drunk through the back streets of Seoul than you are walking home sober in many Western cities. The greatest danger you're likely to face here is being bailed up by a bunch of drunken businessmen intent on practicing their English skills. You'd have to be amazingly unlucky or exceptionally stupid to be the victim of violent crime in South Korea.

Dishonesty and violence not only reflect badly upon the individual, but also on the family and the nation as a whole. Sure, shit happens in Korea but the amount is nowhere near the depressing levels deemed normal in the West. This isn't to say that it's impossible to become a statistic, it's just generally a safer place to be when you're young, drunk and stupid.

Generosity is another area where the locals shine. In Korea it's hardwired into the people and it's evident everywhere you look, regardless of a person's age or status. It's the grinning old ladies in the market who urge you to have one more free sample and then chuck an extra handful of produce in after the deal is struck, and the Kindergarten students who happily share their snacks with the whole class, even though it often means the bag is empty before it gets back to them.

This generosity runs through all facets of life and society. It's drinks distributed, dinners bought and time spent without preconditions. It's Korean language lessons provided by fellow teachers on their lunch break. It's stopping to fill up your gas tank at a quiet country service station and having a little granny grab you by the hand and lead you over to eat lunch with her in the shade. It permeates all levels of society and is one of the defining characteristics of Korean culture.

If you have friends or family planning to come over, be prepared to only see them occasionally during their visit, because they'll be inundated and overwhelmed by offers to show them around. Amongst your Korean friends and co-workers lie hordes of instant tour guides just waiting for the chance to proudly show off the local sights and their English skills. It's not uncommon for visitors to be hijacked in the street by friendly locals, especially if they have a tendency to stand around looking lost with a map in their hands. More than a few tourists have received a free guided tour of the city when all they really wanted was directions back to their hotel.

Your guests will be wined, dined and showered with gifts, leaving the country with sore feet, extended waistlines and overweight luggage. If you're not careful they'll depart with the nagging suspicion that you didn't really want to see them, so be firm and ensure that you get some quality time as well.

It's these positive qualities, this wealth of spirit that comes naturally from the heart, that makes it such a special place to live. Koreans really do see you as a guest and feel it's their personal responsibility to ensure that you have a rich and rewarding stay. They genuinely want you to feel welcome and will go to amazing lengths to ensure that you do. Of course there'll be moments when you want to run for the hills to avoid another temple trip, but when it's all said and done it'll be these things, these little acts of kindness and hospitality that will remain with you long after your time in Korea has passed.

INTO THE UNDERBELLY

By this point in the book, you could be forgiven for thinking that the author is some kind of unrepentant Koreaphile, one of those born again citizens of the world who fall in love with an exotic location at the price of being blind to its faults. While you'll probably meet a few of these fruitloops during your stay (a foreign male wearing traditional Korean clothing is always a dead give away), rest assured that the author is operating under no such illusions.

You've no doubt had a gutful of majestic mountains, ancient temples and curious customs, and are beginning to wonder just what's the catch with South Korea? At some deeper level you know that it can't be all barbeques, beer and efficient public transportation. No country can live through decades of colonization, oppression, war, dictatorship and rapid industrialization without paying some sort of price. You can feel it in your bones, a lingering suspicion that beneath the surface lies another, less wholesome reality.

The following chapter isn't the most appealing, but if you're going to live in Korea for any amount of time, you need to be aware of the full picture. To truly understand the country, to say you've seen it from all sides, you have to delve deep into the underbelly.

As a wise man once said, every ying has its yang, and nowhere is this more true than in South Korea. For every ancient temple or village church you'll find nearby a dozen houses of ill repute, be they room salons, hostess bars, coffee houses, brothels, singing rooms, barber shops or massage parlors. Here the major sin involves sex, and most men at one point or another find themselves engaging in some form of prostitution. The sex industry is estimated to be worth over twenty two billion dollars or four percent of the gross national product.

Most men have their first sexual experience with a prostitute during their military service and many find the habit hard to kick. It's believed that over two thirds of Korean men engage the services of sex workers at some time during their married lives, and if the anonymous surveys are to be believed, at least twenty percent of young men pay for sex on a monthly basis. It is conservatively estimated that at least half a million women are trapped in this unsavory trade, though the number is thought to be double that figure if underage girls and illegally trafficked foreign nationals are included in the total.

This situation isn't particularly surprising when you stop to consider the country's deep Confucian core. When the traditional social setup segregated married men from their wives, limited social contact through a strictly enforced female curfew, and made it a criminal offense to seduce the neighbor's wife, a culture prone to the lure of prostitution was born.

Humans have always managed to find ways to satisfy their desires, especially when the people in question have been horny old men in positions of power. Those perceptive gentlemen in antiquity agreed that while it might be disruptive to conduct amorous affairs within the boundaries of respectable society, it needn't be a problem if they discreetly confined their infidelities to a certain class of women.

This of course isn't anything new. The Western world has long been locked in a similarly destructive relationship involving sex and vulnerable women. The only real difference being that while it certainly goes on back at home, the client base isn't as large, the service industry so obvious, or the government and general public so openly tolerant of the situation.

Of course, as with anything unfortunate in Korean society, the blame always gets pinned on the Japanese. Koreans will tell you that it wasn't until the Japanese occupation that prostitution took off. While it's a documented fact that the Colonial administration legalized brothels and brought over Japanese women to work in them, it's also true to say that the customers weren't only Japanese, nor did the lucrative industry dry up and blow away when liberation arrived.

Others like to point the finger at those interfering imperialists, the Americans, as they do make a handy scapegoat whenever people discuss their woes. Millions of US soldiers served in Korea and pumped countless fortunes into a burgeoning sex industry (no pun intended). Large communities, known as camptowns, sprang up around military bases, providing mundane services like laundries, bars and restaurants, as well as introducing countless women to a life of sexual slavery.

The big issue of concern for most foreigners isn't the historical roots of the problem but the current situation of tacit approval that exists towards the sexual exploitation of women. Most Korean men don't really see that there's a problem and many women view it as a necessary evil. People are content to ignore the moral and ethical implications and overlook the medical, social and psychological costs because to do otherwise would require them to acknowledge the fact that the nation as a whole is complicit in condoning this state of affairs.

The commonly held fantasy that the majority of individuals willingly choose to engage in prostitution also helps to avoid the touchy issue of crime and corruption. The greater part of these women, and the businesses they work for, are controlled by criminal elements, and this source of illicit and highly lucrative income is safeguarded from police interference through a culture of bribery. This corrupting influence on government, combined with a society unwilling to examine itself, has created an industry of staggering proportions. Though it is a poor joke to make, it's true to say that in the land of the blind the one-eyed man is king.

You only have to live in Korea a short time to note that while displays of natural passion are frowned upon, covert sources of illicit sexual activity are everywhere to be seen. There are coffee girls in vinyl pants trotting into shops and apartments with those suggestive thermoses by their sides. There are singing rooms and hostess bars where women wait to serve drinks and other less salubrious needs. There are massage parlors where a tug comes with the rub and barber shops that guarantee satisfaction with every shave. There are hotels that rent rooms by the hour and whole sections of cities dedicated solely to the purposes of prostitution. Sometimes it seems like half the female population is on the job in some form or another.

This wasn't written to scare you off, but to point out that like every other place on the planet Korea has its share of problems. If you are a female visitor you probably won't have much exposure to this part of the underbelly, but gentleman would be advised to think twice about late night offers of fun and adventure.

A certain teacher once opened his door late one evening to see who was causing the racket. After a variety of threats were made, he reluctantly agreed to join his drunken Korean friends for a trip to the hot baths on the provision that they never came to his apartment again after midnight. On the way there they mentioned that the establishment provided professional massage services and that they thought he should experience this important cultural activity. He should have known better, but they somehow managed to convince him that it was all above board.

The first part of the night was completely legitimate and consisted of a relaxing soak in the hot baths followed by a session with a highly skilled blind masseuse. Her English was quite good and they had an interesting discussion regarding Korean society and its treatment of the disabled. She informed him that her husband was also blind and that they considered themselves to be very fortunate in that their work allowed them the opportunity to be financially independent, unlike most other people with a physical or mental disability.

The evening then took a distinctly disturbing turn for the worse when upon exiting she thanked him for the opportunity to speak English and informed him that his girl would be in shortly. When he made it quite clear that he had no intention of using such services his friends in the nearby rooms were informed of this strange behavior.

They were quite astounded that a healthy young man would refuse such a thing and sought to set him right. They explained that it was "only play sex" (what ever that meant) and that he needed to relax, as they themselves were married men and had no qualms with what they were doing. Eventually they gave up trying to convince him of his folly and went back to their special massages. Needless to say the journey home was a little uncomfortable, but the teacher was left in peace after that particular episode.

Domestic violence is another issue of concern. While this phenomenon is by no means restricted to South Korea, it is exacerbated by a Confucian worldview that continues to regard women as being subordinate to men. Traditionally this has meant that husbands, fathers and brothers had the right to physically punish the women in their care for any real or imagined wrongdoings.

While the Korean legal system has changed over the last century, public opinion regarding a man's right to beat his wife has moved at a slower pace. Many older men still view physical and verbal abuse as their prerogative and can't understand why it's anybody else's business. The fact that Korea has a binge drinking culture that emphasizes quantity over quality probably doesn't help matters. It should be noted that the Korean government has recently taken great steps toward remedying this situation by initiating media campaigns to educate the public about domestic violence. Regrettably for those women at risk, entrenched misogynist beliefs don't disappear overnight.

Accurate statistics concerning domestic violence are hard to come by in a society that places a strong emphasis on maintaining face regardless of the cost. Medical practitioners, neighbors, co-workers and family members are uncomfortable with the thought of becoming involved, and often the victims themselves are reluctant to take action against their spouses, thus the majority of assaults go unreported. There is also a reticence on the part of law enforcement agencies and the judicial system to lay charges and convict.

Women with children are caught in an especially difficult position, in that even if they somehow manage to find the courage to divorce their abusive husbands, they are unlikely to gain custody of their children due to a Confucian bias that favors men in these sorts of legal proceedings. Thus many women, who might otherwise flee, remain trapped in dangerous relationships through fear of losing their children. Things are changing, but it's a sad fact that during your time in Korea you'll come across more than a few women who've walked into doors.

The fate of the physically and mentally challenged is also fairly depressing. While there are plenty of bumpy strips for the blind and lowered curbs for wheelchairs, the people who might use them are conspicuously absent from the scene.

This is again because Koreans are caught in an unyielding net of face, and a blind daughter or legless son continues to be viewed as a stain on the family's reputation. This has resulted in whole sections of the population being segregated from the greater community, either kept hidden at home or given away to some government institution. It's ironic that the only time you're likely to see disabled people out in force is on December the third, when the world celebrates the International Day of Persons with Disabilities. On this lone date they are ironically permitted to attend a parade or party in celebration of their existence, however limited and controlled it might be. It's truly a terrible situation and one that is especially heartbreaking when you consider the physical, emotional and psychological pressures these people already endure.

A certain teacher once stopped for lunch at a small family-run restaurant in the mountains and witnessed this kind of thing first hand. The day was sunny and the place busy, so he quite happily allowed himself to be seated at a table a fair distance from the main building. While he waited for his meal a middle aged man emerged from a small shed amongst the trees and slowly wandered over to join him.

They started to talk and it became clear that his dining companion was a son of the proprietors and that he suffered from cerebral palsy. He explained in remarkably fluent English that he had never been to school and that every word he'd ever learned had come to him via radio, TV and videos. He spoke of how these random encounters with diners were his only opportunity to speak English and how glad he was that they'd had the chance meet.

Their pleasant chat was broken by a terrible scream, as an appalled and aging mother ran towards them waving a broom. Scolding her son for daring to leave his room and bothering the customers, she began hitting him about the head and shoulders, ignoring the horrified pleas from the Westerner to stop. Mortified with shame, the man silently shuffled back to his place of exile amongst the trees.

This incident left a lasting impression on that teacher and he hopes that by sharing this disturbing incident some good may come of it. Not only can you discuss the plight of these people in your classes in an effort to raise awareness but you can also become directly involved. Ask your boss to put you in contact with the right government office, NGO or community group to see if there is the possibility of volunteering. One of the most damaging aspects of this kind of segregation is the social isolation, and by giving a small amount of your time you have the ability to radically alter someone's life.

South Korea is probably not the best place to suffer a breakdown either, as it lags far behind in its treatment of the mentally ill. This refers not only to the medical side of the equation but to the social side as well. Most Koreans regard mental illness as a shameful phenomenon, one so frightening and distasteful that by mere association with the afflicted they are in danger of becoming tainted. This harsh attitude results in a doubly damaging blow. Not only are sufferers reluctant to seek medical help for fear of discrimination, but they also face the very real danger of being abandoned by their friends and family, the very people whose support they need to overcome their illnesses.

In terms of actual medical care things aren't much better. Modern and innovative psychiatric methods are only just beginning to make inroads into South Korea, which means that the majority of patients are still suffering from the blunt trauma of heavy sedation, isolation and restraint. Conditions in the country's psychiatric wards are similar to those found in the West forty years ago and visitors have likened them to a never ending scene from One Flew Over The Cuckoo's Nest.

Again Confucian values are intertwined with this outdated system, allowing fathers to commit disobedient children and recalcitrant wives without a great deal of checks and balances. Once delivered to these institutions, patients have limited recourse in terms of appealing their incarceration, influencing modes of treatment and gaining their release. Human rights activists point out that this is one area where the country's laws are shockingly negligent and are in need of urgent and dramatic reform.

Then there's the suicide. South Korea has the highest rate of any OECD member state, with suicide being the number four cause of death in the country. The fatality ratio is just under 30 persons per 100,000, which translates to roughly 12,000 members of the community lost per year. That might not seem a lot, but consider that for countries like Canada, Australia and the US the rate is about half that number.

Especially worrying is that statistics indicate that this trend is growing at an ever-increasing pace as the country continues to modernize. Since the early eighties the rate of suicide has more than quadrupled. The factors behind this alarming increase are complex. While some have been around forever, like mental illness, homosexuality, domestic violence and child abuse, they remain taboo subjects within Korea. This in turn makes discussion of their relationship to suicide difficult to address. Their very forbidden nature means that those suffering from depression and anxiety often choose to take their own lives before exposing their families to public ridicule and shame.

A large proportion of these suicides are people unable to openly express their homosexuality in a staunchly conservative society. Most gays and lesbians are forced to deny their sexual orientation and marry straight partners for the sake of their families and personal reputations. The few brave souls who are openly homosexual face outright derision, discrimination and social ostracism both at home and in the wider community.

Try putting those shoes on for a moment and taking a short stroll. Imagine it, you either settle down with a person you have no sexual chemistry with for the rest of your life, or choose a path whereby the majority of your friends and family will despise and reject you.

Others factors influencing the suicide rate stem from a rapidly changing, stressful society. Students are pressured to achieve top grades. Employees chase after promotions and tenuous jobs. Housewives balance a myriad of tasks and struggle to please the in-laws. The elderly seek to find meaning in a culture that is slowly losing a place for them. Poorly paid farmers search in vain to find wives in a land that no longer values their labor. Influential celebrities are placed on impossibly tall pedestals. The list goes on and on. Almost any demographic you can identify is finding that the fruits of modernization come with an increasingly bitter aftertaste.

When it comes to crime and punishment there isn't a great deal going on. If you ignore drink driving, prostitution, domestic violence, gambling and the odd bout of illegal fishing, the average citizen doesn't have too much to fear. Of course the nation has its share of crime but it's highly organized and behind the scenes, unlike the West where just about anyone is free to rob a gas station.

Known as Kkangpae, these gangsters can be identified by their short haircuts, tacky designer suits and ugly tattoos. Apart from driving menacing black cars and parking them illegally, they tend not to cause too much trouble for the average foreign visitor, as their goal is not to attract police attention. If one does approach you it's probably out of curiosity or a desire to improve their English. Becoming a tutor for the Korean Corleones probably isn't that dangerous, providing you remember to hand out lots of stickers and never scold your students.

They're still a fairly traditional mob, far too busy paying bribes, blackmailing government officials, smuggling contraband, laundering money, running brothels and squeezing nightclubs to worry about kidnapping foreigners. Equally fortunate for the locals is the fact that they don't go around shooting up churches, killing police officers or delivering pony heads to politicians.

So there you have it. Not quite the deluge of diabolical doings you secretly suspected but enough to dispel any thoughts about Shangri-La. Hopefully this chapter hasn't put you off teaching in South Korea because comparatively speaking the rest of the world is in far worse shape. The basic message is that while South Korea isn't exactly a paradise, neither is it a risky environment for foreign nationals. Saudi Arabia might offer better pay, but who wants to swap barbequed pork, cold beer and cheap cigarettes for an alcohol free zone filled with cane wielding morality police.

NAZI HIDEOUTS IN THE HILLS

At some point in your travels you may find yourself wondering about the sinister road signs marked with swastikas that dot the landscape. If you were lost in the backwoods of Bavaria they might be cause for concern, but here in good old South Korea you can rest assured that you haven't stumbled across directions to some kind of Third Reich retirement village. What you've discovered are merely signs that point the way to the nation's Buddhist temples.

But why use the swastika? It seems an ironic contradiction for that particular symbol to be associated with an ancient belief system dedicated to peace and non-violence. While it's true that any twelve year old can connect the dots to the Nazi Party, few know that it has a past that stretches back over thousands of years. It's one of the oldest symbols known to man, and has been used by such diverse groups as the Hopi Indians, the ancient Egyptians and the Celts of pre-Christian Europe.

Though for most Westerners it symbolizes intolerance, fanaticism and genocide, the swastika also possesses a rich and noble history. In other times and places it has represented humanity, prosperity, fertility, good luck and the four sacred directions. In Korea today it stands for fortune, happiness and the wheel of life. The word itself derives from Indian Sanskrit and means "to be well".

If you look closely at the symbol on those road signs, you'll see that it is turning in a clockwise manner, whereas the Nazi design turns in the opposite direction. Hindus, Jains and Buddhists all employ this dynamic symbol in the decoration of their temples, artworks and holy scriptures.

Buddhism is both a philosophy and an ethical framework. It is a way to live one's life and a guide to understanding it. Many practitioners consider it a method to experience and interpret reality rather than a religion per se, which is why it's completely possible to be Jewish or Christian and a practicing Buddhist.

To help you more fully understand and appreciate Korea's Buddhist heritage, a woefully inadequate summary of Buddhist history and thought has been compressed into a few pages for your reading pleasure.

The story of this peaceful movement, which has over 400 million followers, began around 563 B.C. in the town of Lumbini, in present day Nepal. The person we now refer to as the Buddha, or Awakened One, was originally a wealthy prince, one Siddhartha Gautama, of the ruling Shakya clan. He lead a pampered, easy life, until, as teenagers often do, he snuck out of the palace one evening and experienced all the things his father wanted him to avoid.

What he met with on his short jaunt outside the walls wasn't the usual parental nightmare of palm wine, betel nut and fast chariots, it was something much more profound. In the darkness he witnessed three simple things; an old man, a diseased person and a decaying corpse. These three alone might have driven him back to the comfort of the palace, but it was the final encounter of the night, a chance meeting with a wandering sage, that changed the course of his life forever.

These experiences struck deeply, and led Siddhartha to the inevitable conclusion that he too would experience the pain and suffering of age, sickness and death. This seemed a terrible thing for any young man to calmly accept, yet the Yogi he had spoken with did not appear perturbed that this was the fate of all living things. He decided to follow the Yogi's path in order to free himself from these fears. He abandoned his cushy, royal life and set out from the palace so that he might understand the origin of suffering and find a way to overcome it.

He became a wandering Hindu holy man, studying Yoga, meditation and the art of mooching for his dinner. He and five other associates shared a hard life of physical austerity and discipline, each attempting to master their own body and reach the elusive goal of enlightenment.

After six years and close to death, he had a breakthrough whilst staring at the strings of a broken lute. He realized that humans were like the strings; wound too tight and they would eventually snap, left too loose and they would never produce a true note. It was only between the two extremes that the possibility of enlightenment lay. Thus was born the Middle Path or Way, which would eventually become the guiding principle of Buddhism.

Siddhartha renounced his extreme practices and was soon abandoned by his five friends, who believed he had given up his quest for knowledge and transcendence. Unperturbed by their lack of faith, he sat down under a Bodhi tree and vowed not to move until he found the answers he sought. His meditation was long and deep, but under a full moon in May he eventually achieved enlightenment and perceived the nature of life, death, and the laws of cause and effect. It was from this point on that he became the Buddha or Awakened One. He spent the rest of his life sharing the wisdom he'd discovered.

His message spread far and wide for a number of reasons; people liked the fact that it taught that a person's life and future lay in their own hands, that there were no gods playing dice, and that the teachings and priesthood were open to all, regardless of their social caste or sex.

The man himself claimed no divinity or special status. He continued to speak publicly and educate people until his death at around the age of eighty. Though the man has been gone more than two and a half thousand years, his message continues to resonate around the globe.

Buddhism has four Noble Truths. Put basically, they are that life is suffering, suffering arises from desire, to reduce desire is to reduce suffering and that by following the Noble Eightfold Path people reduce suffering, both in their lives and in the world at large.

The Eightfold Path is kind of like the Ten Commandments, except that you don't burn in hell for all eternity should you happen to screw up. These guidelines are merely there to help people pursue a balanced life of learning and self discovery. They are Right Understanding, Right Intent, Right Speech, Right Action, Right Livelihood, Right Effort, Right Mindfulness and Right Concentration.

As it spread across Asia Buddhism changed, altered in form by the cultures and countries that accepted it, yet never losing its deeper message. Today there are three main branches of Buddhism and many smaller sects. There is Theravada in India and south-east Asia and Mahayana in places like China, Korea, and Japan. It was here that Zen Buddhism flowered, while later in the Himalayas it evolved into Vajrayana or Tibetan Buddhism, a rich mixture of Tantric ideas, shamanism and Mahayana beliefs. It's interesting to note that unlike Christianity or Islam, these great schisms or splits never led to wars between their respective followers.

Buddhism is said to have arrived in Korea from China in 372 B.C. It was quickly granted royal patronage and in time came to incorporate indigenous beliefs and practices, maturing over the course of centuries, until the famous monk Chinul established the Chogye sect. It's a Zen variation of Mahayana Buddhism, and remains today the dominant Buddhist sect, representing 90% of the country's Buddhists.

In an irony the monks probably failed to appreciate, Buddhism itself proved to be impermanent, and during the late Koryo Dynasty (935-1392), it began to fall from favor. Internal corruption and the adoption of Confucianism as the official state ideology under the Yi Dynasty (1392-1910), led to repression and persecution. Privileges were withdrawn, temples were closed, land and assets seized and the building of new facilities banned. This is why most of the old temples you see today are hidden deep in the mountains, far from the urban centers and the Confucian elite who controlled them.

Many of these temples are approached by a staircase of exactly one hundred and eight steps. This particular number is highly auspicious and occurs again and again in Buddhist practice, from the number of times a bell is struck to how many beads complete a Buddhist rosary. The number represents all of the defilements that afflict the mind and body and which must be overcome if enlightenment is to be attained. Thus the stairs with feet upon them symbolize the true seeker's nature ascending towards Nirvana, shedding faults and desires as it approaches the goal of non-suffering. Others believe it's just a cunning way to wear out the kids so they don't fidget during meditation.

Rising slowly, you pass through three different gates. The first is the Single Pillar Gate and in crossing it you symbolically leave behind your worries and begin your journey. The second is the Four Heavenly Kings Gate, which is guarded by fierce looking protectors whose job is to deny entrance to those not pure of heart. The last is the Salvation Gate, the final one which opens on to Buddha's land.

When visiting don't expect a neutral, unobtrusive decorating scheme that merges seamlessly with the forest beyond; instead prepare yourself for the equivalent of a retinal orgasm. Color, so much color! Who would have thought seekers of wisdom would use pastel turquoise so extensively. This quite unexpected shade matched with a rusty maroon is the dominant combination, accented in places by complex patterns utilizing the traditional cardinal colors of red, green, black, white and yellow. Few exposed surfaces escape the tireless brush unadorned.

What's not painted is probably stone, one of the country's few abundant natural resources. Granite is harder than steel and was used everywhere. Long before sleek kitchen countertops became renovation must haves in the West, Korea was utilizing this heat, stain and scratch resistant stone for all kinds of projects, from the foundations of new buildings to statues of the Buddha. It continues to be used extensively today, from common street gutters to fancy tombs.

Two things you'll often see made from this material are stone lanterns and pagodas. Lanterns in the shape of Lotus blossoms symbolize the wisdom of the Dharma, guiding people to a brighter world. The stupa design comes from pre-Buddhist Indian grave mounds, the type that at one point held the cremated remains of the historical Buddha. It now represents the concept of the Buddha and his teachings and is usually found near the central area of the temple.

After leaving the third gate you'll often see a large, two storey, semi-open building. This is the Bell pavilion and usually contains four instruments. This oversized percussion group announces and regulates the life of the monastery. The Dharma Drum, Wooden Fish, Cloud Shaped Gong and Brahma Bell all serve a different purpose. Korean temple art is highly symbolic; nothing is meaningless or just for decoration.

All earthbound creatures are called to awareness by the large skin-covered wooden Dharma drum. The two drum skins come from a cow and a bull, and so symbolize duality and its harmonization. The Wooden Fish Drum stands for all those beings that inhabit the waters. Their eyes which never close echo the dream of the studious monk. The Cloud Shaped Gong is for all the souls upon the air and is rung at mealtimes. The sound of the great Brahma bell carries relief to all who are suffering in the world and is rung in the morning and evening.

The main hall forms the center of the temple. It's also known as the Golden Hall due to it usually housing a gilded image of the Buddha at the back of the building. On the right side usually hangs a scroll painting of the Guardians who protect Buddhism and its followers, and on the left is a memorial area commemorating the deceased. Other buildings around the temple precincts are dedicated to past and future manifestations of the Buddha; Bodhisattvas—beings who have achieved enlightenment yet remain on earth to help others, and Arhats—the Buddha's awakened followers.

Last on the list can be one, or sometimes three, small individual halls dedicated to the Three Sages. These are the potent face of native beliefs, so powerful that they were absorbed, not lost, when Buddhism was introduced, and which remain important to this day. They are the Lonely Saint, Sansin the Mountain God and the Seven Star Spirits or Big Dipper.

The elaborate wooden halls, sometimes more than a thousand years old, are sweet with countless offerings of incense, the floorboards worn smooth over centuries by the passage of bare feet. Large wooden columns stretch up into the darkness, supporting horizontal beams and clusters of brackets, all painted in colorful repetitive patterns. Doors and windows often incorporate complex wooden lattice work featuring floral or geometric motifs. The roofs are usually hipped and gabled, with dull black tiles offsetting the elaborate decoration below.

These beautiful temples are open to all, Korean and Westerners alike. Famous temples like Pulguk-Sa and Haein-Sa are certainly impressive and worth the journey, but hidden in the hills everywhere are jewels just waiting to be discovered. Visit on your own during a weekday and sit in silence, absorbing the age and atmosphere of these ancient centers of meditation and devotion.

Regardless of your religious flavor or fervor, everybody gets Buddha's birthday off. The celebration is held on the eighth day of the fourth lunar month, usually falling in May. The Government even grants pardons for penitent cons on this day.

The celebrations at the temples on Buddha's birthday are not to be missed. What they lack in calm they make up for in color and activity; rarely seen scroll paintings are brought out of storage, free meals are provided, and everywhere hang countless delicate red and green paper lotus lanterns, inscribed with prayers and wishes. Night falls to the gentle chanting of monks, bells and drums ring out, and the wooden temple walls glow softly in the warm light of countless candles.

In cities and villages across the country, parades take place. Long lines of men, women, and children form, lanterns held aloft as they walk along the darkened streets. Floats with symbols of the Buddha, smiling teenage Bodhisattvas atop decorated farm vehicles, massive paper lanterns that somehow defy the flames within, and propane powered fire breathing dragons light up the night. It's kind of like a peaceful Asian Saint Patrick's day without the Guinness fueled drunks and ugly hats.

Throughout the rest of the year the temples are filled with monks and nuns quietly going about their daily routine. Traditionally the training to become a monk or nun could last as long as ten years, but recent changes have reduced it to a four year course, after initial training at a temple. Monasteries have kitchens, living quarters and lecture halls on site, usually set away from the main places of worship and meditation.

Monks and nuns are usually happy to answer questions but they aren't tour guides, so don't expect perfect English. Most of the larger, older temples have large signs in English explaining the various buildings and historical objects.

Below most temple grounds are small stores which sell a wide range of merchandise. Those of you who think that Pope clocks and Jesus-themed dish towels are the height of cool will be in seventh heaven browsing the many stalls and stands. Some of it makes for neat souvenirs and many of the Buddhist bracelets and bags are quite beautiful. Incense made from local plants according to traditional recipes also makes a good purchase.

Mixed in among the vendors are restaurants that sell fantastic food and drinks. A good choice is the Sanchae Bi Bim Bap, though strict vegetarians may wish to ask for no egg. The little teahouses scattered throughout these commercial zones are great places to wait for the bus back to town.

A few things to keep in mind when visiting a temple; don't show too much skin, if given a meal eat it all, be quiet, take off your shoes when entering a building, step over—not on—a threshold and don't take pictures inside the temples. Basically all you need to do is show a little respect and you'll be fine, nobody is going to lop an arm off if you bow in the wrong direction.

So when you see the red swastikas, stop in and say hello. It doesn't matter whether you're a recent Catholic convert, a geriatric Jew or a merry Muslem, you're always going to receive a friendly welcome when exploring Korea's Buddhist heritage.

CONFUCIUS SAYS . . .

Korea is the last stronghold of Confucian culture. Far from its origin in both time and space, it is only here, on this once isolated peninsula, that traditional Confucian practices remain basically intact, though how far into the twenty first century this unique situation will endure is anyone's guess. China, the land of its birth, suppressed and destroyed much of its Confucian heritage during the turbulent years of the Cultural Revolution.

This period in Chinese history was marked by the catastrophic campaign of "casting away the four olds"; old ideas, old culture, old customs and old habits. All of the traditional systems that had guided and governed life in the Middle Kingdom for thousands of years were swept away, as there could be no other competing institutions of faith, no other structures of power and authority in the new China the Communist Party was forging.

Buddhist, Taoist and Confucian centers were specifically targeted for destruction; buildings and monuments demolished, documents and artifacts destroyed and religious leaders led away to re-education camps, prisons and unmarked graves. The direct descendents of Confucius had already sensed the way the wind was blowing and fled the country in the 1940s.

The last two decades have witnessed remarkable changes in China, with the Communist Party now more intent on honoring

Mammon than Marx. When Deng Xiaoping announced that to get rich was glorious, a new revolution had begun. This surprising U-turn in economic theory has brought many benefits, including a face lift to the town of Confucius's birth and a growing festival for tourists, but it's unlikely that cosmetic surgery will revive the old master in any meaningful way.

Other areas of Asia adopted Confucianism, but none with the sincerity or fervor that Koreans displayed. In earlier times, the Chinese, in honor of Korea's strict observance of Confucian rites and protocol, referred to it as the Land of Eastern Decorum. Today, no other country continues to maintain Confucian traditions and ceremonies in the manner in which Korea does.

To truly understand any current situation, one must first learn about its history and the context in which it arose. The man you know as Confucius lived in China from 551 to 479 BC. K'ung Fu-tzu was born into a poor family of minor aristocrats, and spent the majority of his life traveling and spreading his message of ethical and social reform.

Confucius lived during a period of strife and instability. China was divided into many small warring states, each controlled by feudal lords who paid little heed to the emperor. These petty despots acted as they pleased, with scant fear of repercussion. The general population suffered greatly, and many scholars sought for ways in which society could be rendered whole again.

Though his teachings were not widely accepted whilst he was alive, by the time of the Han dynasty, 206 BC to 221 AD, Confucius's philosophy had become the basis of Chinese education, society and governmental law. This state of affairs would remain basically unchanged until the end of the Qing dynasty in 1911 AD.

Confucianism arrived in Korea over two thousand years ago, and by the fourth century AD scholarly centers for its study and dissemination were operating in a number of regions. By the seventh century, official delegations were traveling to China and Confucian culture was well established. It was not until the Yi dynasty, when Confucianism was formally adopted as the state ideology, that it came to fully dominate Korean life.

Confucianism is not a religion, though it brings comfort and psychological security to many millions of people. It is perhaps best described as a system of ethical beliefs for the harmonious management of society. Central to these beliefs are the proper relationships between people. These emanate from righteous behavior, empathy, and the active cultivation of both virtue and education.

Inherent within this system is the strong belief in patriarchal authority and filial piety. The ruler and subject, father and child, husband and wife, teacher and student, elder and younger sibling, boss and employee, and all other hierarchical relationships are bound and governed by the same ethical framework. Only friends of the same age, sex, social status and education are considered equals.

This system was not developed to provide individual happiness and freedom but to maintain social cohesiveness and stability. The desires of one are sacrificed for the good of the whole. Whereas in the West, personal choice and freedom of expression are seen as the right of the individual and the driving force of society, the same behavior is viewed traditionally in Asia as narcissistic self interest and a negative influence upon the common good.

In concept, this interdependency between people was supposed to be mutually beneficial, a kind of benevolent paternalism that Confucius believed would change society for the better. However, as time progressed it came to resemble a rigid hierarchy of inequality, under which women and the lower classes saw their rights and privileges eroded.

As is often the case with great ideas that change the world, lesser minds and the passing of time return things to the status quo. Eventually the message itself was lost and only the words and ceremonies remained, mere echoes of their former power and promise.

Things did not begin to change until around the turn of the century, when pro-Japanese reformers initiated modifications to the legal system that put all classes on the same level before the law, pronounced slavery illegal and abolished the traditional government entrance exams that were based on Confucian texts. Without these changes the majority of Koreans today would not enjoy the lifestyle they lead, but don't expect them to thank the Japanese anytime soon.

The colonizers continued the process of reform, though for the most part it was for their own immediate benefit and personal gain. Korea is now a democracy and the days of feudal obedience are long past but Confucian ideals still influence many aspects of life in Korea. Young people continue to seek their parents' input and approval, whether it's choosing a university course or a marriage partner. Eldest males often look after their parents in old age and younger children submit to the orders of their senior siblings without serious complaint.

Everything from marriage ceremonies to burial practices are laden with Confucian overtones. The body was, and still is to some degree, viewed as a gift from the ancestors, and so to demean or destroy it is to insult those who have gone before, thus the elaborate mourning rites and ancestor memorial services. This also explains the reticence most Koreans feel even today about tattoos, body piercing and other practices which harm the body. (Drinking yourself brain dead and screaming Karaoke songs until you're tone deaf obviously doesn't count!)

On a superficial level this means that almost every single thing you experience during your stay will be influenced by the venerable old sage. In learning to observe the world through Confucian tinged glasses, you'll be better equipped to understand the things that happen on a daily basis and thereby avoid some of the frustration that comes with living in Korea.

Smile when students raised on a diet of American sitcoms berate you for callously putting your grandparents in an old people's home. Bow your head with shame when your doctor chastises you for having the arrogance to inquire about a second opinion. Accept with grace and humility the delay when your position in the queue is pushed back by a gang of groaning grannies. These are all just accepted facets of Confucian culture and whining about them won't change a thing.

You really shouldn't complain, because it's Confucianism that provides the cushy jobs. Without its ubiquitous influence there'd be no competition between parents to have the best educated boys in the apartment complex and it's Confucianism that engenders the respect and gratitude Koreans feel towards education. It provides nylon socks on teacher's day, leaves cups of tepid coffee in the staffroom and curbs the proliferation of foul mouthed fiends that are the bane of teachers in the West.

A little time spent observing the lives of the elderly will leave you with no doubts as to who has the better deal. All members of society from the smallest children to the richest businessmen defer to them and value their experience. Old people in Korea possess respect and power, unlike many of our own elderly citizens who get shuffled off into retirement villages, where they exist in a twilight limbo-land punctuated only by weekly baths, bland meals and standardized greeting cards.

Korean children also benefit by having grandparents in the home; cashing in on bedtime stories, fresh Kimchi and lots of good old fashioned spoiling. Working parents enjoy free babysitting and meal preparation, though wives who inherit bossy mothers-in-law tend to stress the merits of less traditional domestic arrangements. Korea is changing under the pressures of modern life and the family structure is beginning to alter, but it will take a long time before Master Kung's legacy has vanished completely from the land of the morning calm.

Confucianism permeates Korean life. Trying to live there without understanding it is like attempting to voyage to the moon without caring about the role oxygen plays. Once you begin to recognize and accept its influence you will be on the road to better mental health and happiness. Of course, no matter what you do, there will always be days when you'll feel like radioing someone back at mission control and saying "Houston we have a problem". When this happens just remember that if you're suffering a little confusion, chances are it's just Confucian.

RED CROSSES AT NIGHT, CHRISTIAN'S DELIGHT

Newly arrived visitors to Seoul, looking out at night across a neon horizon littered with glowing red crosses, might be forgiven for thinking that the local Christians offer all night prayer sessions for the spiritually sleepless, but what they're observing is just a reflection of how enthusiastically Koreans have adopted baby Jesus and made him their own.

Unlike the rest of Asia, which for the most part has been a little slow on the uptake, South Korea is by far the most Christian nation on the block. Statistics place most of the neighbors at about 2% Christian, whereas the Hermit Kingdom, depending on who you're quoting, is somewhere between 25 and 30% holier than thou. Which raises an important question, namely, why is Korea so different?

To understand how a small Confucian/Buddhist peninsula jutting out from the mass of Asia became one of the most quickly converted countries on earth, you have to, as the great Bob Marley once said "Know their history, and then you'll know where they're coming from."

The first official traces of Christianity show up with that fun-loving war freak Hideyoshi and his invasion of 1592. Some of his soldiers were recent converts and they brought along a Jesuit priest to offer spiritual guidance as they raped and looted the countryside. This did surprisingly little for the new faith's popularity, and things stayed pretty static on the local religious front for another couple of centuries.

It wasn't until 1770, when envoys to the Chinese court brought back Chinese Catholic literature, that Koreans began to take an interest in Western religious practices. In 1783, a group of scholars anxious to learn more about Western culture urged the son of the Korean ambassador in China to learn all he could about the odd god.

He returned home in 1784, distributed his collection of Christian literature amongst the neighbors and told the curious scholars everything he'd learned. He obviously had some favorable things to say, because these gentlemen began to discuss with their friends and families the new religion, and before long they were preaching the gospel, teaching the catechism, and baptizing babies like there was no tomorrow.

That these guys got fired up on God wasn't anything new, in fact it's a perfectly understandable reaction to learning that your immortal soul is in danger of eternal damnation. What was different was that unlike almost every other 'convert the heathens' scenario being played out around the world at that time, Christianity in Korea was introduced and disseminated by locals.

Catholicism spread amongst a limited number of intellectuals but not without opposition. Most scholars and government officials were offended by the new religion, as it clearly ran against long established Confucian values and beliefs. Especially galling was the fact that the Catholics viewed the traditional practice of Jesa, or ancestor veneration, as a form of pagan idolatry. This became a sticking point for many Koreans considering conversion, that and the fact that failure to perform Jesa was punishable by life imprisonment or execution.

These facts however didn't slow the growth of the fledgling church and by 1801 there were believed to be over 10,000 practicing Catholics in Korea. Things came to a nasty impasse around that time when the reigning King died and the Queen Regent took the reins. One of her first acts was to denounce the new religion and label the worshippers as traitors. The fact that many of the new converts were members of political groups deemed subversive surely had nothing to do with Catholicism being deemed a "cult of evil learning". Besides faulting them for having a confusing virgin mother goddess, and priests with bad haircuts, she also threw in charges of immorality, heresy and the practice of black magic.

As everybody knows, all good religious fanatics dream of sweet martyrdom and the Queen Regent's proclamation helped bring about that painful reality. The Shinyu persecution, as it became known, killed over 300 Catholics and locked away thousands more. Like it had with the Romans before them, harsh persecution merely ground the seeds deeper into the stony soil and ensured Christianity an enduring place on the Korean peninsula.

The next few decades were relatively quiet, with the church keeping a low profile to avoid confrontation with the state. Periodic killing sprees occurred, but it wasn't until 1815 that the next batch of martyrs was sent to heaven prematurely. This was followed by a lull in state-sponsored mayhem until they decided to cull the rising numbers in 1827. (You have to remember that this was all back in the days before computer games and television.)

Though hemorrhaging under the government's policy of "kill all Christian devils", the Catholic Church remained eager for more punishment and requested that the Chinese Bishop send them an official priest to minister to their spiritual and seemingly suicidal needs. In 1831 the Chinese found a risk taker in one Father Liu Fangchi and sent him to care for the Lord's people in the land of the morning calm. He was joined by a pair of French priests and just as importantly, two local lads, who became Korea's first indigenous priests.

Murder and martyrdom fluctuated over the next couple of decades, depending on who was in power, but things really took a turn for the worse during the 1860s. Previous government opposition to Christianity had primarily focused on its menace to traditional society, but as Japan yielded to American gun boat diplomacy and Russia flexed its growing muscles, Korea became understandably suspicious about the intentions of the West, and her local Christians became guilty through association.

The persecution of 1866 was the pinnacle of paranoia. More than 8,000 Koreans were tortured, starved and cruelly executed, a huge blow to a church that only numbered some 18,000 believers. Things didn't let up until King Kojong ascended the throne in 1873. While his reign was marked by a period of poverty and instability, the focus of the new monarch was on bigger issues, and the church was able to slowly recover during the following decades, though these years were not without hardship.

The 1870s, '80s and '90s saw religious regrowth at every turn. Priests were trained, bibles printed, orphanages opened, local nuns ordained, and new places of worship consecrated. The Catholic Church maintained this steady growth even as the Japanese increased their stranglehold on the peninsula by carefully implementing a policy of neutrality towards the evil empire. By the end of the first decade of the twentieth century, adherents of the Catholic Church numbered over 70,000, a remarkable figure considering the brutal persecutions that had dogged the movement over its century of religious struggle. Little did they realize that the greatest threat to their spiritual franchise would come from fellow Christians.

As with all things questionable in Korea, the first Protestant to set foot in Korea was a Japanese bible thumper, who hit the port of

Pusan in 1883. It should however come as no surprise that it was those meddling Americans who really got the ball rolling in 1884, when two different evangelical operations, the Presbyterians and the Methodists, set up shop in Seoul after an agreement had been reached between Korea and the United States that guaranteed the safety of foreign missionaries.

It's hard to say how things might have gone for the newcomers had it not been for a lucky break in the form of a botched assassination attempt on the life of Prince Min, the designated ambassador to the United States and the Queen's nephew. Dr. Allen, the new Presbyterian missionary, also happened to be the medical officer at the US foreign affairs mission in Seoul. He lived near the scene of the attack and was able to offer emergency first aid to the victim and save his life. His quick thinking earned him heartfelt gratitude and the prestigious position of royal physician.

In a single fortuitous moment the course of Christianity in Korea was altered, for in winning the confidence of the government, Dr. Allen earned the Protestant missionaries much needed respect, and in 1885 he gained permission to open the first Western hospital. Allen's actions created a more favorable environment for saving souls, and over the next few years more and more protestant missionaries from around the world arrived to do the Lord's work.

Things turned ugly again in 1888 when the Catholic Church arrogantly began construction of a cathedral in a location deemed too close to the royal palaces and shrine. When politely asked by the King to find another site, the Catholic Church ignored the royal request and proceeded with laying the foundation. The King's reaction was swift and not particularly surprising; he banned the spread of Catholicism and once again simmering anti-Western sentiments rose to the surface. Riots broke out and people were killed as nasty rumors spread through the country that foreigners ate Korean children, a blatant lie but not inconceivable after years of eating Kimchi.

Due to this hostile and often hazardous environment, the evangelical missions quickly came to realize that the safest way to gain new converts was through doing good deeds. They started schools for both boys and girls, opened hospitals and medical colleges, ran orphanages and set up institutes to care for women, the aged and the infirm. Education was then, as it is now, extremely important to Koreans, and it was through this avenue that the missionaries really started to gain the public's trust and confidence. By 1910 the various religious groups ran over 800 schools and had a student population of over 40,000, twice the number of those enrolled in government schools and academies.

A decision that would later serve the Christian agenda well would be the use in these schools of Hangul, the native script, over traditional Chinese characters. This not only made it easier and far quicker to educate children, it also had the benefit of providing all students with a unifying identity. Later, as Japanese attempts to destroy and malign Korean culture intensified, this common thread would prove to be a rallying point and source of pride for Korean nationalists.

Relations between the occupying powers and the Christians gradually lost any semblance of neutrality, and the Japanese came to perceive the Christians as one of the few organized groups that could oppose them. Events such as the Conspiracy Trial of 1911 and the Independence Movement of 1919, both of which had an unusually high proportion of Christian participants, provoked the Japanese into outright oppression and persecution. Hundreds of men and women were imprisoned, tortured and killed, and dozens of churches were burned to the ground. These deaths left a lasting impression amongst Koreans that the church was not about serving foreign interests, but about promoting and defending the Korean people.

As Japan fought its war with China, it became clear that it needed a solid base on the mainland to conduct operations and Korea turned out to be the perfect location. To ensure security and loyalty, it was decided that Korea had to be completely Japonified. The country became a giant prison and all its resources became the property of the empire. Men became soldiers and manual laborers, women were reduced to sex slaves and servants. The Korean language and script was banned, traditional names were replaced with Japanese ones, and every other degrading idea that could be justified under the goal of total assimilation was put into practice.

Japan believed that a unifying religion would help the cause, so they enforced Shintoism and the glorification of the Emperor upon the nation. Christians and Buddhists alike were ordered to pay their respects and participate in the ceremonies and rituals. Shinto shrines were erected in Christian schools, churches, private homes and public places. The occupying government installed puppet leaders and restructured churches in order to make them more docile. Missionaries that refused to endorse the moves were expelled, and any locals who associated with foreigners were liable to be accused of espionage. Thousands of Korean church leaders refused to play along and were locked up, many of them dying before liberation forces could secure their freedom.

The end of World War Two did little to ease the suffering and precipitated, with the help of two super powers who don't need to be named, a civil war that tore apart an already devastated peninsula. Like the Japanese before them, the Communists in the north identified the Christian community as a threat and acted accordingly. Many Christians fled south to safety, but as the war intensified thousands were executed in Communist purges.

By the time the Korean War ended, the country was a tragic wasteland. Millions of people were dead or displaced; whole cities lay in ruins; bridges, roads and railway lines were destroyed; fields were littered with live munitions and over one hundred thousand children had lost their families.

Into this desperate situation poured millions of dollars of aid, mainly from the USA and other Western nations. Christian organizations ministered to the physical and spiritual needs of the people and in the process won more hearts and minds. They set up food programs, cared for orphans, arranged adoptions, helped amputees and supplied clothing, shelter and medicine free of charge. These actions saved the lives of countless Koreans and many converted to Christianity during those troubled years.

The following decades saw the various churches grow in leaps and bounds. Christian groups continued to provide support to the poor where the government failed to do so, whilst maintaining their reputation for freedom through their involvement in the democracy movement. By this time Christianity had become a powerful enough force to be able to persuade both the army and industry to allow priests and ministers to serve alongside the soldiers and workforce. Church groups set up radio and television stations in order to better communicate their message. The number of converts grew so quickly that through the '60s, '70s and '80s, the percentage of the population that identified themselves as being Christian doubled every ten years.

Today Christianity is thriving in South Korea, to the point where it now exports its own missionaries to save the rest of the world. This spiritual success story has its roots in two hundred years of oppression, social unrest, war and rapid social change. Knowing how it all came about probably won't convince you to accept Jesus Christ as your savior, but it will explain how every village with more than ten houses came to have a church, and why all those creepy red crosses light up the night time sky.

TO SUMMON TEN THOUSAND SPIRITS

If you pause to consider Korea's four main spiritual movements, you'll notice that one continually gets discredited, disparaged and ignored. Why Shamanism should get the cold shoulder is perplexing, especially when you compare it with the competition.

Christianity appeals with the promise of eternal life but its obsession with sin scares off potential converts. Buddhism rocks with its message of non-violence but the chanting gets monotonous. Confucianism, with its focus on social harmony, works well in theory but sucks if you aren't the oldest male offspring. And poor old Shamanism has only these few minor points to recommend it . . .

- A foundation of ancient nature worship that sits comfortably with recent global shifts regarding the environment.
- A domination of female Shamanic practitioners, which provides a refreshing change of leadership in a deeply patriarchal society.
- A purported ability to reconcile the dead, heal the mentally ill and personally intercede with the spirit world.

- Frenzied drumming, ecstatic dancing, colorful costumes, mysterious rites, scary swords, bronze bells, beautiful paintings, delicious offerings and those unattractive yet strangely appealing pig's heads.

What's not to like?

It would seem to the outsider that Shamanism has quite a lot going for itself and deserves more recognition and respect than it currently receives. How does a mysterious pre-historic religion with so much to offer, end up being seen as an embarrassing load of superstitious claptrap? How does a nation come to be ashamed of an integral part of its own culture, one that has faithfully served it in times of crisis for countless centuries? To fully answer these questions you'll need to learn more about Shamanism and its long history of repression.

Shamanism can be defined as a spectrum of traditional rituals and beliefs relating to the spirit world and its inhabitants. A Shaman is a person who has specialized knowledge and abilities in regards to interacting with the spirits. Their main role is that of intermediary, messenger and associate. A Shaman acts as an employee for members of a community, in order to influence conditions and events believed to be controlled by the spirits. They may be engaged in intimate family concerns such as marriage, birth, sickness and death, or act on behalf of a whole community to manipulate desirable outcomes such as plentiful rains, bountiful crops or successful fishing and hunting activities.

Unlike other Shamanic cultures around the world, in Korea the Shaman is almost always female. She is commonly referred to as a Mudang, though this is a derogatory term that is not appreciated by the practitioners themselves. A more respectful traditional term is that of Manshin, which translates to "ten thousand spirits". This title refers to the ten thousand spirits that are capable of being summoned by the Shaman. Male Shamans are called Paksu.

Within The Republic of South Korea there are two basic types of Shamanism. In the north it consists of women who have been driven by the spirits to become Shamans, often at great physical, social and mental cost. This variety of Shaman typically works with individuals to solve specific problems. In the south of the country the role of the Shaman is usually hereditary, being passed from mother to daughter, with the focus more on agricultural and communal issues. These geographical distinctions are blurring though as Korean society becomes more mobile and less bound by tradition.

Shamanism has been around for many thousands of years and was practiced in Korea long before the Buddha was a gleam in his mother's eye. The ancient agricultural communities that dotted the peninsula were pre-literate, thus a firm date for when Shamanism became established in Korea is impossible to give. Whether it arrived with the nomadic Asian tribes that first settled the land or arose later on its own accord will probably never be known.

By the time Buddhism appeared on the scene, Shamanism permeated every aspect of Korean life. The Buddhists were pragmatic proselytizers, so instead of attacking Shamanism they took the soft approach and incorporated many of the important Shamanic spirits into what would later become Korean Buddhism, thus winning over converts without directly alienating large portions of the population. A trip to any Korean temple today reveals how deep and lasting this union has been. Images of dragons and spirits decorate the buildings, and outside the main Buddhist structures there are almost always three chapels dedicated to the Mountain spirit, the Lonely Saint and the Seven Star Spirits.

Acceptance and assimilation is one thing, outright persecution is another. When the Neo-Confucian bandwagon rolled into town, things started to go downhill quickly. Any new religious movement is bound to look down its nose on the competition, but one that was imported, male orientated, literate and bureaucratic was definitely going to have trouble sharing the stage with an indigenous, female run, oral based, agricultural folk religion. The new kids in town quickly moved to persecute and marginalize Shamans, going so far as to declare them outcasts and banning them from entering the capital, though this was never really enforced due to Shamanism's intimate ties to everyday life.

The Neo-Confucian patriarchs might have scorned the Shamanic beliefs of the local peasants in public, but when there was trouble in their own households it wasn't the wise old sage they turned to for help. No sir, it was the ancient spirits of home and hearth, land and sky, that were invoked in times of misfortune and despair. When there wasn't a male heir forthcoming it was to the Birth Grandmother they turned. When the Kimchi rotted or the soy sauce soured it was Taegam, the Overseer Spirit they placated. When the clouds held back their life giving waters, it was the Rain Dragon they humbly beseeched with prayers and offerings. When invaders threatened and war raged, it was the fierce looking Chi U whom they asked for protection. When disease ravaged the countryside, it was Cho-yong, the Home Guardian, whom they begged to watch over their children. When a new structure was built, it was Song-Ju, the deity of construction, they paid their respects to. Confucius was ok for a bit of social engineering, but when push came to shove it was the Manshin and her spiritual connections that Koreans depended on.

Even the royal family, the pointy bit at the top of the social pyramid, was not immune to the Shaman's power. Queen Min, the last Queen of Korea, who lived from 1851 to 1895, had her own Manshin in order to produce male heirs and keep the family safe. The queen regarded her so highly that she attempted to elevate her to the rank of Princess. That action failed however due to the royal courtiers developing back problems when it came to bowing down before a lowly female fortuneteller.

By the time Christianity began to blossom, Shamans had been pushed down to the lowest rung on the social ladder, sharing the space with such illustrious occupations as prostitutes and butchers. Though this at first may seem a harsh judgment, it can also be viewed as an ironic salute. By placing the Manshin in such esteemed company, the government was basically stating that the services Shamans provided were on par with sex and steak, which, when you consider the average person's wants and needs, is quite the compliment.

The local Catholics had already been giving Shamanism a bad rap for decades, but it was the arrival of Protestant missionaries at the end of the nineteenth century that really spelled trouble. These guys came with narrow minds, heavy hearts and some seriously 'holier than thou' attitudes. They'd risked life and limb to travel across the seven seas in order that Christ's love might be known by the millions of heathens that lived in spiritual darkness. In their biased eyes, God's eternal love and salvation was being held back by a load of superstitious bunk. They couldn't openly attack Confucianism due to its relationship to the king, but Shamanism, already marginalized and persecuted, offered the perfect target for their religious propaganda.

Their conversion program resembled any modern political campaign, in that for every good thing they said about themselves they found two damaging things to say about the opposition. They painted the Manshin as either savvy charlatans preying on the uneducated for monetary gain or evil harlots in league with Satan, hell bent on leading the innocent into temptation, sin and eternal damnation. They railed against what they perceived to be superstition, devil worship, sorcery, the veneration of idols and the channeling of demons. They saw in the Shamanic practices of Korea all the terrible acts that the Bible warns of in Deuteronomy.

"Let no one be found among you who practices divination or sorcery, interprets omens, engages in witchcraft, or casts spells, or who is a medium or who consults the dead. Anyone who does these things is detestable to the LORD."

As more and more Koreans found themselves being introduced to Christianity, through its medical, charitable and educational fronts, so too did they imbibe the pro-Western outlooks of their patrons. They came to wholeheartedly believe that Western clothes were more stylish, Western medicine more effective, Western education more beneficial, Western science more inventive, Western music more harmonious, and Western art more realistic. Most importantly for Shamanism, Western religion was promoted as the only guaranteed path to heaven.

Along with a love for all things Western came a sense of shame and embarrassment regarding many aspects of Korean culture. Bowing, long hair, traditional clothes, ancestor veneration, Shamanism—all of these things were seen as old fashioned and primitive. The Christian modernists felt strongly that Korea would never be treated as an equal by the outside world until the nation had been purged of these backward practices.

As if Shamanism didn't have enough enemies to contend with, they soon had the Japanese on their case. The Imperial occupiers sought to remake Korea in their image, and part of that process involved forcing the state religion of Shinto upon the beleaguered nation. The poor buggers not only had to speak the language of the occupiers and take on Japanese names, they even had to start praying with them.

Now for once you might have thought that things were looking up for Shamanism, seeing that Shinto is primarily animistic and polytheistic, worshipping everything from mountains to ancient emperors. A betting man might have wagered that the Japanese would leave the Shamans alone but that wasn't the case, as the Japanese didn't deal well with anything that looked remotely like resistance. They banned ceremonies, destroyed offerings and brutally imprisoned anyone caught defying Japanese martial law.

The Second World War ended, the hated Japanese got the boot and Korea won its freedom, but the long suffering Shamans found little to celebrate. The first President of Korea, Syngman Rhee, like the various presidents and military strongmen that followed, was of the opinion that Shamanism had no part in a modern, progressive nation. The fact that he was a Christian convert with a Western wife no doubt had something to do with the decision to continue the Japanese policy of harassment and repression.

Meanwhile up North, both before, during, and after the Korean War, the communists followed a more severe policy of incarceration and execution. The communists conceptualized faith in anything other than revolution as opposition, and attacked all forms of organized religion. Amongst the waves of refugees who fled south were hundreds of Shamans and their own unique Northern traditions.

The Korean War ended in a truce, but the years that followed were no kinder for the Manshin. President Park Chung Hee followed the course of action laid down by his predecessors and actively persecuted Shamans during his long dictatorial reign. Manshin were harassed, their families ostracized and Shamanic activities forcibly suppressed by government agencies. It was only during the 1980s that Shamanism was recognized at a government level as being an integral part of Korean culture. Since that time the official conditions of the Manshin have changed for the better but they still face abuse, discrimination and censure, especially amongst the Christian community and the media.

Korean Shamanism has evolved over an extended period of time and each ritual and rite comes with its own highly specialized set of clothing and props. All of these unique articles are necessary in that they set the scene and become the stage when the spirits appear. Each object has a particular role and all are required if there is to be a successful outcome to the ceremony.

One of the most important elements in a Kut, the shamanic ceremony, is the musical accompaniment. This typically consists of a wooden drum and bronze gong, but at larger or more intensive ceremonies these core instruments may be joined by additional drums, gongs and flutes. The unique rhythmic pulsing of the music leads both the Manshin and audience into a different reality, separating the mundane from the miraculous. It is this discordant, ecstatic crescendo of sound that signals the arrival of the spirits.

Big pointy spears and swords are another sign that a Kut is in progress. The cold iron blades belong to the martial spirits and signify power, strength and aggression. They are a symbol of the Manshins' ability to dominate, vanquish and expel unclean demons and ghosts. Apparently a rusty five foot trident being swung about by a possessed Korean pensioner is enough to make even the undead think twice about sticking around.

The psychedelically bright costumes are more than just eye candy, they are the uniforms of the possessing spirits. Different entities are denoted by, and attracted to, certain colors, thus in the course of a single Kut several changes of clothing may appear. They are worn one on top of another so as to allow the Manshin to continue the ceremonial action with only minimal wardrobe delay.

As well as multi-colored robes, Manshin also wear various types of headgear. These differ in color and construction, acting as another clue to inform the audience as to which spirit is present. The Shaman will often have in her hands a fan or set of bells, to dispense blessings or disperse the spirits when they are no longer required.

Though Kuts can be held at any location, it is necessary for the Manshin to create an acceptable setting for the participants, both physical and spiritual. This consists of hanging images of the spirits, along with various pennants, ribbons and ropes around the area. These act to demarcate the ceremonial area and provide the spirits with a focal point in which to manifest themselves.

The most important physical elements are the various altars that display the offerings dedicated to the spirits. Different altars are needed for different types of spirits. Just as you wouldn't want to piss off a vegan friend by frying their tofu in the same pan as your bacon, so too do the Manshin avoid offence by separating the various spirit offerings. While heavenly visitors must be tempted with sweet fruit and rice cakes, their counterparts in the underworld demand sacrifices of flesh and strong wine. It should be noted that after the spirits have consumed the ethereal essence the living conveniently get to eat whatever remains.

Kuts can last anywhere from a few hours to over seven days depending on the type of Shamanism and the particular ceremony being carried out. Only those practitioners with outstanding stamina and dedication are capable of performing all day. Most Manshin only tackle a section in coordination with other Shamans. Some Kuts are held on a regular basis in order to bring about prosperity, fertility and general wellbeing, whilst others are held to solve a particular problem affecting a family or individual. Certain Kuts can have as many as twelve parts, but most are divided into four sections, each dealing with a particular class of spirits.

Usually the first to be called upon are the Literary spirits and other non martial entities. These can be genuine historical figures as well as those from stories and legends. Literary spirits may be asked for help concerning examinations and schoolwork, whilst other spirits like the Birth Grandmother may be invoked for the procurement of a child.

The Ancestors follow, and like many elderly family members they tend to be a pain in the ass. Wandering relatives from the astral plain are often the cause of grief for their descendants, and this part of a Kut usually seeks to learn of their grievances and find solutions the living can implement. The standard problems are untended graves, poorly conducted ancestral rites, and the inappropriate actions of children and grandchildren. The promise of behavioral changes by the descendants and a suitable offering is usually enough to placate them

Next come the Martial spirits or Generals, all Type A males with major chips on their shoulders. These guys are the personification of rough and tough, and when their support is gained it's good news for the Manshin. Their mastery of weapons and experience in war, combined with their fearsome exteriors is enough to drive away even the most persistent ghost or demon. They are the most physically demanding of the spirits that possess the Manshin and their appearance is not to be mocked or treated lightly.

Last, but certainly not least, come the rituals for the dead. These lengthy ceremonies involve the Shaman carrying out certain actions so that the deceased can reach heaven and the world of the living remains free from negative influences. The Manshin's job may be to simply accompany a departed soul to paradise, or conduct a complicated rescue mission to hell in order to free the trapped spirit. During the ceremony the Manshin must not only channel those martial spirits who are capable of braving the underworld, but also those who guard and control it. Both kinds of spirits place great physical and psychological demands on the Manshin, and it is only very accomplished Shamans who can bear this pressure and free the imprisoned soul.

Another impressive ceremony which may sometimes be witnessed at a Kut is the knife ritual. This ceremony is intended to demonstrate the Shaman's supernatural abilities and her access to spiritual power. She will often do this by licking razor sharp blades or drawing them with force across her arms and face. After this she may climb a ladder made from blades or dance upon a small platform of knives. Though it seems impossible, the same could be said for fire walking or a dozen other strange phenomena that science has yet to explain. You may be tempted to write this off as mere chicanery, but care should be taken if you intend to prove this by grasping one of the blades yourself. More than a few disrespectful tourists have gone off in search of stitches after foolishly attempting to discredit the spirits.

The smoking of multiple cigarettes is another common display of power. It's not unusual to see a Manshin heartily puffing away on half a dozen Marlboros only to see her reverse them so that the hot bits are inside the mouth. This disturbing display is likely an updated demonstration of the Shaman's ability to control fire, or it may just indicate that the nicotine patches are not doing their job.

The real show stopper of any ceremony centers around the acrobatic abilities of a large dead porker. If the big pig can be balanced for a short period of time upon a wooden pole as thick as a child's wrist, it's a sign that the spirits are in agreement and that a successful outcome is forthcoming. This is no easy task, considering that your standard swine weighs about the same as your typical couch potato (try propping your unconscious roommate on a broom handle and you'll see what the Manshin are up against). The balancing bacon need only hang there for a few short moments, but if this should prove impossible, it spells trouble for the patrons. To overcome such difficulties the Kut must either be abandoned or higher spiritual powers called upon.

Between Kuts, some Manshin supplement their income by practicing fortune telling. Koreans, like most people, find the thought of a little inside information hard to resist and visit fortune tellers in the same way Westerners seek a tarot card or palm reading. This kind of advice is often sought by parents. Important issues like education, marriage, jobs, and the procurement of fat bottomed male grandchildren are all cause for a quiet trip to the Manshin.

Most of this future gazing occurs in the privacy of the fortune teller's house. These services are discreetly advertised by the presence of a tall bamboo pole that rises visibly above the inner courtyard. Much stigma still surrounds Shamanism and fortune telling and it's a brave and self confident Korean who will openly discuss their use of a Manshin.

In order to accurately interpret another's future, the fortune teller needs to know the birthdates of those seeking help as well as their current situation. Numerous methods are then used to interpret the advice of the spirits. Common ones focus on the significance of numbers, the pattern of falling objects, and the direction of floating ashes or smoke after an offering has been burnt.

Today there are a plethora of online fortune tellers promising to predict the future from the anonymous comforts of home. With the click of a mouse and the right credit card information, anyone can catch a glimpse of the future in perfect secrecy. Of course the chances that any of these sites are being operated by authentic Manshin is highly unlikely.

This crass commercialization is just one of the many difficulties faced by genuine Shamans today. Living in an increasingly urbanized culture that's growing ever more detached from the land, it seems unlikely that Korean Shamanism as it's understood today will survive beyond the next few decades.

Of course there will still be colorful performances put on for the benefit of tourists, new buildings to bless and fortunes to tell. No doubt young boys will continue to learn the frenzied beat of the drums and young girls the complicated ceremonies but it won't be the same. For without real belief, without a deep sense of the mysterious and spiritual, it will become just another bit of cultural flotsam, a quaint but meaningless relic from the past, bobbing on an endless sea of modernity.

Maybe this analysis is too hasty, perhaps Shamanism, which has endured so much over the last three millennia, will manage to adapt and survive. It's hard to say what will happen, but if you should find yourself living in Korea, you'd be foolish not to go and experience this most ancient of spiritual activities. Hopefully this chapter will give you some insight into this unique religion and help you to understand its uncomfortable place in Korean society. At the very least it should discourage you from licking the knives or disrespecting the pig!

THE WAR THAT NEVER ENDED

If you cast a glance back over the course of Korean history, it seems that every great sorrow that has befallen the nation has emanated from those naughty neighbors to the east. Nowadays the Japanese are a pretty meek bunch, content to limit their world domination plans to having a Nintendo Wii in every home and a fuel efficient hatchback in each garage, but there was a time not so long ago, when the heady draught of nationalism intoxicated the little rascals to the point where they thought that enslaving the rest of Asia was a pretty good idea.

Their occupation of the kingdom of Korea in 1905, after nearly a quarter of a century of unjust treaties, murder and intimidation, set in motion a chain of events that would ultimately end in a clash of wills between the two dominant political philosophies of the twentieth century. The cost of that conflict was immense, resulting in the needless deaths of millions, the utter destruction of a country, and the permanent division of its people.

The Japanese, like most colonial powers, didn't have much empathy for the locals and basically did whatever they wanted. All manner of insult and atrocity was heaped upon the Korean nation; their language was forbidden, art treasures stolen, royal family murdered, archives burned, natural resources plundered, judiciary corrupted and the people themselves raped, beaten and abused. Throughout the Japanese occupation there were numerous acts of resistance, political protest and sabotage, but the martial efforts of an agrarian society headed by a bunch of literary scholars was never going to beat down a culture that spawned ninjas and samurai warriors.

During the occupation years various nationalists and freedom fighters fled to the safety of countries like the US, Russia and China where they established groups opposed to Japanese rule. The Chinese and American groups eventually joined forces under Syngman Rhee and worked to garner American influence and support. The Russian clients however, were more hands on, organizing and supplying armed resistance units within Korea. One of these guerrillas was Kim IL Sung, who would later flee Korea and fight with the Russians in Europe. (If the name seems familiar you might be thinking of his fashion conscious son, Kim Jong IL who until recently ran the fun loving republic to the North.)

But it wasn't until the end of the Second World War, as the American and Allied forces worked their way across the Pacific, that the Korean people began to harbor any real hopes of emancipation. When the atomic bombs exploded over the cities of Nagasaki and Hiroshima, it must have seemed that freedom was finally at hand, but the great powers that were punishing the Empire of the Sun each had their own plans for Korea.

As the Russians pushed down into Korea in the summer of 1945, the Americans came to the belated realization that they needed to establish their own zone of influence if they were to have any control over the country's political future. With the reds already in the North, the Americans felt it prudent to divide the nation into two distinct zones, where each could accept the surrender of their mutual enemy without stepping on each other's toes.

A proposal was made to use the 38th Parallel, which neatly sliced the peninsula in two, as the dividing line, leaving the Americans with Seoul and the rice fields of the South, whilst the Russians got Pyongyang and the industrial centres of the North. This state of affairs suited both countries and so it was incorporated into General Order Number One, the protocol for the surrender of the Imperial forces of Japan. Each foreign army was then free to disarm the Japanese and get down to the real work of convincing the local population that their ideology was best, despite the fact that they'd both promised earlier in the war that the Korean people would be left to settle their own political affairs.

While this temporary division gave the Soviets more time to consolidate their influence in the North, the Americans hoped it would give Rhee and other non-communist nationalists a chance to gather strength amongst the people of the South. Within months, Kim IL Sung was installed as the leader of the provisional communist government, while the Americans anointed Rhee as head of the nationalist administration. An unpopular Rhee, and a pro-American government riddled with Koreans who had collaborated with the Japanese, fuelled support for the communists, which in turn led to violent protests, repressive crack-downs and an ever increasing authoritarian stance in the South.

Meanwhile up North, the Soviet-backed temporary government began a series of land reforms in order to feed itself and the army it was secretly building. Kim wasn't one for originality and so he dutifully followed the communist program; executing wealthy landowners, jailing businessmen and seizing these newly liberated assets for redistribution.

Whilst America had entered the country with no plans to leave troops permanently stationed there, it was becoming increasingly obvious that without American military and financial aide the country would come under communist control, something neither Rhee nor the Americans wished to see happen. In 1947, the problem was brought before the United Nations (UN). The

US proposed holding elections then withdrawing, the Soviets proposed withdrawal then elections. Although many countries agreed with the Soviet proposal, good old US pressure won out. The specter of limited financial aid for re-building a post war Europe frightened most voting members into speedy compliance.

The Northern administration naturally rejected the UN decision and so on the 10th of May 1948, the South alone held its first election. Not surprisingly, Rhee and his questionable cronies took the majority of the votes. On the 1st of August 1948, Rhee declared himself president of the Republic of Korea (ROK). In a tit for tat response Kim IL Sung named the country the Peoples Democratic Republic of Korea and awarded himself the top post. Many Koreans resented the US led division of the country, Rhee's repressive tactics and the way the elections had occurred without the participation of the North. Throughout 1949 and early 1950 demonstrations, civil unrest, and violent guerrilla attacks plagued the South.

On January 12th 1950 the US announced its Communist Containment Policy. In the Pacific a defensive line would be drawn that stretched from Alaska through to Japan, Taiwan and the Philippines. Countries lying west of the perimeter would be left without protection. (You don't need to be a geo-political wunderkind to guess what happened next.) The North, under Kim IL Sung, naturally viewed this policy as an opportunity to unify the country under communist control without the threat of major US involvement and so proceeded towards a military solution.

At 4 am on the 25th of June 1950, the North Korean Peoples Army or NKPA launched a coordinated assault on an unprepared and unsuspecting South. Surprised ROK units and their American advisors were swept back by a series of well planned and executed attacks. The crafty NKPA even re-laid train tracks across the 38th Parallel under the cover of darkness so as to expedite the transit of soldiers to the front.

The fall of Seoul in a few short days was not only due to the proficiency of the North but also the ineptitude of those protecting the South. When the Americans abandoned the city they left the enemy 1,500 vehicles, 10,000 litres of fuel and massive stores of food and ammunition. In a similar show of stupidity, when the ROK command detonated the bridges over the Hann River they left 44,000 of their own troops on the Northern bank to be slaughtered.

As cities and towns fell, communist infiltrators took up the numerous positions that became vacant. Previous government employees from judges to clerks were shot or imprisoned alongside money lenders and wealthy land owners. Anyone with formal duties, from policemen to postmen, were classified as enemies of the state and hunted down. Those who had worked for, or had had any contact with the American embassy or the US military were executed on the spot. Mass shootings took place outside all the major towns and nightly disappearances of whole families became the norm. About the only group in Korean society who didn't need to worry were the illiterate peasants who made up the bulk of the rural population.

On the 26th of June the US Pacific Command based in Tokyo was ordered to provide air and sea support for the retreating ROK army—this entailed a naval blockade and the bombing of NKPA positions south of the 38th Parallel. On the 27th of June the UN Security Council at US insistence passed a resolution for UN members to help the Republic of Korea to repel the enemy and restore peace and security. With this decision, the US and her allies gained the international approval necessary to push back at Soviet aggression. Sadly, neither party had any clue as to how far and how fast things would escalate into full scale war.

On the 30th of June 1950, at General McArthur's urging, President Truman signed the executive orders necessary for the introduction of ground troops into the field. Within 24 hours American soldiers were dying in the rice paddies of Korea in a vain attempt to slow the NKPA, but it soon became apparent that a safe haven would be necessary if the country was not to be abandoned. Pusan in the south, with its large deep water port, was an obvious choice and fortification behind a strong defensive perimeter was quickly begun.

During the autumn of 1950 Pusan saw an unending flow of men and materials, whilst the sky above throbbed with countless missions to bomb and strafe any enemy positions that dared to expose themselves during daylight hours. By September, McArthur had the numbers, and against the advice of the Joint Chiefs of Staff, he arrogantly ordered a seaborn invasion to retake Seoul, via an amphibious landing at Inchon, coinciding with a mass breakout by American and UN troops back in Pusan.

McArthur's goal was to catch the enemy off guard, cutting off their supply and communication lines and trapping them between his two converging forces. When word of the Inchon landings reached the NKPA, panic spread quicker than lice in a kindergarten. What began as a disorderly withdrawal quickly blossomed into chaos. The retreat became a rout; entire units were chopped up by UN air attacks as they attempted to flee along roads leading to the North.

The plan was brilliantly executed and within 2 weeks nearly the whole of Korea below the 38th Parallel was again under non-communist control. Seoul however was in pretty rough shape, and the majority of the towns and villages between it and Pusan were hurting. Tens of thousands of Koreans were left without shelter and many would die over the coming winter due to exposure and malnutrition.

With victory fresh upon their lips, the Americans felt that they were in a strong enough position to kill two birds with one stone—punish the communists by taking back the North and reunifying the country under democratic rule. The unspoken question was would the Soviets allow this to happen.

On October 1st, McArthur demanded the full and unconditional surrender of the North. Oddly enough, no response was received. By October 7th the Americans had crossed the 38th Parallel and were hurrying to catch up with the ROK army. There was very little formal resistance and no real front as the two forces raced north. It appears that Kim Il Sung had fallen for the same trick as the South had only months earlier, and in failing to foresee an armed invasion he'd forgotten to make plans for that contingency.

The Soviets predictably cried foul and proposed a ceasefire and the withdrawal of foreign troops but no one at the UN was listening. Things were going so well in fact, that many US personnel actually thought they'd be home by Christmas. Sadly lacking in historical perspective, the Americans were destined to learn the hard way that predictions of that nature are notoriously difficult to fulfil.

As the ROK, US and UN forces pushed north, the communist block ran its own sombre calculations. Although the Soviets knew that they could not survive an all out nuke fest, neither could their pride allow a new communist state to fail. While they couldn't directly intervene for fear of initiating a larger war with the West, they gambled that China with its neighbourly status could step in without expanding the conflict beyond the Korean peninsula.

On October 1st Mao declared that if the US took the war further north, he would be forced to intervene, as a hostile American presence so close to its own border posed a menace to China's internal security. The Americans assumed that this was nothing more than a bit of empty sabre-rattling and continued on with their offensive, oblivious to the danger poised above them.

The Chinese swiftly responded by moving troops south, night marching whole units of men across the border into the deep valleys of North Korea, where they remained motionless during waking hours. The Americans with their day flying spy planes never caught a glimpse of them, and consequently wrote off Mao's words as nothing more than a bit of commie bluster.

By the 15th of October, over 100,000 Chinese troops were hidden and waiting. These 'volunteers' were hardened peasant guerrilla soldiers from World War II and Mao's civil battles to gain control of the mainland. Towards the end of October almost 300,000 Chinese soldiers were waiting silently in position. These troops possessed three major advantages; they did not need roads to move, they carried their own supplies and most importantly, they were completely unknown to the enemy.

On October the 26th, just 65 km from the border, the Chinese struck, and then after several days of heavy fighting, retreated into the hills. As days passed with no further Chinese attacks, the US let themselves believe that it had been nothing more than a final bluff to stall the inevitable UN victory.

On November 24th McArthur gambled on this assumption and ordered a final offensive to take the North. Victory however, would end up belonging to the Chinese. Through excellent reconnaissance and battle experience gained by the NKPA, the Chinese knew their enemy well and were prepared to exploit any weakness in order to win.

The Chinese fought hand to hand, attacked at night, kept off roads, used captured arms and avoided large scale battles; all tried and tested tactics which suited the steep terrain and an enemy unfamiliar with guerrilla warfare. They fought with abandon, often sacrificing numerous soldiers in order to triumph in any given engagement. Their superior numbers swamped a weary, over-stretched opponent and entire US and ROK units were slaughtered.

By December 1st, it was obvious that the war had taken a dramatically different turn. The American and UN forces were taking heavy casualties, which combined with a poor supply situation meant that a full scale winter campaign in the North was not a viable option. McArthur, uncomfortable with the word retreat, repeatedly urged the government to unleash the full nuclear might of the US military upon the Chinese, but thankfully Truman thought it best not to start World War III.

On December 3rd McArthur accepted the unavoidable, and bitterly stated to his superiors that a withdrawal back to the 38th Parallel was necessary. With better terrain, infrastructure and 250,000 men at their disposal, the Joint Chiefs of Staff agreed that back in the South it might be possible to hold and maintain a line against the Chinese, whereas to remain in the North would be suicide.

As part of the official retreat a scorched earth policy was enacted to deny the enemy shelter and food. It certainly hurt the Chinese, but it was even worse for any Korean peasants still alive in the area. This decision carried out at the beginning of winter resulted in the deaths of countless civilians.

As the Chinese neared the 38th Parallel it became their stated, if somewhat unsurprising, policy to attempt reunification on behalf of their Korean brethren. On January 4th Seoul was back in communist hands. They pushed on to the 37th Parallel, but with flatter terrain and better roads the Americans dug their heels in. As the battle stalled, the UN began to wonder when and where the war would ever end. While it was rapidly losing faith in the US dream of complete reunification, it could not afford to desert Korea, as that would give the communists a green light for the rest of Asia.

While McArthur still wanted to win the war and teach those commies a thing or two, Truman was coming to the realization that containing the battle to the peninsula and finding a way to peace might be a situation that he and the America public could live with. By February 1951, the Chinese and NKPA had been stopped in their tracks and were slowly being pushed in the other direction. The US under UN pressure agreed that peace around the 38th Parallel was an acceptable if somewhat ironic solution to the war.

By March 18th US and UN troops were back at the Hann River, standing amongst the remains of Seoul. Less than 1/5 of the pre-war population huddled in the devastated ruins of the city and those that had survived were starving. By the end of March, the front was once more north of the 38th Parallel. During the spring of 1951 McArthur aired his own opinions on how the war was being conducted a little too publically, and on the 11th of April he was relieved of his command and replaced by Lieutenant General Matthew Ridgeway. McArthur had failed to remember that military heroes are replaceable when they embarrass their political masters, especially when elections are imminent.

On the 22nd of April a massive offensive was launched. Air, artillery and napalm were thrown at the enemy in enormous amounts, the purpose of which was to inflict heavy loss of life in order to push the enemy still further back and encourage them to consider more peaceful alternatives. (An interesting fact to note—more shells were fired in Korea than in the entirety of WWII.)

During the course of the war prisoners had been taken on both sides, though the communists had a way of accidentally shooting soldiers in the act of surrendering. While it's true that ROK and US troops also committed atrocities in the field, the UN on the whole honored the Geneva Convention and treated their POWs respectfully. More than 100,000 Northern prisoners ended up being housed on Koje Island in the South of the country.

As to be expected, both sides hoped to influence their guests into abandoning their previous political convictions for the purposes of propaganda. The Americans attempted to achieve this by giving their prisoners all the material comforts communism couldn't provide, while the Chinese took the simpler, more cost effective route of starvation, medical neglect and daily indoctrination classes.

Throughout April and May the Chinese sacrificed some 60,000 men in fierce battles just above the 38th Parallel in an attempt to push the line of control south again. These attacks failed and the high casualties only weakened their fighting capacity, preparing the way for the inevitable peace talks. In early May the US formally stated at the UN that they could live with a truce along the 38th Parallel. It was obvious to the Chinese and Russians that the war was slowly turning against them and that an all out war with the West over Korea was not an option. On June 23rd the Soviets at the UN made their own speech where they too stated that a ceasefire along the 38th Parallel could be viewed as a step towards peace.

On June 30th Ridgeway asked the leaders of the North if they were ready to walk the talk. Rhee of course was not a happy camper. He'd sacrificed the lives of his countrymen in a costly effort to reunify the country and now his partners were giving up on the plan just when the tide was turning again. Rhee demanded that the Chinese retreat back to their border and that all NKPA units disarm and surrender. They didn't of course, which left the southern administration with little choice but to accept the US initiative, as they no longer had the money or munitions to continue the fight alone.

On July 1st Kim IL Sung agreed to begin talks at a place called Kaesong, a few miles south of the 38th Parallel inside communist lines. Both parties met on July 8th and agreed to full negotiations on July 10th. The UN idea was to freeze the fighting, draw up a demilitarized zone (DMZ), exchange prisoners and establish an international commission to discuss the issue of a truce. While it sounded fairly simple and straightforward, it would prove to be a complex and time consuming procedure that would stretch out far longer than anyone could imagine.

The meetings began, and it soon became clear that reaching an agreement wasn't going to be easy. The communists insisted on the 38th Parallel even though in most places the UN forces were above it. The UN by this time desperately wanted to cease the war, while the communists were willing to delay talks if there was any benefit to be gained. Peace seemed tantalizingly close but in reality it was more than 2 years distant.

Talks were later transferred to Panmunjom inside the neutral zone, where the setting was a little more even. While negotiations dragged on, each side continued to bleed out onto the fallow fields and empty hills. Over the next 24 months half as many men as had died in the first year of the war would lose their lives.

On the 17th of November 1951, the ceasefire line was agreed upon. This ended large scale battles but it did not stop the killing, for without fear of losing ground the Chinese could afford to maintain their practice of delaying negotiations through a policy of attrition. Down South, remnants of NKPA and pro-communist militias conducted small ambushes and attacks, while skirmishes continued along the ceasefire line. US and UN soldiers found themselves in the unenviable position of defending a front that could no longer advance.

The sticking point at Panmunjom became the issue of prisoners. The North wanted all Chinese and NKPA prisoners returned without question, while the US said only those who wanted to go would be sent. This was in essence a problem of appearances. The leaders of the free world didn't want to be seen forcibly repatriating prisoners to a Stalinist state, while the North knew it would lose face if some of its 'volunteers' chose not to come home.

The UN held some 132,000 prisoners, of which almost 50,000 stated that they did not want to return. The North was forced to admit that they held only 12,000 soldiers, leaving tens of thousands of UN and South Korean soldiers unaccounted for. By October 1952, the US was sick of the bullshit. It withdrew from talks, stating that no more discussions would take place until such time as the North wanted to end the war. Unfortunately, while the talks could be put on hold the killing could not. During this time more than 2,500 men per month died for nothing more than political obstinacy.

In November 1952 Truman lost the election and the hawkish Republicans under Eisenhower were in. Attacks on UN outposts and bases along the 38th Parallel increased in an attempt to pressure the new US government into softening its prisoner policy. Men died, the policy did not. The Americans opened their camps on Koje Island to the public in an attempt to pressure the North into doing the same. The denial of Red Cross visitations within their own POW camps in the North did little to improve their reputations.

On March 5th 1953, Joseph Stalin died. Along with facing difficult questions like how you mourn a genocidal tyrant who has killed millions of his own people, the Russians were dealing with internal issues of stability and continuity within the Communist Party. The Soviets needed no external concerns distracting them from the task of appointing a suitable successor and so put pressure on China to encourage the North Koreans to make peace.

On the 28th of March 1953, the Chinese stated that they would accept a neutral commission to interview and separate prisoners. In April they agreed to the return of sick and wounded soldiers.

While talks continued slowly towards peace, the North escalated its attacks along the line of control. It seems they just had to get in a few more punches before they could accept that the bout was almost over.

On June 4th an agreement on the issue of prisoners was finally reached. POWs desiring repatriation would go home. A neutral body would seek homes for those prisoners who refused to return to their country of origin, aided by the Red Cross and other concerned organizations. The only kid not coming to the party was Rhee, as a truce that left his enemy alive and a country divided was not the happy ending he'd been hoping for. In order to pacify Rhee, the US government agreed to provide the South with long-term food, military, and financial aide.

On July 27th 1953, after more than three years of bloodshed, the armistice documents were signed by UN and North Korean representatives. While the fighting ended that day, most people fail to recognise that the conflict never did. All that was signed was a truce, so technically speaking, both sides remain locked in a state of war.

Part of Rhee's demands included the proviso that American troops would remain on Korean soil until such time as political reunification occurred. Rhee refused to sign the actual armistice agreement and no Korean president since then has done so. While not particularly admirable, this stubborn streak explains why South Korean men to this day are still expected to serve in the military.

The war left the country divided and destroyed, with an economic outlook only slightly better than post partition Bangladesh. Over the years South Korea has recovered and prospered, but the North remains a stagnating state filled with starving peasants and empty factories. All wars are deplorable but few have resulted in such long term suffering. Millions of families were broken, orphans became a dime a dozen and a truly homogenous people were separated for the sake of political ideology. Most Koreans still dream of unity but that goal remains even more distant today than it did on the 27th of June 1953.

That basically sums up how things got to be so screwy; the following are just a few facts on how things stand today.

In South Korea the war is known as the 625 War—the June 25th War. In the North, where they tend to be a tad more formal, they refer to it as the Fatherland Liberation War, which you have to admit has a certain Stalinist flair about it.

The most visible sign of division is the DMZ. It crosses the 38th Parallel on an angle west and south. It is 238 km long and 4 km wide. A military demarcation line goes down the middle indicating where the front was when armistice was signed. Ironically, it now constitutes the largest intact biosphere anywhere on the Korean peninsula, though the landmines scattered throughout its entirety tends to limit the breeding populations of any animal that weighs more than a kilogram.

Soldiers still patrol inside the DMZ on their respective sides and are limited to light weapons and the odd axe, though that hasn't stopped hundreds of soldiers from dying there over the decades. Two villages remain inside the DMZ, each basically maintained for the purposes of pissing the other guys off. Tourists are allowed to enter the DMZ from the South on special guided tours. Flags, camouflage pants and inflammatory comments shouted at North Korean guards are not recommended.

While the surface upon which the DMZ rests is clearly delineated and controlled, the situation beneath the earth is a different story. Over 17 illegal tunnels have been discovered and no doubt more remain to be found, as the North is nothing if not industrious.

These tunnels aren't your average worm holes; instead they're compact engineering wonders, complete with concrete bunkers, electric lighting and all the comforts of a Stalinist home. Some have even been found to contain light rail systems built to move men and weapons. A few are big enough to transport entire divisions in the space of an hour.

Other oddities you might notice during your stay in South Korea are air raid drills and pristine, yet oddly deserted, beaches. The air raid drills happen irregularly and the only action required is that when you hear the siren you get off the street immediately and take shelter in a building—which probably isn't a bad idea considering the fact that the whole country lies within easy reach of conventional missiles. As for those lovely-looking beaches closed off by the military, don't be like a certain teacher and set up camp under the cover of darkness. Trying to convince freaked out teenage soldiers with live weapons that you aren't a North Korean infiltrator isn't cool at two in the morning.

Other than that it's all pretty much hype and hot air. Sure the North would like to reunite the country by force and send the majority of South Koreans to the coal mines, but the reality is that with America still standing guard and China reminding them to play nice nothing much is going to happen.

Ok, so every year they fire on a few South Korean crab boats, sink the odd navy frigate and test missiles in the airspace above Japan, but after so many decades it seems highly improbable that any major new chapter will be written while you're visiting. (Yes, the shelling of that island in late 2010 did kill a few people but half of them were southern military personnel conducting their own live fire exercises in a disputed marine area.) The North is far more likely to keep up with its sly as a fox routine, milking the UN for all the aid it can get and playing on its axis of evil/bad boy reputation whenever the world starts to ignore it.

South Korea has been stuck with this problem child for decades and unfortunately the North continues to display signs of arrested development. With each passing year the economic disparity between the two states yawns ever wider, while the rhetoric from the North remains the same, meaning that the future possibility of reunification is pretty much zero.

That said, most South Koreans still consider the people of the North to be relatives and genuinely desire some sort of reconciliation, so it's probably a good idea not to offer your own opinions on the subject unless pressed to do so. In short, the new head honcho next door is probably as mad as his dad but he's still family, so watch out how you speak about those neighbors to the North.

EVERYTHING BUT THE KITCHEN SINK

The final installment, as the title implies, is a foolish attempt to catalog every other interesting fact that didn't find a place in the preceding chapters. The following bout of literary diarrhea is not guided by any semblance of order, logic or aesthetic principles. It's merely a compilation of randomly organized information that couldn't be omitted due to the author being an intellectual packrat of the lowest order.

It's intended as a series of social snapshots, a collage of Korean culture, each part capturing some unique aspect of life in this most amazing of countries. Some may inform, some may disturb, and others may make you ask why the hell they were deemed relevant. If just one helps to explain the strange, weird or wonderful thing that's happening down the street or around the corner, then this closing round of whack-job wisdom was worth including. Enjoy.

Fishing. Koreans like doing it, and so they should, considering how much of the stuff they eat. What makes it worth noting here is that while Korea has its fair share of rivers, most of them are small, polluted and damned up the ying yang. To make up for this lack of suitable habitat those indomitable Koreans have come up with a number of options to ensure that the sport continues.

One is just to ignore reality and keep fishing from the rivers, eating the few toxic minnows they manage to catch. Another is to construct large indoor fishing tanks in the middle of residential areas so that people can pay for the convenience of not having to leave the city.

The last, and in this humble author's opinion, the best, is to stock small rural dams with fish and then surround the perimeter with large comfortable lounge chairs. There's something wonderfully surreal about driving through the countryside and spotting a group of professionally garbed fishermen comfortably ensconced in black vinyl recliners, casting away beneath a clear blue sky.

Birthdays. Most are celebrated in pubs and cafes by singing Happy Birthday in Korean while attempting to eat aesthetically pleasing cakes with chopsticks. This in itself is both challenging and fun, but what makes birthdays in Korea really interesting are the parties that are held when people turn one and sixty.

To reach the ripe old age of one traditionally signified that a child was out of the danger zone, and parents continue to celebrate this fact by holding a special party to which their friends and relatives are invited. The main entertainment is a fortune telling exercise involving a piece of thread, a pencil and some cash. These objects are set in front of the child and whichever he or she grabs predicts their path in life. The thread symbolizes a long life, the pencil scholarly devotion and the cash suggests a firm grasp of all things financial.

Guests are expected to bring a gold ring as a gift for the child, the jewelry acting as a kind of fiscal reserve in times of need. A bit of baby bling also adds a little color and contrast to those huge nude baby portraits that Korean parents love to hang in their living rooms. (Why anyone wants to display their child's genitals at 4X magnification is a mystery best left to cultural anthropologists.)

The other big bash is when Koreans make it to sixty. This special day, known as a Whangap, is considered extremely important, as it marks one whole zodiac cycle. One circle of the zodiac takes twelve years to complete and in Asian astrology five circles represents a full cycle. This is meaningful in that it symbolizes rebirth, a significant concept in a country still deeply influenced by Buddhist thought.

The event itself is huge, with all the children, relatives, friends and neighbors attending in order to pay their respects. In a society fixated with seniority, nothing else says you've made it to the top of the totem pole like a fancy Whangap party with hundreds of guests vying for your attention.

Weddings. Koreans basically have two of them, a traditional Korean ceremony followed by a Western one with all the white satin and pearls a girl could ever dream of. Many are held at private wedding halls. The term hall though is a bit misleading, a more accurate description might be multi-story wedding center equipped with smoke machines, disco balls, gilded baroque décor, dubious foreign 'ministers' and a comprehensive catering service.

On the subject of weddings, you need to know that if invited to attend a ceremony the standard gift is cold hard cash in a white envelope. While this might seem a little impersonal, it's actually not a bad custom, in that it will mostly go towards covering the high costs of the wedding. Anything left over will then be directed towards practical purposes such as assembling a mortgage deposit.

Penis Trees. Occasionally while walking in forested areas close to urban centers you may come across a projecting limb or stump of a tree that has been carved to resemble a very large, anatomically correct penis. It will more than likely possess a disturbingly high polish.

Information on these trees is difficult to access but it seems likely considering Korea's obsession with producing male heirs, and the ancient relationship between fertility and mountain spirits, that some kind of shamanic rite or ceremony occurs at these places. As to what actually goes on between Mr. Pine and the hopeful mothers is anybody's guess.

Names. Don't be alarmed if on the arm of Mr. Kim is Mrs. Park, because Korean women don't give up their family names when they enter the blessed state of matrimony. The order of a name is also different. Thus with the famous folk hero Hong Gil-Dong, Hong would be the family name, known as the ireum or seong-myeong and Gil-Dong would be the first name. In Korean culture there is no such thing as a middle name or a decorative hyphen.

When it comes to last names, be prepared for a little confusion in class as over fifty percent of your students will be Kims, Parks, Lees, Choes or Jungs. The other half will come from about 245 other variations. Most of these names are ancient, Confucian culture not looking favorably upon change.

Each of these family names is divided into clan groups that correspond to a city or village of origin. People who share the same family name are considered to be related, no matter how distantly, and thus are believed to be of the same blood. Strong taboos against clan intermarriage exist and while it's no longer against the law to marry another person with the same last name, it's still frowned upon.

Pigs. Not only do Koreans cook their sweet flesh in a multitude of mouthwatering ways, their heads also feature prominently in the act of opening a business, building a house or buying a new car. The ceremony involves placing the steamed head on a table surrounded by food and other offerings, and then bowing as you stuff the mouth full of cash. No one can explain the exact origins of this custom but everybody knows that it's just what you have to do if you don't want the business to go bankrupt or the wheels to fall off. (The pig's thoughts on the ritual are equally unknown but vegetarians and animal welfare experts assume they aren't too happy about it.)

Scary looking totem poles. Known in Korean as Jangseung, these carvings were created to protect the entrances of villages from evil spirits. The male is called "The Great Male General in the Sky" and the female is known as the "The Great Female General Underground". Their power in recent years has been diminished by the church and the production of miniature souvenir replicas, but older people in the countryside still respect them as guardians of supernatural power.

Ying and Yang. Yes, that nifty tattoo on your butt cheek does seem to feature prominently on the Korean flag. In Asian philosophy it represents the universe, which traditionally is understood to consist of two opposing yet complimentary forces, Eum and Yang or as you know them, Ying and Yang.

Eum is symbolized by the blue section, and represents among other things the earth, the moon, the night, water and women. The red part respectively stands for the sky, the sun, the day, fire and man. Eum and Yang were included in the design of the flag to demonstrate that only through an acknowledgement of opposites and a process of compromise can a nation reach a state of harmony and balance.

Whacking Elderly Ass. You may notice if you get up early and explore the hilly parks that surround most Korean towns a tendency for the elderly to rhythmically beat their butts against trees and other inanimate objects. If you can resist the urge to run away you'll find that this isn't some kind of creepy masochistic ritual but rather a step in their daily callisthenic routine. Stick with them and you'll see a range of stretches and other exercises performed on the various pieces of odd looking equipment that fill these parks. The exact purpose of the bum whack isn't clear.

Maybe it loosens up the muscles, drives off lactic acid or realigns the spine. Who can tell?

New Year's Eve. Basically the same as home. Involves copious amounts of alcohol, public urination and unrealistic resolutions. The only thing that differs is that in addition to a countdown at midnight, Koreans also get to listen to a gigantic bronze bell.

The big bell, which once marked the closing of the city gates, is housed in a wooden pavilion in central Seoul. It is struck thirty three times by thirty three citizens to announce the arrival of the New Year. This isn't just because Koreans are partial to threes, it's because the number thirty three holds special significance in Korea. After the numerologically inspired ding-donging, the guests join hands and sing a heartfelt song whose lyrics voice the peoples' hopes for reunification. To be chosen as one of the thirty three is a great honor and more than a few people would gladly trade their eyeteeth for the chance to help ring in the New Year.

Ginseng. If there is one agricultural product that is synonymous with Korea this would have to be it. Ginseng is the root of a specific plant—Panax Ginseng—and it is one of the country's most valuable crops. Etymologically the name Panax derives from the Greek, meaning "all heal", and Ginseng, appropriately enough from the Chinese term "Ren Shen", meaning "man-root". It is an important ingredient in Asian medicine, traditionally associated with good health and longevity.

The Korean name for Ginseng is Insam. Translated literally it means human root. This makes perfect sense when you see it, as it often bears a striking semblance to a skinny, bleached torso. Most Korean Ginseng is grown commercially in fertile valley fields under heavy black shade cloth, but the more expensive variety, wild mountain Ginseng, can only be found high up in shady mountain glades.

The cost of a large, mountain Ginseng root is so enormous that instead of eating it or grinding it into medicine, most buyers stretch out its value by storing it in alcohol and having a straight shot at regular intervals. In this way, with judicious topping up, a single wild root can last for many years.

Medicinal Mineral Water. For most Westerners mineral water is overpriced H2O in a fancy bottle, but for many Koreans it is an important medicinal product that has featured for centuries in their understanding of health and well being. At the base of different mountains are springs whose waters contain a variety of dissolved elements. These highly mineralized solutions are believed to be efficient remedies in the treatment of internal disorders, especially those of the liver.

Although local water treatment facilities provide a clean, safe product, many Koreans still don't trust the liquid that comes from their tap, preferring to augment the official supply with water gathered from local mineral springs. To be honest, the water in question often tastes weird, as if it's been sitting in a rusty pipe for the last decade, but your friends and coworkers will swear that it's good for you. Some springs have such a high iron content that the rocks around the outlet are stained red from mineral deposition.

Though it may not appeal to Western palates, its popularity makes sense when you consider it from an historical perspective. In the past the average Korean peasant would have had very limited access to dietary iron and other important trace elements. The water from these medicinal springs may have partially filled that nutritional gap.

PC Bangs. Koreans love computer games. Koreans love to do things together. Therefore, it makes perfect sense that Koreans love to play computer games together. Of course online gaming was invented so that you could play against other people from the comfort of your own home, but for most Koreans that's a bit too isolated and antisocial. They prefer to sit side by side in what are known as PC Bangs—computer rooms, and play online games such as Starcraft, Warhammer and Lineage until their wives or mothers drag them home.

Over one third of the population is involved in online gaming; some estimates place the figure as high as 17 million people. If the nation can be said to have a hobby, then this is it. And with these kinds of numbers, it's big business. Where else would you find cable TV channels dedicated to online gaming, and a professional tournament circuit where players can look forward to pulling in prize money worth hundreds of thousands of dollars.

You're welcome to enter a PC Bang and use the computers for email or other non gaming purposes. The cost is low and the patrons, if they ever look up, will probably smile and say hello. Just be aware that it will be dark, noisy, and rank with the combined odors of cigarettes, cheap coffee, instant noodles and the sweaty funk of repressed teenage angst.

Hangover Soup. Koreans love to drink delicious soups almost as much as alcohol, a fact which explains why the local hangover cure comes served with a spoon. The wise cultures of the East realized centuries ago that one of the best ways to feel better after a heavy night's drinking is to replenish the body's water supply. However being Koreans they couldn't just drink two liters of water and go back to bed, they had to boil up a unique mixture of beef, bean sprouts and vegetables that not only soothes the stomach but pleases the palate. In any large town or city you'll find numerous restaurants dedicated solely to the purpose of restoring the workforce to maximum efficiency via hangover soup. It's quite tasty stuff, but whether it's worth braving the belligerent stares of the other customers in order to try some is open to debate.

Comments. Koreans like to make observations about certain foods and implements that will become very annoying to you after a few months. For some reason Koreans think that all foreigners don't like chilies, can't stand garlic and have never handled a set of chopsticks in their lives. You'll want to punch someone around the 100th time you hear one of these inane statements but it's probably best just to smile and find your happy place.

Baby Bums. If you are observant you may notice what appears to be a large bruise on the lower backs and bums of Korean babies. This is not the sign of widespread child abuse but rather a curious genetic anomaly. Almost all babies born in Asia have what's known as the Mongol spot, a benign birthmark that usually fades away during childhood. It also occurs in people of Native American, East African and Turkish descent.

Traditional Korean folklore puts the cause of the Mongol spot down to the hefty paddling given to babies by the mythical grandmother spirit. Before babies are born it was believed that they lived for a while with this magical grandmother, and that when it was time to go down to earth they were reluctant to depart. This resulted in a firm spanking, which is why babies emerged howling with a big blue bruise on their backsides. Modern science, in all of its poetic beauty, lays the blame on melanocytes encapsulated in the dermis during their passage from the neural crest to the epidermis, which is really just a fancy way of saying that a few pigment producing cells get lost along the way.

Konglish. Great name for a book but in the big picture it wasn't important enough to warrant a whole chapter on the subject. Of course for those of the zealous persuasion the improper use of English in Korean society represents the most insidious foe you'll ever face, but for most teachers its just one of those things you learn to live with.

Konglish comes in two forms. It can be a mispronounced word that still carries the original meaning, such as Bideo for video, or as it's more commonly understood, it can be an English word that has come to possess a new and sometimes entirely different meaning. Some of these meanings are only slightly altered whereas others are almost unrecognizable.

Of course from a linguistic perspective all languages are in a constant state of flux and no new words that supplement a living language can be objectively described as wrong or incorrect. English speakers certainly have no right to judge, seeing that the majority of their vocabulary and grammar was appropriated from a variety of other language sources. So try not to get too worked up over Konglish, because while it's a battle you can fight, it's not a war you can win.

Here are a few classic examples. Enjoy.

Eye shopping—window shopping
Service—free product or service
Fighting!—a cry of encouragement
Cunning—cheating
Skinship—kissing, intimate physical contact
Flash—flashlight or electric torch
Apartu—apartment
Fancy shop—a stationery store
Hip—bum or bottom
MacGyver knife—Swiss army knife
One Shot!—bottoms up
Overeat—to vomit
Pocketball—the game of pool
Handphone—cell phone or mobile phone

White faces and Weird Hats. Like the rest of humanity, Koreans want to be something they're not. In the West it's all about an idiotic obsession with turning pasty white into glowing bronze, while in Korea the focus runs in the opposite direction. All kinds of nasty chemical whiteners and makeup exist to disguise or erase the dreaded tan. The same goes for the neo-Amish bonnets, gloves and forearm protectors you see. It all stems from an historical hangover that associates exposure to the sun with poor social status, as once upon a time it was only the peasant women who worked outdoors who ended up brown.

Pocketball. No, it's not a sexual euphemism; it's the Konglish terminology for billiards and pool. Pocketball halls can be identified by a sign on an upstairs wall or window that shows four colored circles separated by two diagonally intersecting lines. Some operate as fee paying clubs but most are open to the public. Cues and balls are provided and you pay by the hour.

Smells. Korea is full of them. Some are good, some are interesting and some are downright disgusting. The good includes mountain passes filled with pines, fruit markets in strawberry season and food stalls steaming away on cold winter nights. The interesting ones are streets dedicated to processing chili powder and sesame oil, traditional medicine shops and incense filled shrines. The bad ones are meat markets in summer, elementary schoolboys after soccer and the sweet stench of sewage.

Nightclubs and Pubs. People in Korea usually go out in large groups due to the custom of many drinking establishments, especially nightclubs, applying a minimum table order upon arrival. This usually consists of six bottles of beer and something to eat, often a large fruit platter. You have absolutely no choice in the matter, but on the upside it does ensure that you're consuming at least two serves of dietary fiber per night.

Wooden Masks. They appear everywhere and come in a variety of shapes and sizes. These wooden masks and their plastic imitations all derive from one small village near Andong, by the name of Hahoe. This village has an ancient history of masked drama, and has become in recent years an important destination for tourists. A visit is definitely worthwhile, for who can honestly resist the chance to witness a millennia old dance that features deranged butchers, lecherous nd pissing bulls.

squitoes and Smoke. During the monsoon season mosquitoes breed up big time in the rice paddies of South Korea. To combat the possible reintroduction of Malaria and Japanese Encephalitis, local municipal workers cruise around at dusk in strange bat mobiles that spew out massive clouds of insecticide. While these machines do have a positive effect on controlling mosquito numbers, it's unknown what the long term consequences are for the crazy kids that rush out to play in the toxic fog.

Banking. Korean banks aren't really prepared to deal with you. Since the 2002 World Cup there are now more ATMs equipped with English options, however the real issue comes when you want to send money home. Certain Korean fiscal laws exist in order to limit the amount of money you can send home in an effort to control illegal tutoring. Theoretically you're not allowed to send home more money than what you receive from your designated employer and you may be asked to provide pay stubs. This doesn't seem to be much of an issue anymore but be advised that sending more than a few thousand dollars may excite your teller's attention.

In addition to this it's a slow, expensive proposition fraught with error, especially at rural bank branches. Be sure to double check all the banking codes and account numbers before you begin, as once the money is gone it can be a pain in the ass to track down a wayward sum.

Designer Garbage Bags. In an effort to reduce the amount of garbage entering Korea's limited landfill sites, the government came up with the idea of special issue garbage bags. This means that only those bags with the correct government designs on them will be picked up by municipal workers. These tiny plastic bags must be purchased in stores and shops. The concept is a good idea, in that if people have to pay for them they'll hopefully sort and recycle their rubbish to decrease the quantity of material that goes into them. That said, human nature will always find a way to circumvent rising costs and more than a few mystery bags of household waste find their way into vacant lots and public parks.

Swimming. A lot of older Koreans can't swim, and those that do aren't really what you'd call competent. Today children are learning to swim at school, but sadly, drowning remains a relatively common cause of death. People don't go under on every outing but be prepared for the fact that you might be the only person on the beach who can co-ordinate a rescue or administer first aid if an emergency strikes.

Riot Police and Big Sticks. If you're visiting Seoul or any of the other big cities, you may chance in your wanderings across groups of riot police training in parks or other public places. Koreans are a very law abiding race of people but they do have a weakness for throwing shit when they get worked up. The Korean police like to counter this inclination with water cannons and the use of long wooden poles that look like giant samurai swords. If you spot squads of riot police beating each other with big sticks it's probably just a training exercise but it never hurts to look around and make sure you aren't in the middle of something about to get ugly.

Go-Stop. Spot a group of old people playing cards in a park and chances are they're playing Go-Stop. Originally a card game from Japan, it's now a Korean tradition in its own right. It's played just about anytime the elderly gather, but it's especially popular during the New Year and Harvest festivals.

The deck or Hwatu, is divided into twelve suits with four cards per suit. Each suit is decorated with a different flower or tree. The game revolves around the matching of suits, thereby scoring points. The name signifies that at certain points in a round the betting can either go on or be stopped. It's a relatively simple game to master but it is a gambling one, so don't ask your elementary students to teach you at school!

Cheggi, Jeggi or Jegi. However you spell it, this fun filled kicking game is definitely within your budget. The Cheggi looks and acts like a shuttlecock from a badminton game, but instead of racquets it's kept in motion with your feet. It is traditionally made from an old coin and strips of handmade paper but nowadays most are manufactured from bright plastic and shiny tinsel.

It's played just like a game of Hacky Sack, in that the goal is to keep the Cheggi in motion with only your feet. One on one it's all about who can kick it the longest. If played in a bigger circle the point is just to keep it up in the air and have fun. If you end up teaching school children, you'll have no shortage of confiscated Cheggis to choose from.

There you have it. No doubt you'll find more weird and wonderful things in Korea but that's ok, as it's part of what makes the place so special. If this book has done its job, you're going to survive your time in Korea and hopefully look back on it as one of the best periods in your life. You'll leave with good friends, great stories and a deeper insight into yourself and the world around you. So don't hesitate a moment longer, get that resume ready and prepare for the ride of your life.

PS: By all means let your friends borrow this book but please don't give it to them. The author has thirteen Guatemalan orphans and seven ex-wives to support, so he needs all the sales he can get.

REFERENCES

Conze, Edward. 1993. A short history of Buddhism. 2nd ed. Oxford: One World Publishing.

Covell, Alan Carter. 1993. Folk art and magic: shamanism in Korea. 3rd ed. Elizabeth, NJ: Hollym International Corporation.

Edwards, Richard. 1987. The Korean war. East Sussex, UK: Wayland Publishing.

Fehrenbach, T. R. 1994. This kind of war: the classic Korean war history. Dulles, Virginia: Lon Brassey Publishing.

Kim, Andrew. n.d. A history of christianity in Korea: from its troubled beginnings to its contemporary success. http://www.tparents.org/library/religion/cta/korean-christianity.htm. (accessed May 26, 2011)

McArthur, Meher. 2010. Confucius. London: Quercus Publishing Plc.

And of course in this era of collaborative knowledge sourcing, Wikipedia and other online dataports were visited to crosscheck information.

ABOUT THE AUTHOR

Matthew Waterhouse was born on October the third, 1977, due to a spirited New Year's Eve party in Toronto nine months earlier. Raised in a loving environment which included lots of books and animals, he went off to university where he spent most of his time daydreaming in the library and playing with his neighbors' cat. After a short stint as a circus strongman, his friends got him a job teaching English in South Korea and the rest, as they say, is history.

The author now lives in the Rocky Mountains outside of Calgary, where he helps his wife manage a rehabilitation center for criminally inclined black bear cubs. He teaches elementary school and writes whenever the muse makes him. When he's not in the land of the maple-flavored munchies he can be found on his parents' wombat farm in eastern Australia, where he manages to consume vast amounts of imported cheese and avoid any form of manual labor.

CPSIA information can be obtained at www.ICGtesting.com
Printed in the USA
LVOW041622251112

308737LV00001B/52/P